First-Grade Essentials

Carson-Dellosa Publishing LLC
Greensboro, North Carolina

Credits

Compiled by: Jennifer Taylor Geck

Content Editor: Elizabeth Swenson

Copy Editor: Julie B. Killian

Layout and Cover Design: Lori Jackson

Cover Illustration: Ray Lambert

 This book has been correlated to state, common core state, national, and Canadian provincial standards. Visit www.carsondellosa.com to search for and view its correlations to your standards.

Carson-Dellosa Publishing LLC
PO Box 35665
Greensboro, NC 27425 USA
www.carsondellosa.com

© 2012, Carson-Dellosa Publishing LLC. The purchase of this material entitles the buyer to reproduce worksheets and activities for classroom use only—not for commercial resale. Reproduction of these materials for an entire school or district is prohibited. No part of this book may be reproduced (except as noted above), stored in a retrieval system, or transmitted in any form or by any means (mechanically, electronically, recording, etc.) without the prior written consent of Carson-Dellosa Publishing LLC.

Printed in the USA • All rights reserved.

ISBN 978-1-60996-474-0
01-335111151

Table of Contents

Introduction 8

LANGUAGE ARTS
Phonics

Let's Go Home..9
Dino Bites ★ 10
Alphabet Ant 11
Ships Ahoy!...12
Animal Sounds ▲★ 13
The Sound Connection...............................14
Circle That Sound 15
Sounds the Same 16
Hear It Last 17
Consonant Stars 18
Fun with Final Sounds 19
Start to Finish ★ ● 20
Show What You Know 21
Sound Review ▲ 22
Bag of Vowels...23
All Cracked Up 24
Hear the Vowel 25
Top of the Box..26
Gus and His Drum......................................27
What Am I? 28
Heading Home ▲★ 29
All Aboard!..30
Seek and See... 31
Long I Art 32
Flying High ★ 33
Give a Dog a Bone 34
Rows of Cubes 35
No Place Like Home ▲ 36
Finish My Name 37
Happy About Y...38
Basket of Vowels 39
Do I Really Need This? ▲..........................40
Flower Power 41
Get Your Head in the Clouds 42
Lovely L Blends ● 43
Friends Get Together 44
The Prince's Prize 45
Rolling Along with R Blends ★ ● 46
Animal Action ▲...47
Star Blends ★ 48
Simply Use an S Blend 49
All Blended Up 50
The Right Kite ● 51
Rhyme Time 52
Frogs in a Pond 53
What's That?..54
Stop, Drop, and Rhyme ▲★ 55
Rhyming Rockets ▲★ 56
Chocolate Chips with Lunch ● 57
Shells on the Seashore 58
Theo's Flower Garden Path 59
Check Out These Sounds 60
Listen to the Fish.. 61
Ring and Sing ★ 62
It All Ends Up Here ● 63
Picking Out Sounds ▲ 64
Do Cows Throw Snowballs? ● 65
Raccoon's Balloon......................................66
Cool Sounds in an Igloo 67
Stirring Up Vowels 68
Ready for More 69
It's My Turn 70
All About Turtle 71

● = Group Work   ★ = Extra Materials   ▲ = Cross-Curricular

Table of Contents

Vocabulary
A Colorful World ★ 72
On Mother's Day ▲★ 73
Wonderful and Great Crossword Puzzle ★ 74
Study and Learn with Synonyms 75
Opposites Attract 76
Antonyms Are All Around 77
Same or Different ★● 78
Double Word Fun 79
For the Love of Words ★● 80
Double Your Word Power 81
Clear About Contractions ★ 82
I'll Brush My Teeth ▲★ 83
He's Hiding! ▲ 84
Way to Grow! ▲ 85
Sunglasses or Sleds? ▲ 86

Reading Comprehension
Busy Birds 87
Leaves and More Leaves ▲ 88
Mixed-Up Story ▲● 89
Time for Art 90
Rainy Day ▲ 91
Some Winter Fun 92
Life on the Farm 93
Wish You Were Here ▲ 94
Welcome Home! ▲ 95
Dress the Snowman 96
My Robot 97
To the Moon! ▲ 98
B Is for Blueberry ▲ 99
Web Spinners 100
Feelings Matter ▲● 101
Is It So? ● 102
We Like to Play 103
Bear Is Busy ● 104

Can You Believe It? ● 105
Be Earth's Friend ▲ 106
A Dog's Life ▲★● 107
Caterpillar Clues ▲ 108
Animal Puzzlers ▲ 109
Fun Fox Facts ▲★ 110
Packing Day for David 111
Which Pet? ▲ 112
Out in the Cold 113
Tell Me Why 114
Fun at the Zoo 115
Anna Is on Time! ▲● 116

Categorization
Sort Them Out ▲ 117
Where to Wear? 118
How Many Legs? ▲ 119

Parts of Speech
The Right Name ★ 120
Helpful Friends ▲ 121
Add Some More ● 122
One, Two, or Three ● 123
What Is Happening Today? ★ 124
People on the Go 125
Gumball Fun 126
Baked a Cake 127
No School Today 128
Matt Was the Star 129
It Looks Like This 130
Toss Around Names 131

Sentences
The Perfect Start 132
Fishing for Answers ● 133
Pet Fair Punctuation 134
For You to Decide 135
Bat Basics ▲ 136

Table of Contents

Writing
The Picture Tells the Story ● 137
Little Acorn Grows Up ▲ 138
In the Future ▲ 139
All About Me 140
All About Me 141
All About Me ▲ 142
All About Me ▲ 143

MATH
Number Sense
Number Art 144
Colorful Critters ★ 145
Apple Insides 146
Animal Travels 147
Watermelon Garden 148
One Hundred Places 149
Take a Step Back 150
Right in the Middle of Things 151
What Comes Next? 152
A Little Less or a Little More 153
One Has Fewer 154
One Has More 155
Could Be More or Less ● 156
Number Train 157
Words for Numbers 158
First in Fire Safety ▲ ★ ● 159
Ducks on Parade 160

Skip Counting
Leaping Lily Pads! 161
Drop by Twos 162
Does the Trash Count? ▲ ★ ● 163
Five Feather Fun ▲ ★ 164
Letters in the Mail 165
Learning to Count On ● 166
Making 10 167

Fractions
Half as Much Fun 168
It Shows This Much 169
Equal Parts Make a Whole ★ 170

Addition
Sums of Shells 171
Double Up 172
Under-the-Sea Addition 173
Apples in All ● 174
Bats Are Everywhere! 175
Add All Three 176
Double-Digit Sums 177
In Outer Space ▲ 178
Presidential Addition ▲ 179

Subtraction
Solving Problems in the Stars 180
Springtime Subtraction 181
Crayons in a Box ★ 182
Exploring Differences ▲ 183
See the Simple Machine ▲ 184
Bees and Flower Favorites ▲ 185
Find the Matching Difference 186
Lucky in Subtraction ▲ 187

Mixed Addition & Subtraction Practice
Pet Problems ★ 188
Bananas over Math ▲ 189
Number Sentences 190
Magnet Math ▲ 191
Gift of Math 192
Make the Connection 193
Staying Healthy ▲ 194

Patterns
Garden Patterns 195
Hearts in a Row ★ 196
Let's Have a Ball! 197

Table of Contents

Berries in Baskets ▲ 198
Growing with Seeds and Petals 199

Fact Families

All in the Family 200
Fact Family Fun 201
Pairs of Number Sentences 202

Algebra

Helping Goldilocks 203
Food Rules! ▲ 204
Hats Off to Math 205
Happy About Math 206
Something Is Missing! 207
Horses in Corrals 208
Butterfly Winters ▲ 209

Place Value

Tens and Ones 210
Place Value Addition 211
Building Three-Digit Numbers 212
Places Everyone! 213
More Than One Way 214

Geometry

Will You Find It Here? ▲ 215
Funny Animal Shapes 216
Cabin Count ▲ ★ ● 217
The Way I See It ★ 218
Practice in 3-D 219
Explore and Explain 220
A Perfect Line? 221
The Same on Both Sides 222

Calendar Skills

These Seven Days 223
This Month or Next Month 224
Seasons of Fun 225
Calendar Setup 226
Calendar Exploration 227

Time

At This Time Today 228
Don't Be Late! 229
Fun Time at the Fire Station 230
Time for the Harvest ▲ 231
Time for Me 232
Rock Clocks 233

Measurement

Toothy Measures ▲ 234
The Measure of Me ★ 235
Measurement Rules! ★ 236
Heavy or Not? 237
Rain Forest Riches ▲ ★ ● 238
Time to Shop 239
Mouse in the Pumpkin Patch 240

Reading Graphs

Vacation Reading ★ ● 241
Apple Orchard Trip 242
Fund-Raiser Fun 243
How We Travel ▲ 244
Zoo Animal Count 245
Sports Are Fun! ● 246
Pet Tally 247
Drink Tally ● 248
Tasty Fruits 249
A Day at the Park 250
Brothers and Sisters ▲ 251
Land or Sea ▲ 252

Data Analysis and Probability

It Takes This Long 253
Classroom Predictions ★ 254
Spin the Spinner! ★ 255
Jelly Bean Probability 256

Table of Contents

Word Problems

Ten-Frame Addition 257
Tasty Problems ▲ 258
Want It or Need It? ▲ 259
Pictures and Numbers ● 260
Ten-Frame Subtraction 261
Seasonal Subtraction ▲ 262
Pumpkin Problems ▲ 263
Celebrating Cinco de Mayo ▲ 264
A Sea of Subtraction ▲ ★ ● 265
Working in Gardens 266
Cleaning Up with Addition
  and Subtraction ▲ 267
Number Line Helper ● 268
A World of Patterns 269
Shopping for Father's Day ▲ ● 270
Healthy Ways ▲ 271
Wonderful Weather Time ▲ 272
Time for Sports! 273
February Activity Planner 274
Math in Our World ▲ ● 275
Math and Me 276

Reproducible Teacher Forms 277
Answer Key 291

Introduction

First-Grade Essentials offers activities for a full year of practice fun! Designed with the busy teacher in mind, the book is full of ready-to-go practice pages. The activities are both simple and engaging and will provide hours of learning fun.

Parents will love *First-Grade Essentials* too! These activities are perfect for basic skills practice at home or on the go. Each book covers an entire year of skills and provides practice tools that children will enjoy. *First-Grade Essentials* includes the following skills:

Language Arts Skills:
- phonics
- synonyms and antonyms
- rhyming words
- reading comprehension
- sequence of events
- parts of speech
- compound words
- contractions
- types of sentences
- punctuation
- writing and composition

Math Skills:
- number sense
- inequalities
- skip counting
- introduction to fractions
- addition and subtraction facts
- column addition and subtraction
- repeating and growing patterns
- geometry
- measurement
- money, time, and calendar
- graphs, charts, and tables
- word problems
- place value

Each activity targets skills that are fundamental to first grade. Many activities also connect with science or social studies curriculum. *First-Grade Essentials* follows national curriculum standards so that teachers can coordinate many of these easy-to-use practice activities with specific units of study.

First-Grade Essentials is teacher tested and includes many helpful features:

- A comprehensive table of contents identifies activities by skill.
- Each activity's skill is identified in the upper right-hand corner for quick reference.
- Icons in the table of contents make it easy to find activities with a cross-curricular connection.
- Every page includes a bonus activity to engage students further.
- Bonus activities that require extra materials or small groups are clearly marked by icons in the table of contents.
- A teacher forms section that is reproducible and perfect for use throughout the school year.

Name: _____

Syllables

Let's Go Home

Cut out the animal pictures. Glue each picture on the correct house to show how many syllables are in the word.

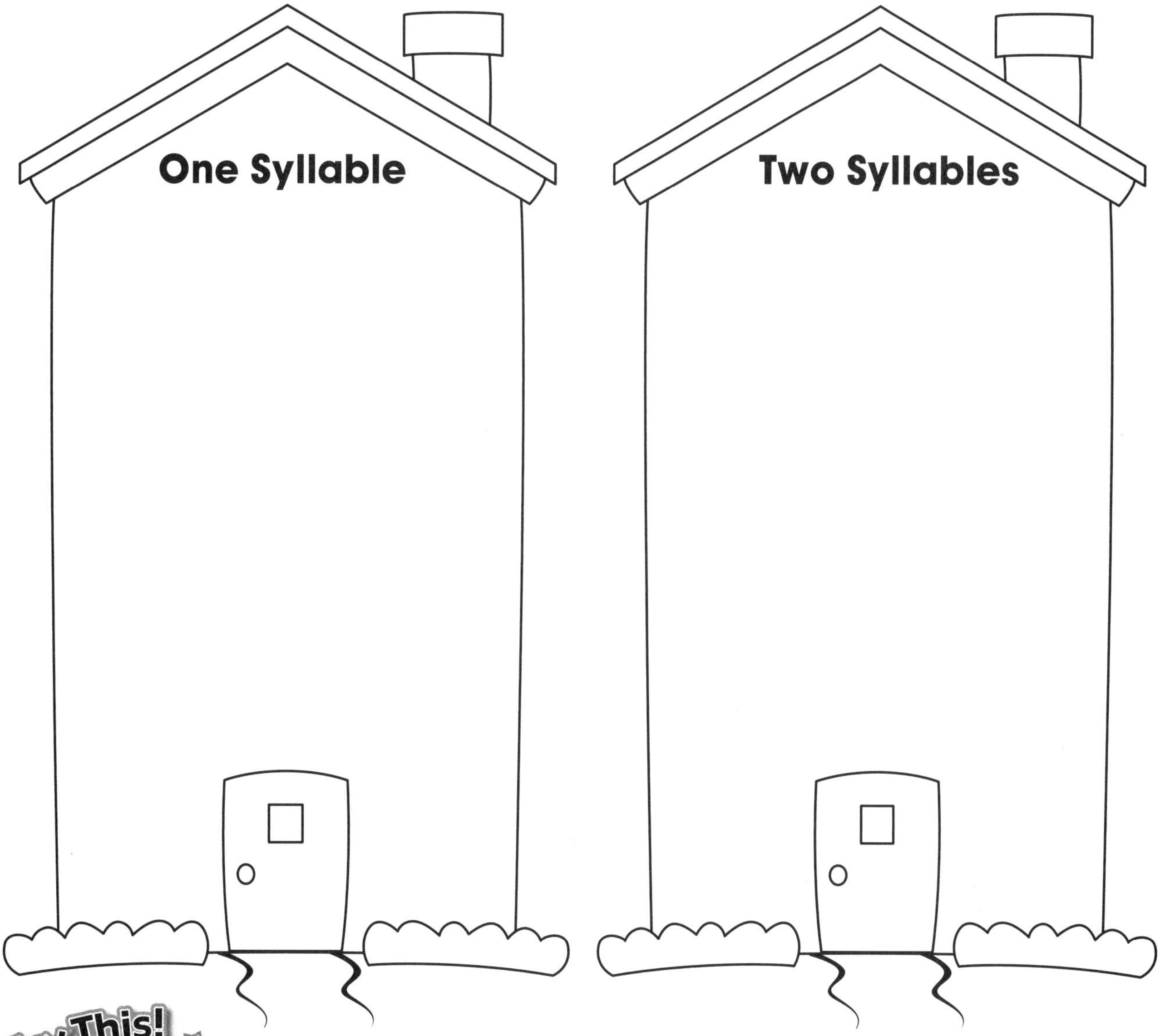

One Syllable

Two Syllables

Try This!

On the back of this paper, draw your home and the people who live in it. Label the people with their names. Write the number above each person that shows how many syllables are in his or her name. How many syllables are there altogether?

 cut

cat   turtle   bird   spider   fish   rabbit

Name: _____   Syllables

Dino Bites

Cut out the words. Glue the words with two syllables on the dinosaur's body.

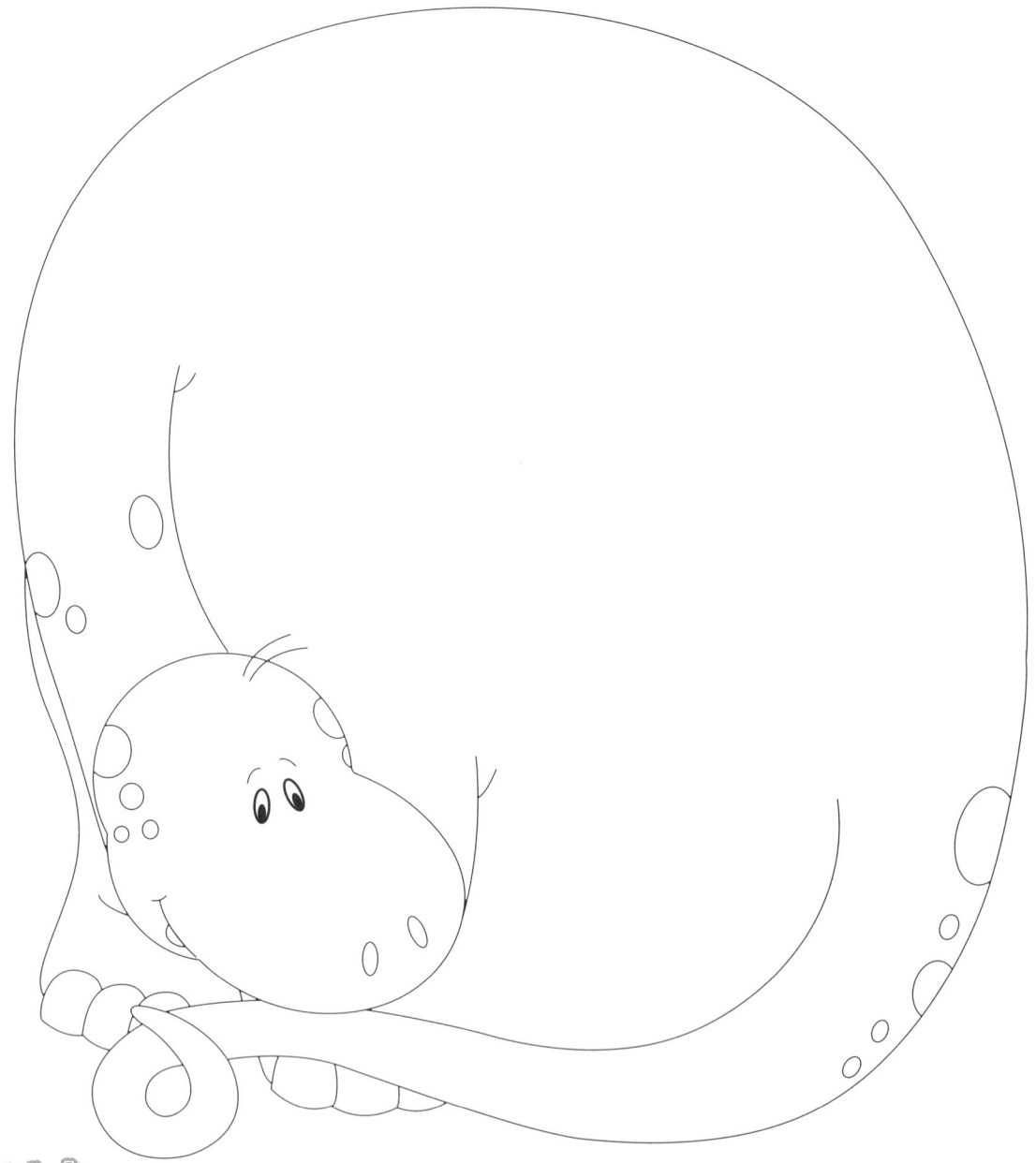

Try This!
Glue the one-syllable words in the center of a sheet of drawing paper. Then, draw and color your own dinosaur around these words.

| bake | muffin | hungry | bowl | kitchen | mixer |

Name: _____

Alphabet

Alphabet Ant

Draw lines to connect the dots from **a** to **z**.

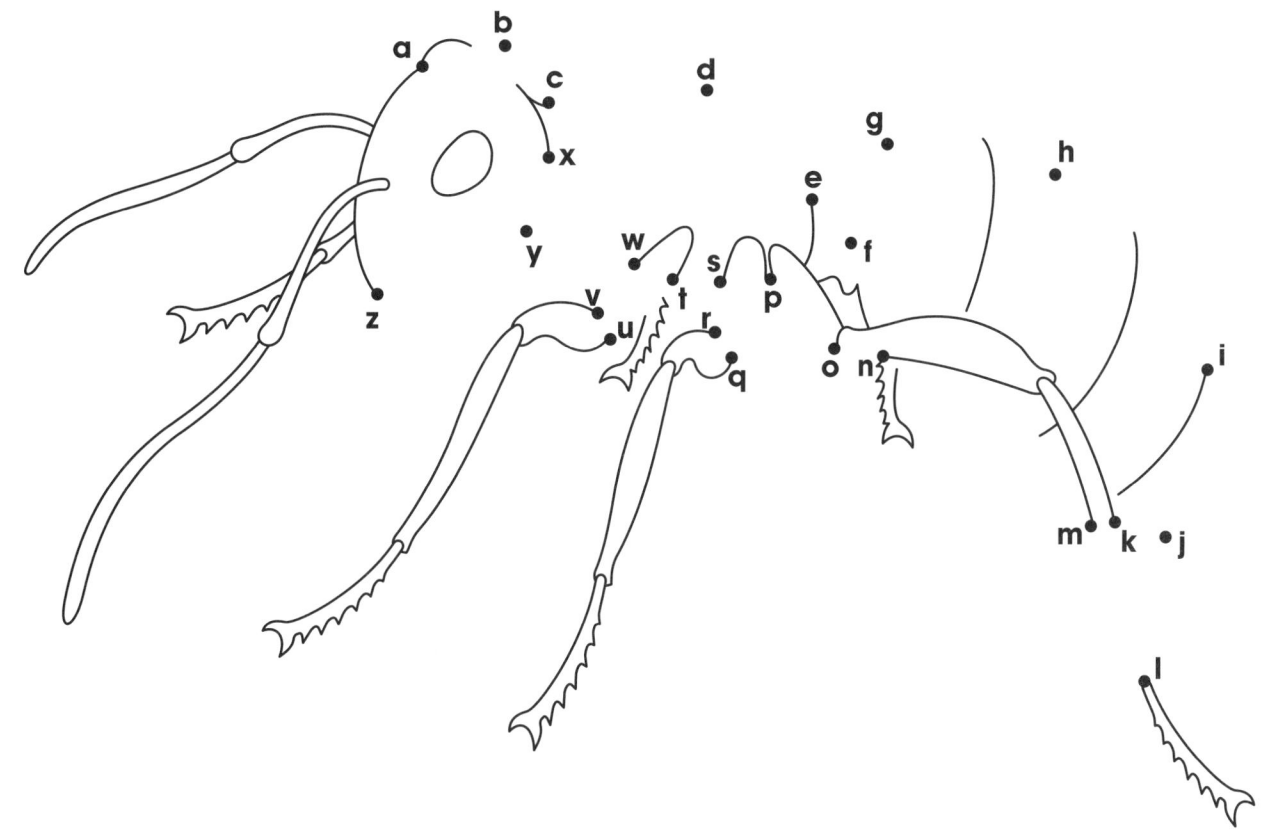

Write the letter that comes next.

J ___   L ___   R ___   T ___   D ___   F ___

Try This!

On the back of this paper, write your first name. Then, write the letter that comes after each letter in your first name. (If you have the letter Z in your name, write an A.) What does your new name look like?

Name: _____   Letter Recognition

Ships Ahoy!

Cut out the letters. Glue each letter on the correct ship. Write five more letters on each ship.

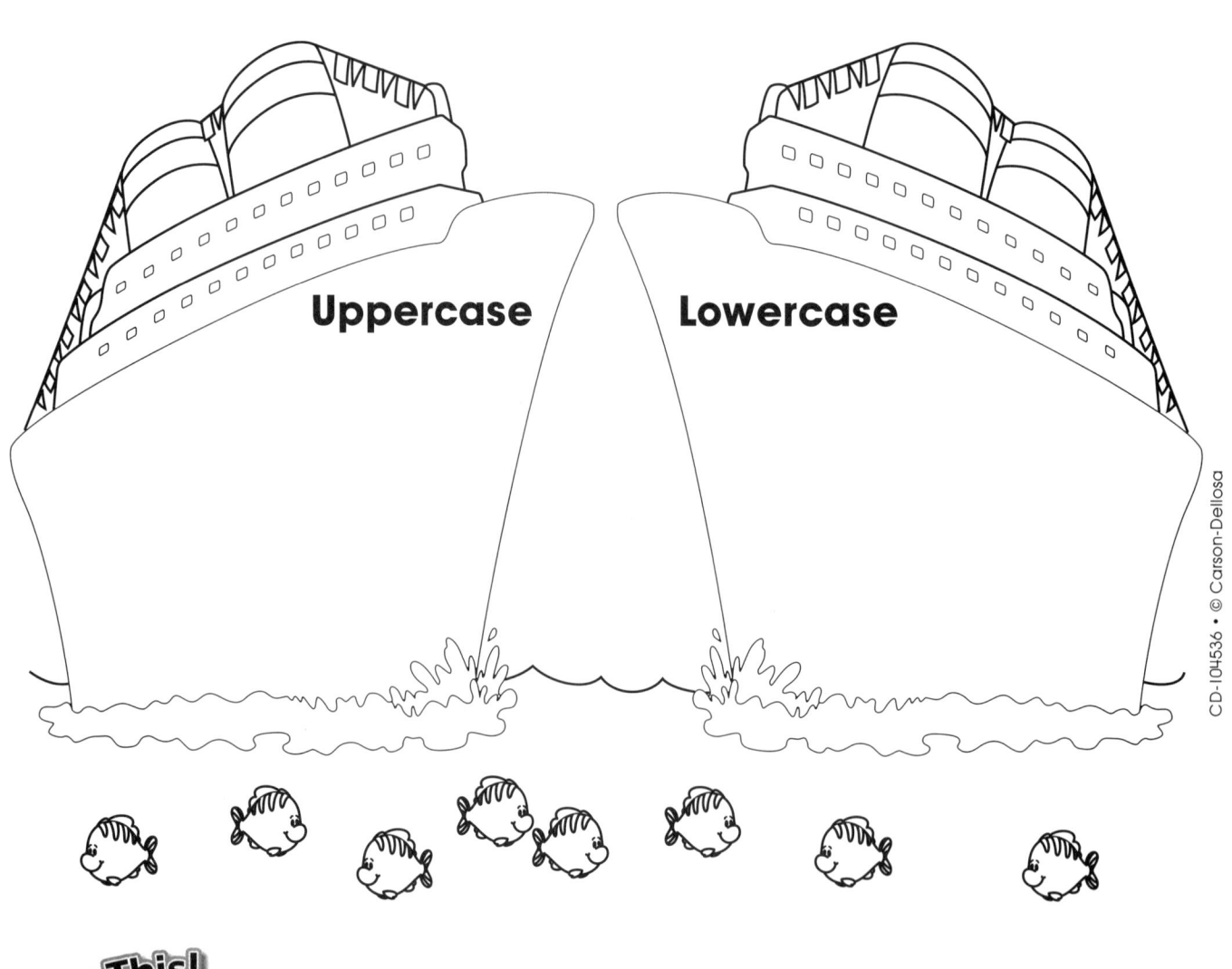

Try This!
Choose a vowel. On the back of this paper, write as many words as you can think of that begin with that vowel. Use the word wall to help you.

G	D	t	b	R	i
L	e	K	q	A	h

cut

12

Name: _____   Initial Consonants

Animal Sounds

Say the name of each picture. Circle the letter that makes the beginning sound.

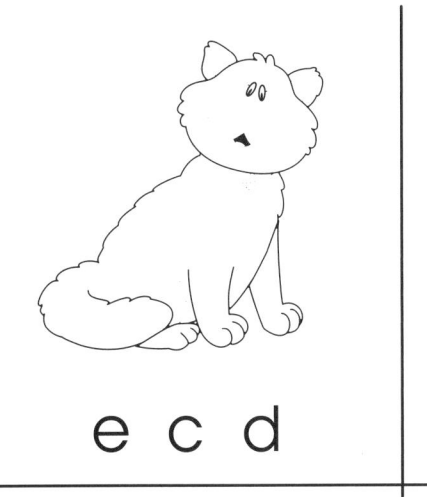

e c d   f p d   f t h

n u m   d j b   g t b

In each box, draw a picture of an animal whose name begins with the letter shown.

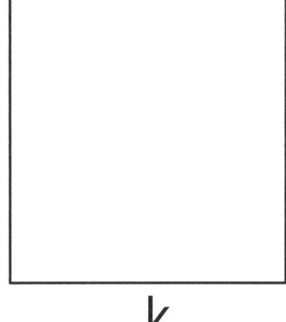

t   s   k

Try This!

Write the names of the animals above in ABC order on a sentence strip.

Name: _____

Initial Consonants

The Sound Connection

Draw a line to match each letter with the picture whose name begins with that letter sound.

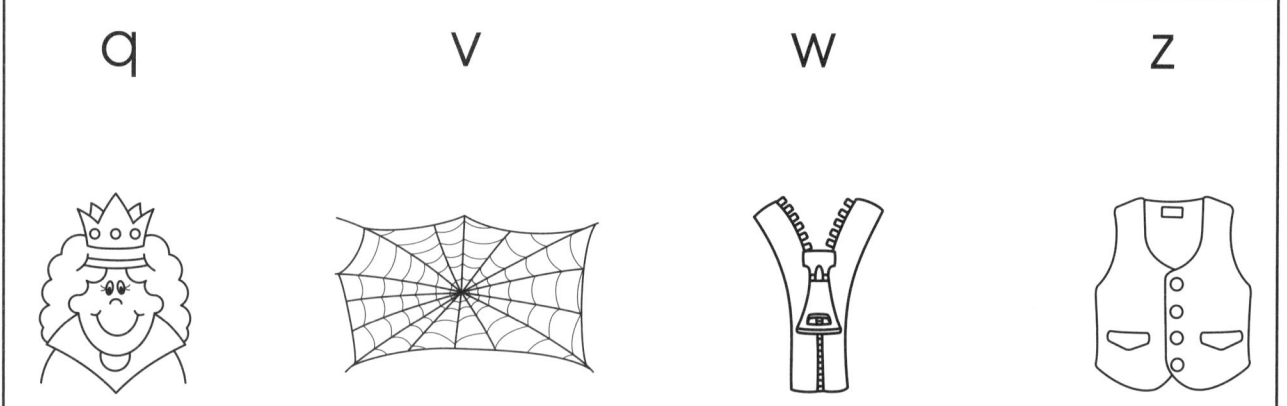

Draw a picture of something with a name that begins with each letter shown.

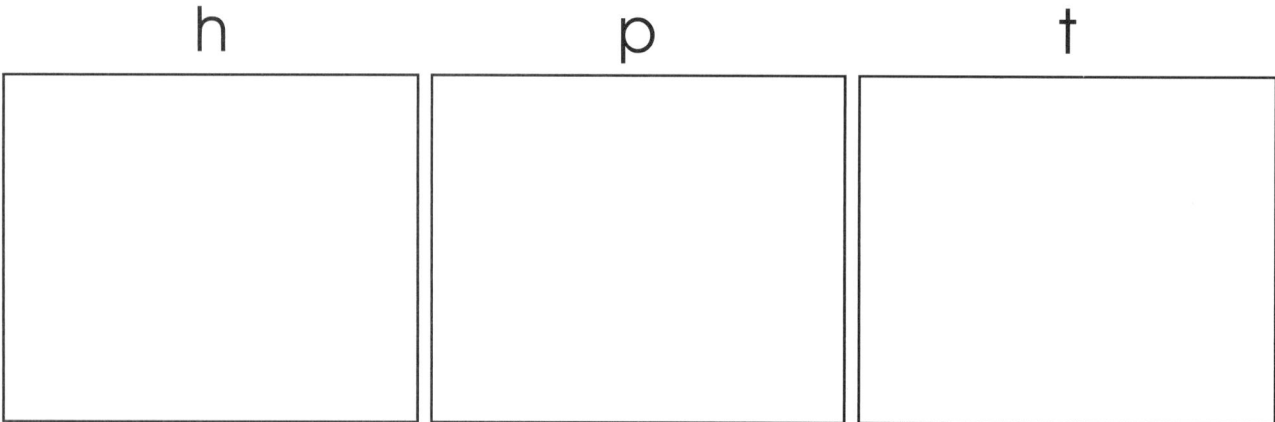

Try This!

Say the name of each picture you drew. Write the letter of the final sound for each word.

Name: _____   Initial Consonants

Circle That Sound

Say the name of each picture. Circle the letter that makes the beginning sound. In the last row, write the letter that makes the beginning sound.

t   z   s   s   c   p   p   m   t

   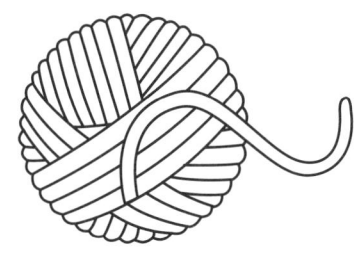   

r   b   f   v   y   w   d   b   f

      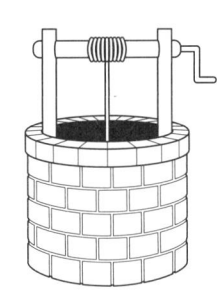

Try This!

Write a secret message using pictures instead of letters. Draw pictures with names that have the same beginning sounds as the letters in the word or words you are writing. For example, draw hat, elephant, lion, ladybug, octopus for the message *hello*.

15

Name: _____

Initial Consonants

Sounds the Same

Color the pictures in each row with names that begin with the same sound as the letter shown. In the final box, draw a picture or write a word that begins with the same letter.

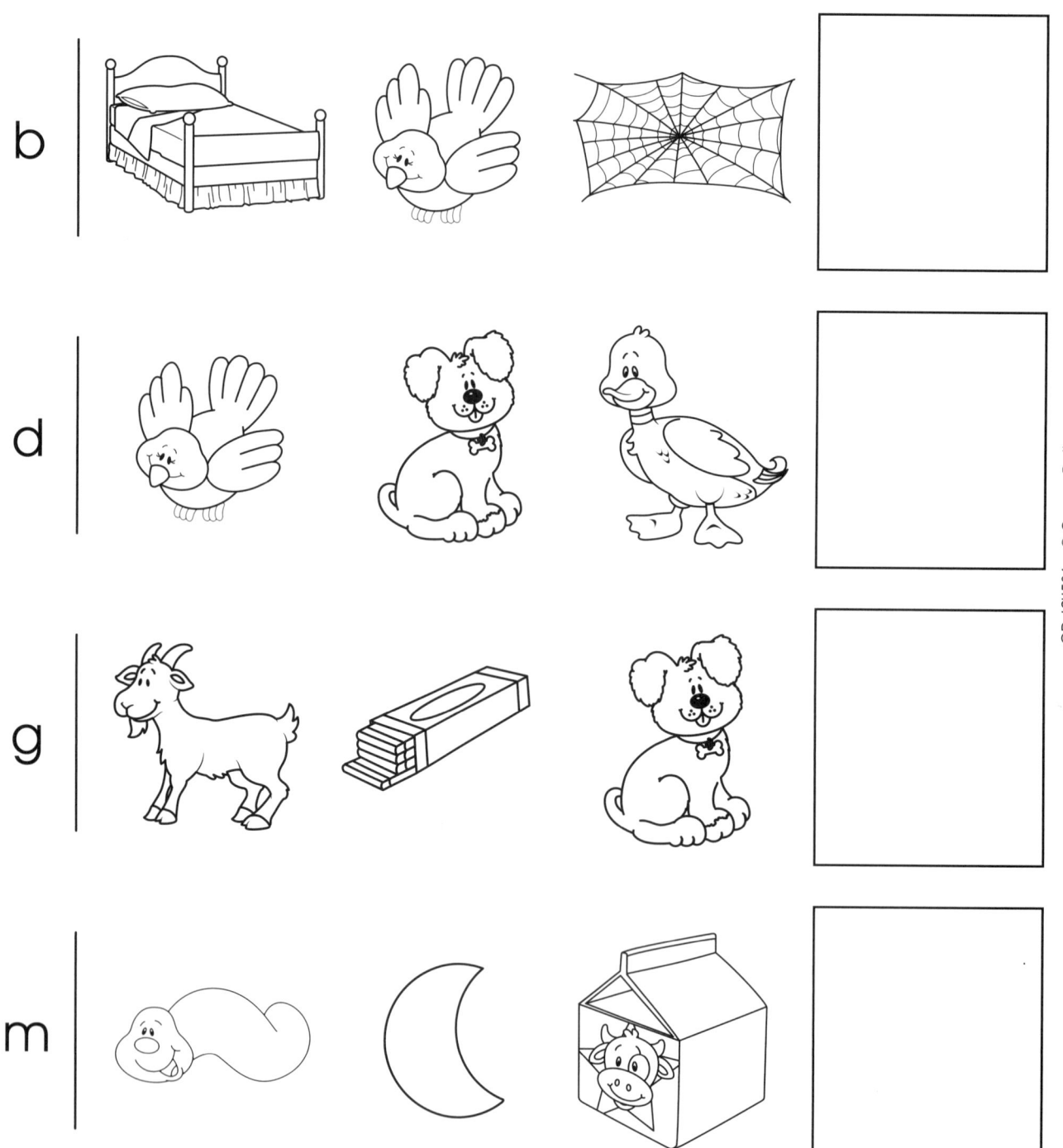

Try This!
Write the letter of the final sound for each word above.

16

Name: _____   Final Consonants

Hear It Last

Say the name of each picture. Circle the letter that makes the final sound.

t n p	x r s	p t r
x f r	r t n	x n r

Say the name of each picture. Write the letter that makes the final sound.

_____   _____   _____

Try This! On a separate sheet of paper, write three sentences using at least three of the above words.

Name: _____   Final Consonants

Consonant Stars

Use the code to color the stars. In each empty star, write a word that has the same final sound as **star**.

| words that end in **d** = red | words that end in **b** = yellow |
| words that end in **t** = blue | words that end in **g** = green |

Try This!

On the back of this paper, write two more words that belong to the same word family as the word on each star.

18

Name: _____   Final Consonants

Fun with Final Sounds

Say the name of each picture and each name. Draw a line to match each picture to the name with the same final sound.

**HELLO
my name is
Scott**

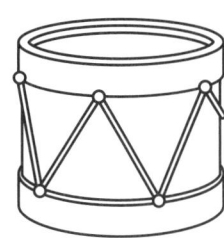

**HELLO
my name is
Taylor**

**HELLO
my name is
Nell**

**HELLO
my name is
Dion**

**HELLO
my name is
Nick**

**HELLO
my name is
Sam**

Try This!
On the back of this paper, list five words that end with the same final sound as your first name.

Name: _____   Initial and Final Consonants

Start to Finish

Say the name of each picture. Write the missing letters.

do___   ___ook   ___ea___

      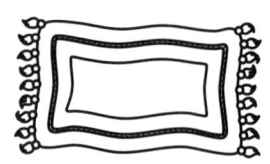

ca___   ___o___   ___u___

Unscramble the letters. Write the words.

x o b   n s u   f n a

_____   _____   _____

Try This!
Draw a picture of three objects. Write the name of each object, but leave off the first or last letter. Ask a friend to complete your words.

Name: _____

Initial and Final Consonants

Show What You Know

Say the name of each picture. Write the first and last letters of each word. Color the pictures with names that have the same vowel sound as **bat**. Circle the pictures with names that have the same vowel sound as **top**.

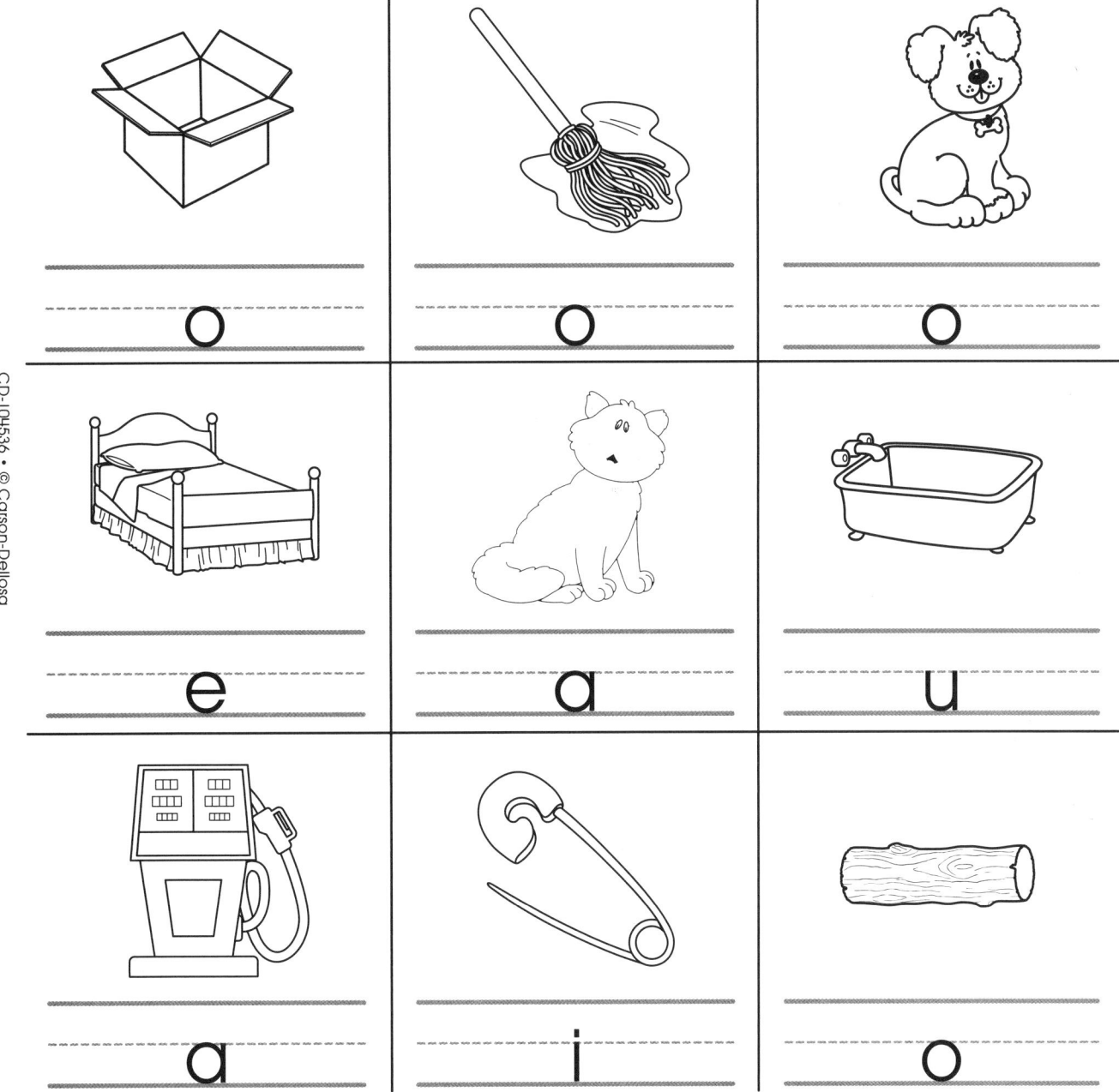

Try This!
On a separate sheet of paper, write the above words in ABC order.

Name: _____

Initial and Final Consonants

Sound Review

Say the name of each picture. Write the first and last letters of each word. Color the pictures that show something living. Circle the pictures that show something nonliving.

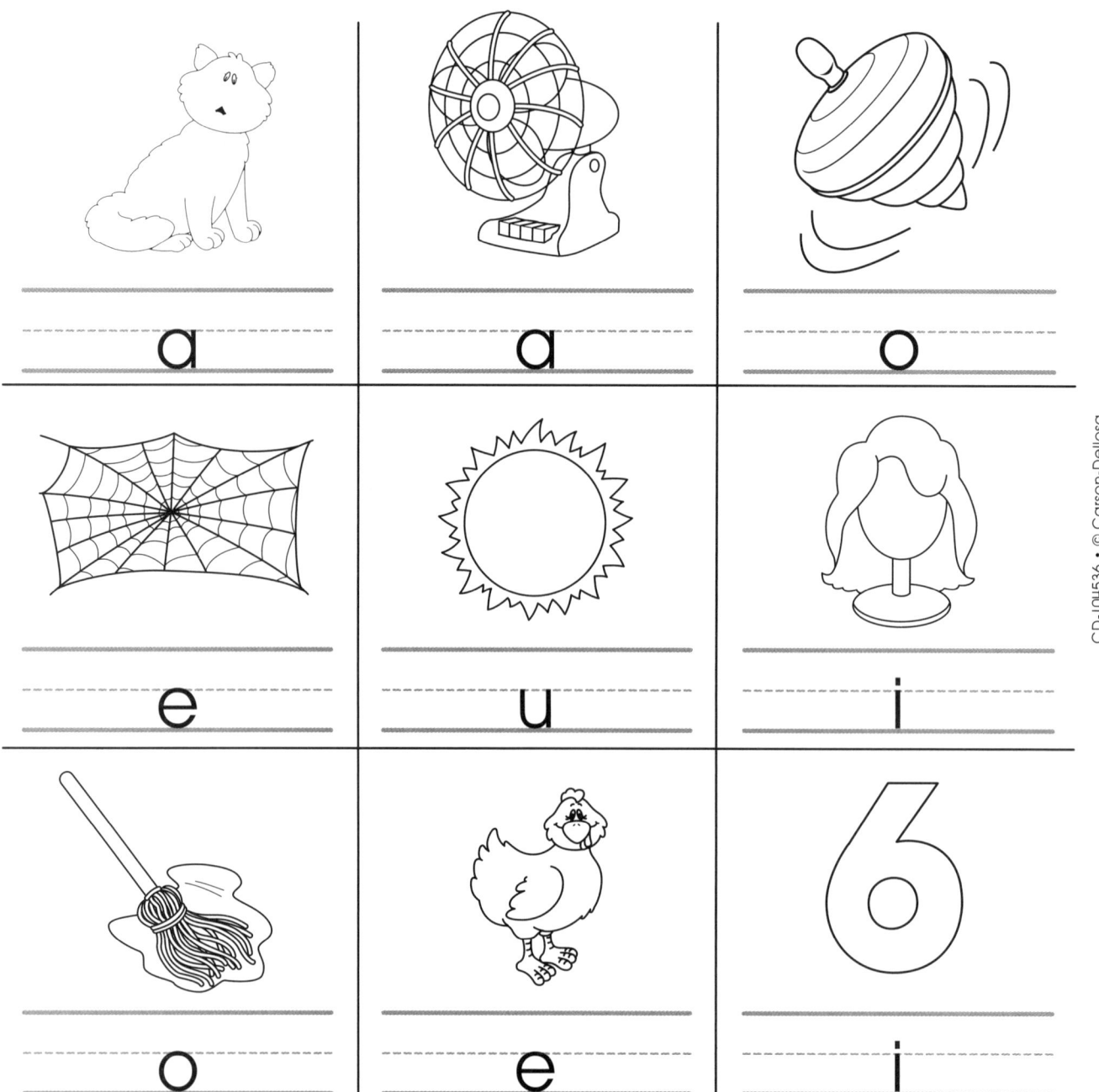

Try This!

On a separate sheet of paper, draw pictures of five items that are in your bedroom. Write the first and last sound for each item. Circle any of your items that are living.

22

Name: _____ Short a

Bag of Vowels

Say the name of each picture. Color the pictures with the **short a** sound. On each empty bag, draw a picture of something with a name that has the **short a** sound.

Try This!

Draw a circle around each picture with the short *i* sound.

Name: _____   Short e

All Cracked Up

Cut out the puzzle pieces. Put the puzzle together and glue it on a separate sheet of paper. Say the name of each picture. Color the eggs with the **short e** sound.

Try This!
On the back of your completed puzzle, list 10 short e words. Circle any words that rhyme.

Name: _____   Short i

Hear the Vowel

Say the name of each picture. Fill in the circle for the letter of the short vowel sound. Color the pictures that have the **short i** sound.

Try This!
Choose two short *i* words from above. Write a silly sentence using both words.

Name: _____   Short o

Top of the Box

Unscramble the letters to name each picture. Color the pictures with the **short o** sound.

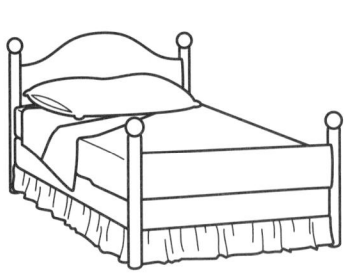
b d e
_____

p m o
_____

o t p
_____

a m n
_____

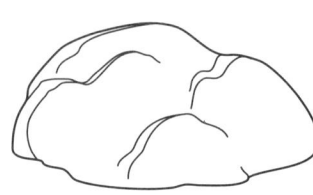
r c k o
_____

c k l o
_____

Try This!

Choose one short *o* word from above. List some words that rhyme with the word.

Name: _____   Short u

Gus and His Drum

Help Gus find his drum. Find a path through the words that have the **short u** sound.

Try This!

On a separate sheet of paper, sort all of the words from the maze by vowel sounds.

Name: _____   Short Vowels

What Am I?

Circle the name of each picture.

fin
fan
fun

can
ran
sand

crab
crib
web

pan
pen
pin

crab
crib
pet

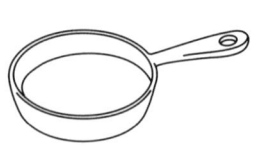
pan
pen
pin

fence
fan
fish

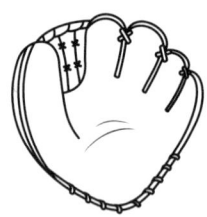
mat
mitt
men

mat
mitt
men

mitt
men
man

Try This!
Draw circles around the pictures with names that rhyme.

Name: _____   Short Vowels

Heading Home

Write **a**, **e**, **i**, **o**, or **u** to complete each animal name. Draw lines to match the animals with their homes.

f__sh

b__t

f__x

h__n

d__ck

Try This!
On a separate sheet of paper, draw one of the animals above in her habitat. Write three sentences about where and how this animal lives.

Name: _____   Long a

All Aboard!

Cut out the words. Glue each word on the train car with the matching picture. Write your own **long a** words in the empty train cars.

Try This!
Use the code to color the train cars.
ay = red   ai = yellow   ae = green

| hay | snake | cave | rain | vase | nail |

Name: _____ Long e

Seek and See

Circle all of the **long e** words. Draw a line to match each sentence to the correct picture.

Jean sees a key in the tree.

Dean reads a book about seas.

Will she eat meat or beans?

What did he see in the stream?

Pete had a dream about sheep.

Try This!

On a separate sheet of paper, write a poem that has at least three long e words. Draw a picture to go with your poem.

Name: _____   Long i

Long I Art

Follow the directions. Circle the words that have the **long i** sound.

Draw a hive for the bees.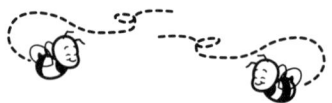

Draw a prize for the knight.

Draw stripes on the kite.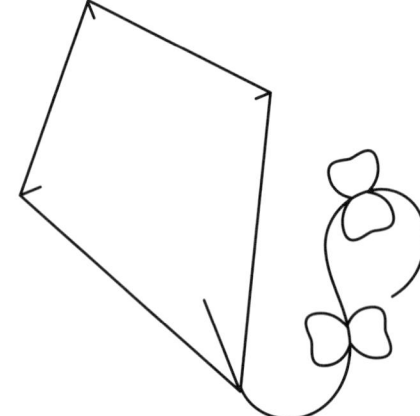

Color nine ties.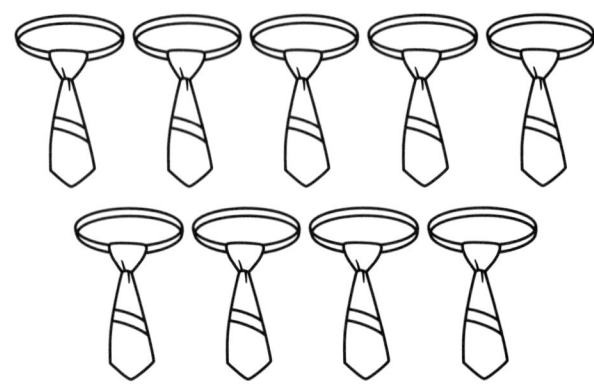

Try This!
On a separate sheet of paper, write a sentence that has two long *i* words. Draw a picture to go with your sentence.

Name: _____   Long e and Long i

Flying High

Use the code to color the kites.

long e = green   **long i** = yellow

Draw a picture in the kite that has either the **long e** or the **long i** sound. Write the name of the picture on the line beside the kite.

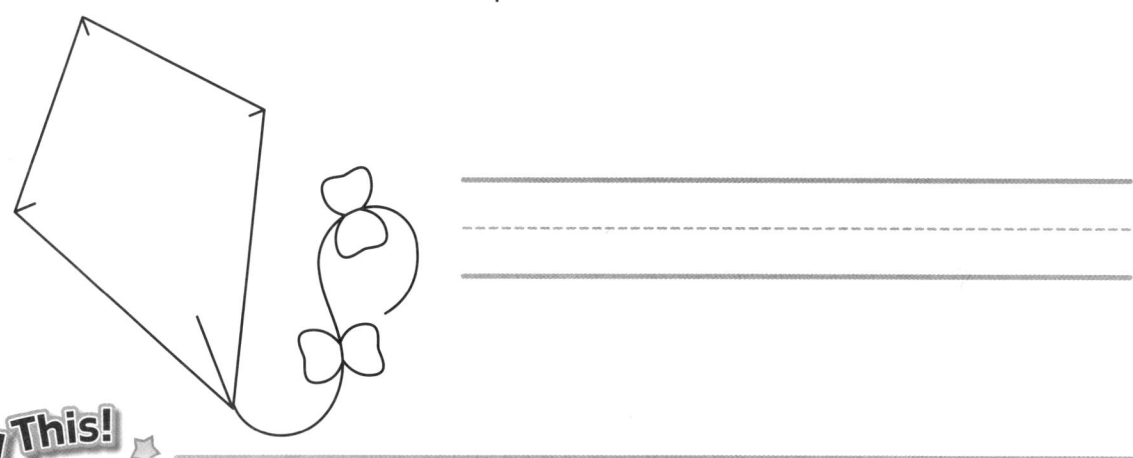

Try This!
Use construction paper and yarn to create a kite. Decorate the kite with long *i* words and pictures.

33

Name: _____ Long o

Give a Dog a Bone

Color the bones with words that have the **long o** sound. Write **long o** words in the empty bones.

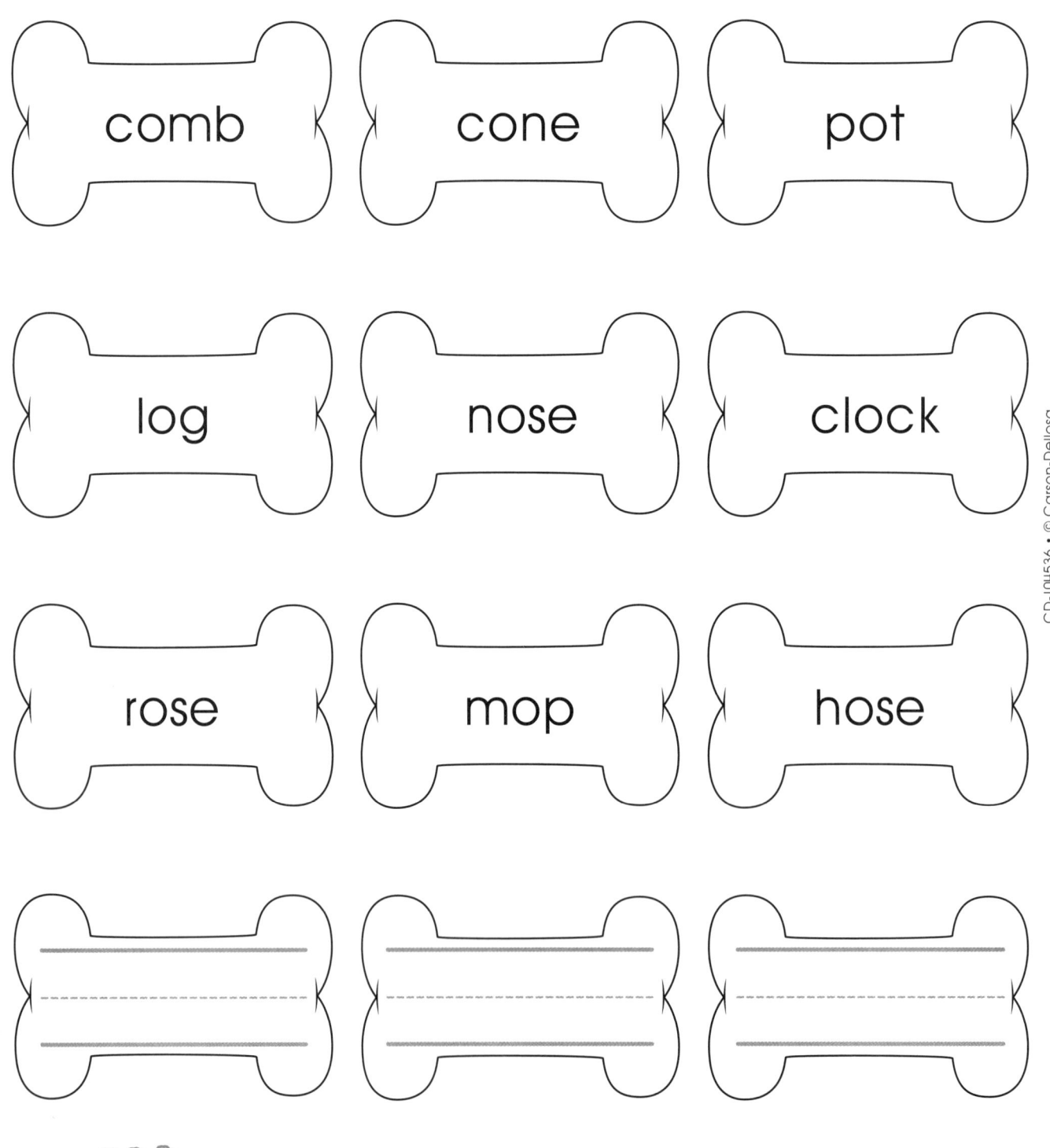

⭐ **Try This!** ⭐
Circle the bones with words that rhyme.

34

Name: _____   Long u

Rows of Cubes

Color the cube blue if the picture's name has the **long u** sound. Circle the row that has the most **long u** pictures.

Try This!
On a separate sheet of paper, draw a row of five ice cubes. On three of the cubes, draw pictures or write words that have the long *u* sound. On the other two cubes, draw pictures or write words that have the short *u* sound.

Name: _____   Long Vowels

No Place Like Home

Use the code to color the homes.

long a = red
long e = green
long i = orange
long o = yellow
long u = blue

goat   mice

Friends Way

lion   bee

Park Place

firehouse

Firehouse Drive

crow   park

Friends Way

toad   snake

Park Place

mule   tiger

Firehouse Drive

Main Street

Try This!

On a separate sheet of paper, write directions from the goat's home to the firehouse.

Name: _____ Long Vowels

Finish My Name

Write the missing vowels for each word. Use the code to color the pictures.

long a = red
long e = green
long i = yellow
long o = orange
long u = blue

 b _ _	 wh _ le	 b _ ke
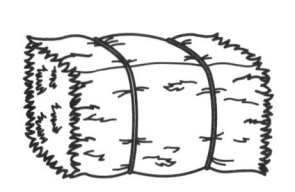 h _ y	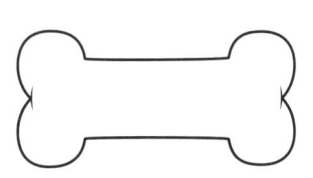 b _ ne	 gr _ pes
 n _ ne	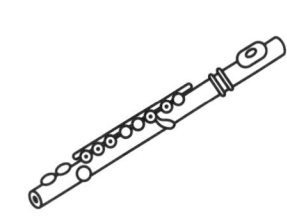 fl _ te	 r _ ke

Try This!

Circle each word above that has a silent e.

37

Name: _____   Y as a Vowel

Happy About Y

Write **y** to complete each word. If the **y** has the **long e** sound, color the happy face ☺. If the **y** has the **long i** sound, color the sad face ☹.

bab __   ☺   ☹

fl __   ☺   ☹

berr __   ☺   ☹

funn __   ☺   ☹

tr __   ☺   ☹

b __ e   ☺   ☹

Try This!

On a separate sheet of paper, sort the above words by the long *i* and the long *e* sounds.

38

CD-104536 • © Carson-Dellosa

Name: _____

Short and Long Vowels

Basket of Vowels

Use the code to color the apples.

long-vowel words = red   short-vowel words = yellow

Try This!

Count how many of the above words have short vowels. Draw that same number of clouds in the sky.

39

Name: _____

Short and Long Vowels

Do I Really Need This?

Cut out the pictures and decide if they are "needs" or "wants." Glue each word in the correct box. Use the code to color the words.

| long-vowel words = red | short-vowel words = blue |

Needs	Wants

Try This!

On the back of this paper, explain the difference between a need and a want. List five examples of each.

fruit	 pet	 soap	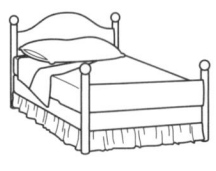 bed
 coat	 game	 gum	 doll

cut

Name: _____

Initial Blends

Flower Power

Use the code to color the flowers. In the empty flower, draw a picture with a name that begins with **pl**.

bl words = blue   **cl** words = green   **fl** words = red

Try This!

On a separate sheet of paper, draw a flower with six large petals. In each petal, draw or write a word that begins with *bl*, *cl*, *fl*, or *pl*.

41

Name: _____ Initial Blends

Get Your Head in the Clouds

Write the letters you hear at the beginning of each word. Use the code to color the clouds.

gl = gray   **pl** = blue

__ __ ant

__ __ ue

__ __ um

__ __ ove

__ __ ate

__ __ ug

Try This!

On the back of this paper, write the above words in ABC order.

42

Name: _____

Initial Blends

Lovely L Blends

Color the picture or pictures in each row whose names have the same beginning blend as the first picture.

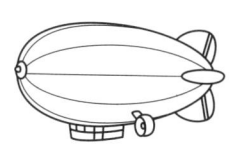

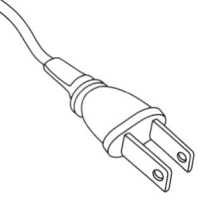

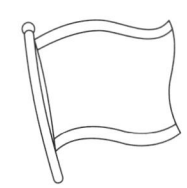

Write the two letters of the beginning blend.

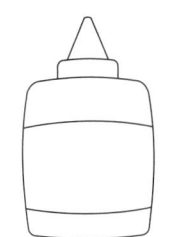

Try This!

Play a game with two or three friends. Look around the classroom or out the window for things whose names begin with an *l* blend. See who can find the most.

Name: _____   Initial Blends

Friends Get Together

Write **cr**, **fr**, **gr**, **pr**, or **tr** to complete each word. Use the picture to answer the questions.

1. Does the ____incess have a ____own? YES NO

2. Does the ____ow have a ____ayon? YES NO

3. Did the ____incess win the ____ize? YES NO

4. Does the ____andma have a ____oom? YES NO

5. Is the ____og on the ____ill? YES NO

6. Is the ____ab in the ____uck? YES NO

⭐ **Try This!** ⭐
On a separate sheet of paper, write a story about the picture above.

Name: _____   Initial Blends

The Prince's Prize

Circle the words in the word bank that begin with the **pr** blend. Find and circle the **pr** words in the word search.

print	rip	person	party	pear
present	prince	prize	part	pretzel

```
p  r  e  s  e  n  t  p
r  n  p  p  b  e  f  g
e  c  p  r  i  n  c  e
t  k  d  i  i  h  a  q
z  s  l  n  m  z  j  b
e  v  w  t  r  d  e  h
l  c  f  p  k  l  g  j
```

Try This!
If you could give a prize to anyone, whom would you give it to and why? Explain your answer and draw a picture of the prize on a separate sheet of paper. Use as many *pr* blend words as you can.

Name: _____

Initial Blends

Rolling Along with R Blends

Say the name of each picture. Draw a line to match each picture to the correct beginning blend.

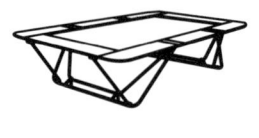

br

cr

dr

fr

gr

pr

tr

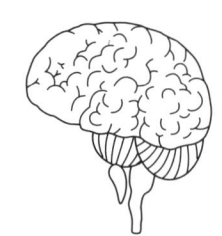

Say the name of each picture. Write the two letters of the beginning blend.

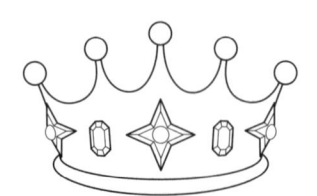

Try This!

Work with a partner to create a collage of pictures with names that begin with *r* blends. Cut out the pictures and glue them on a sheet of paper labeled *r* blends.

Name: _____   Initial Blends

Animal Action

Circle the words with **s** blends in each sentence. Follow the directions in each box.

Draw a snake on a stool.	Draw a swan flying in the sky.
Draw a skunk wearing skates.	Draw a squirrel on a swing.

Try This!
On a separate sheet of paper, make a T-chart to sort the objects in your pictures into living and nonliving objects.

Name: _____

Initial Blends

Star Blends

Write the blend that comes at the beginning of each word.

__ __ider 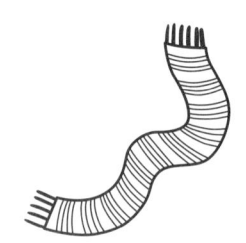   __ __arf 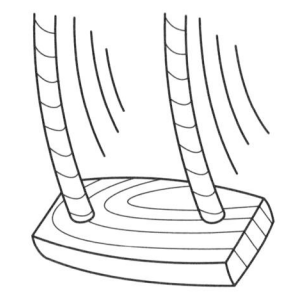   __ __ing

__ __op    __ __ail    __ __ide

Draw a picture in each empty star that begins with an **s** blend.

Try This!

Cut out the stars and glue them to a sentence strip in ABC order.

Name: _____   Initial Blends

Simply Use an S Blend

Circle each **s** blend.

1. ski
2. twenty
3. smother
4. stare
5. tweezers
6. sting
7. smog
8. sneeze
9. spend
10. swat

Write the word from the word bank that completes each sentence. Circle the beginning blend.

11. I need a _____ to mail my letter.

12. That _____ is spinning a web.

13. We went sledding in the _____.

14. Look at the clouds in the _____!

sky
snow
spider
stamp

Try This!

Circle five *s* blend words above. Use the words to write a story on a separate sheet of paper.

Name: _____   Initial and Final Blends

All Blended Up

Cut out the pictures. Glue each picture in the correct box.

Beginning Blend

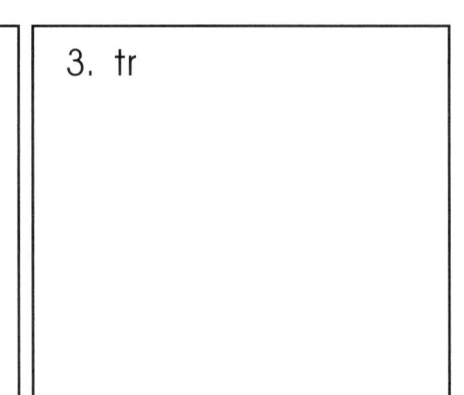

| 1. fl | 2. cl | 3. tr |

Ending Blend

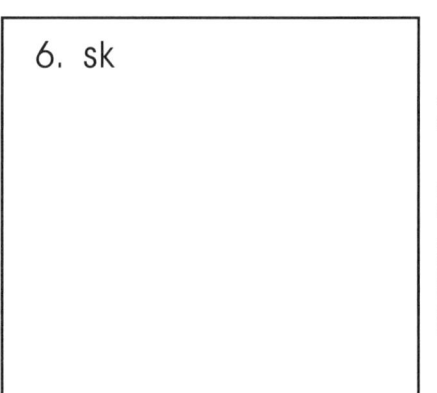

| 4. nd | 5. nt | 6. sk |

Write three words with different blends.

7. _____   8. _____   9. _____

Try This!
Find five to 10 objects in the classroom that have a beginning or ending blend. Draw a picture of each object and write its name.

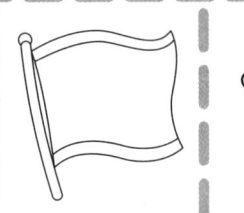

cut

50

CD-104536 • © Carson-Dellosa

Name: _____   Rhyming Words

The Right Kite

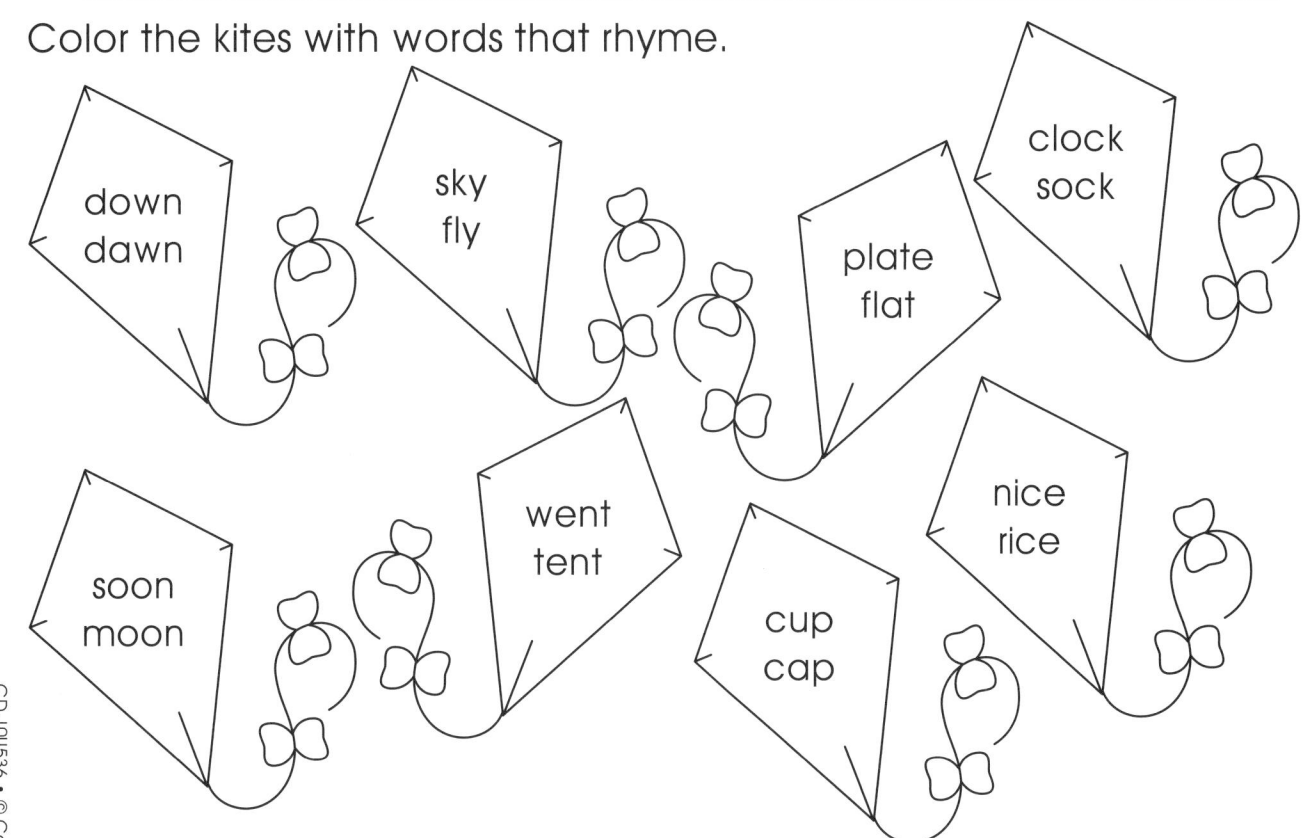

Color the kites with words that rhyme.

- down / dawn
- sky / fly
- plate / flat
- clock / sock
- soon / moon
- went / tent
- cup / cap
- nice / rice

Write a rhyming word below each kite.

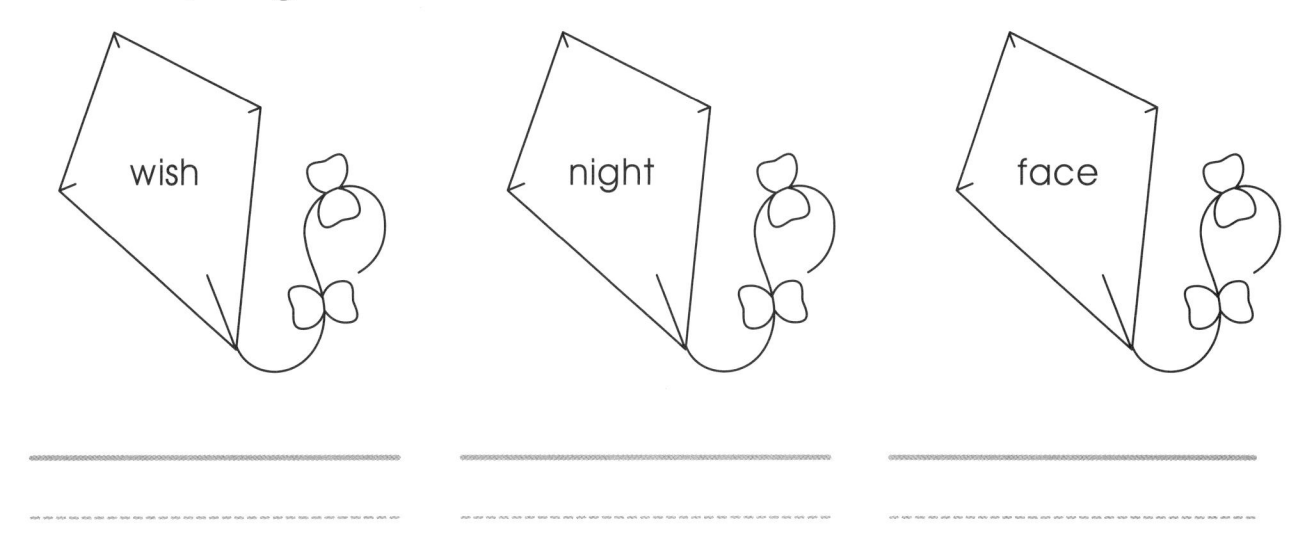

- wish
- night
- face

_____   _____   _____

Try This! Play this rhyming game with a partner. Write a word on a separate sheet of paper. Your partner then writes a rhyming word. Continue playing until you run out of words. The last person to write a rhyming word wins.

51

Name: _____

Rhyming Words

Rhyme Time

Write a word that rhymes with each underlined word. Use the pictures to help you. Draw a line to match each sentence to its picture.

1. She likes to run under the _____.

2. I see a bee in the _____.

3. He can hop over the _____.

4. The cat was on the _____.

Try This!

On a separate sheet of paper, write a sentence with a pair of rhyming words. Draw a picture to go with your rhyme.

Name: _____

Rhyming Words

Frogs in a Pond

Cut out the frogs. Glue each frog beside the lily pad with the rhyming word.

- top
- take
- hole
- leg
- meet
- him

Try This!

On a separate sheet of paper, write as many words as you can think of that rhyme with *frog*. Then, write a sentence using at least two of the words.

cut

- lake
- swim
- egg
- hop
- eat
- pole

Name: _____ Rhyming Words

What's That?

Write the word from the word bank that completes each rhyme. Finish the pictures to match the rhymes.

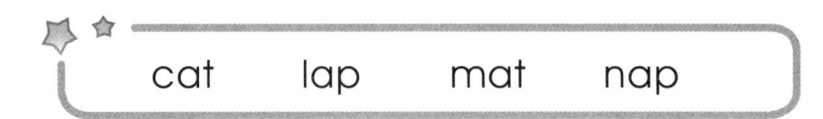

cat   lap   mat   nap

What's that?

Tom saw a _____ .

Pat the cat

sat on a green _____ .

Pat was tired, so he took

a _____ right on top

of grandpa's _____ .

Try This!
Write your own rhyming story. Draw a picture to illustrate each rhyme.

Name: _____

Rhyming Words

Stop, Drop, and Rhyme

Cut out the fire hydrants. Glue each fire hydrant beside the paw print with the rhyming word. Write your own words that rhyme with the word that has no match. Make your rhyming words about fire safety.

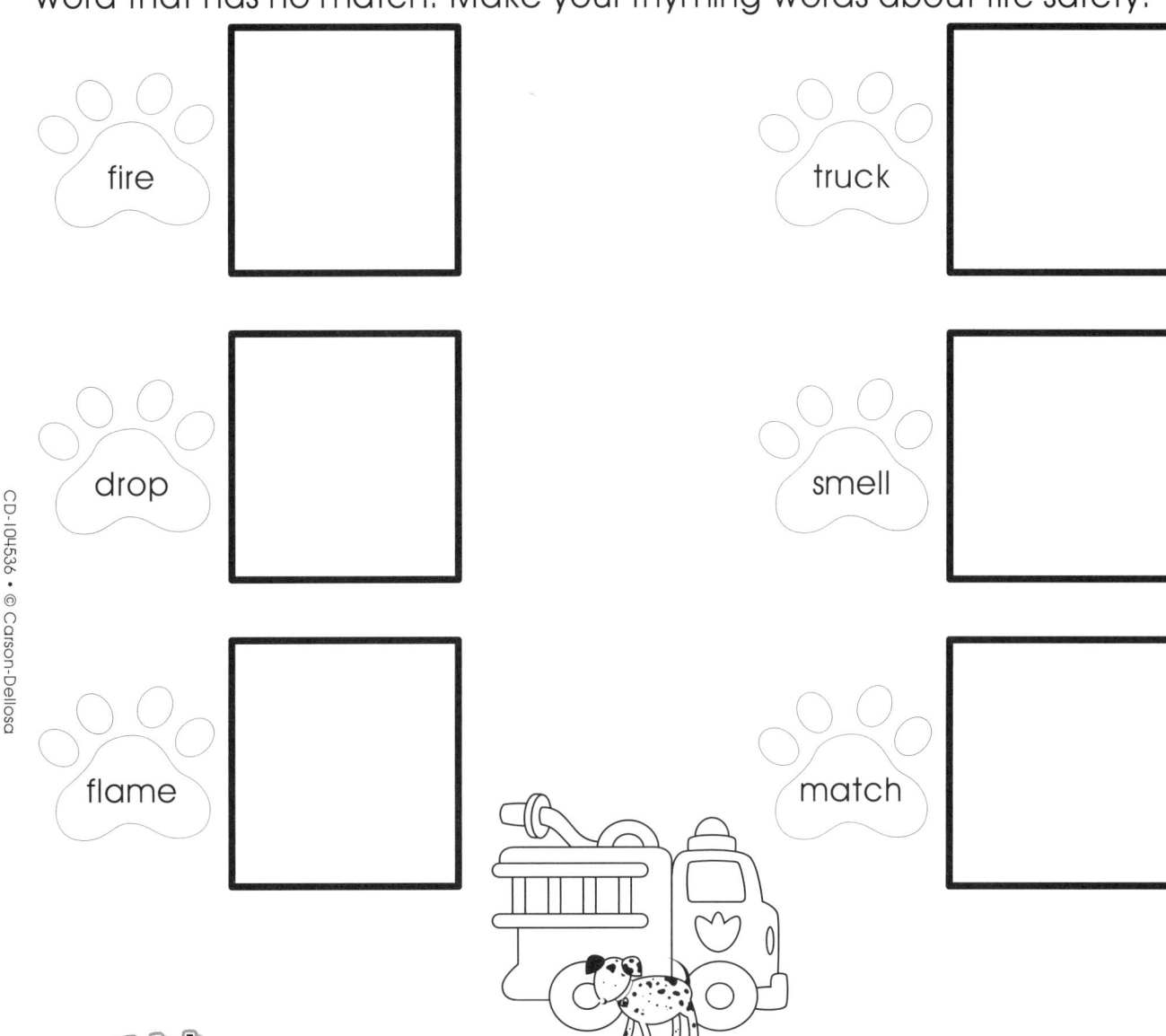

fire

truck

drop

smell

flame

match

Try This!

Create a fire safety poster. Use the words from above and from the word wall.

✂ cut

| wire | catch | stuck | game | bell |

Name: _____

Rhyming Words

Rhyming Rockets

Write a rhyming word from the word bank for each rocket.

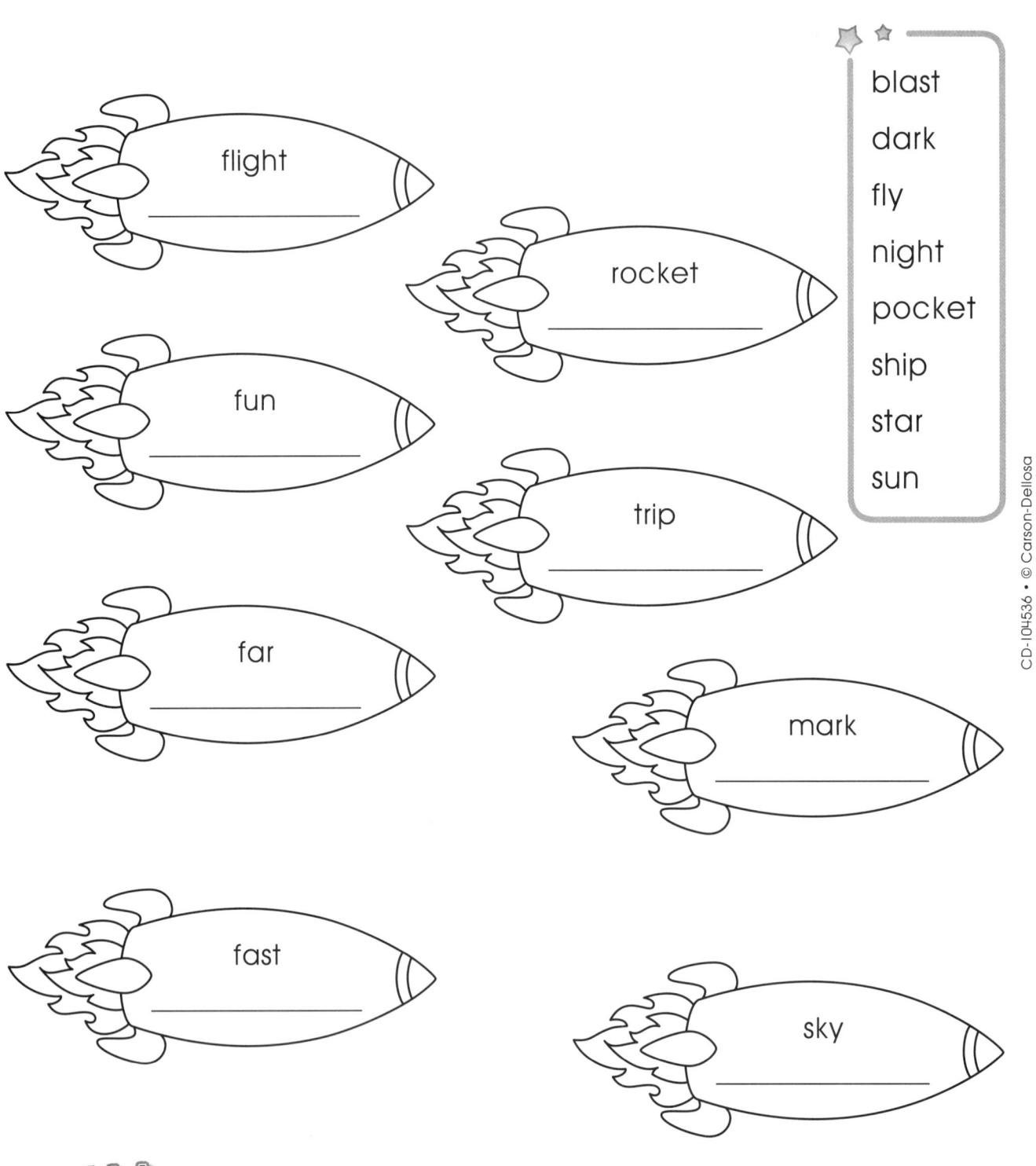

Word Bank:
- blast
- dark
- fly
- night
- pocket
- ship
- star
- sun

flight _____

rocket _____

fun _____

trip _____

far _____

mark _____

fast _____

sky _____

Try This! On a sheet of construction paper, draw a picture of our solar system. Label each planet.

Name: _____

Digraphs

Chocolate Chips with Lunch

Cut out the cookies. Glue each cookie on the correct cookie jar.

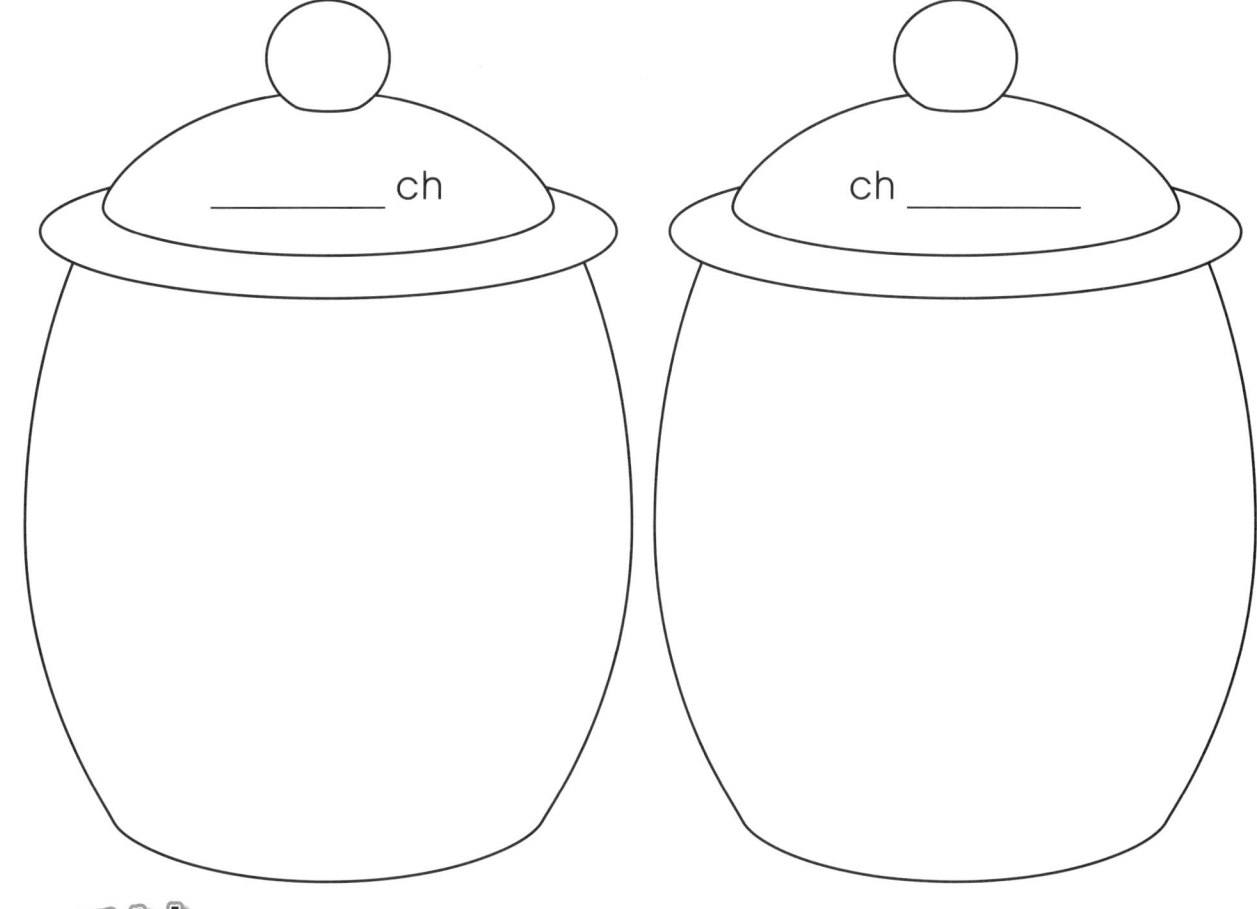

_____ ch

ch _____

Try This!

Work with a partner to create a healthful lunch menu. Draw or write your menu on a separate sheet of paper.

| check | cherries | watch |
| match | chair | sandwich |

Name: _____

Digraphs

Shells on the Seashore

Say the name of each picture. Use the code to color the shells.

> words that begin with the **/sh/** sound = pink
> words that end with the **/sh/** sound = brown
> words that do not have the **/sh/** sound = yellow

In this shell, draw a picture of something that has the **/sh/** sound in its name. Use the code to color the shell.

Try This!

On a separate sheet of paper, draw pictures of three things you might see at the beach that have the /sh/ sound in their names. Write the name of each picture.

58

Name: _____

Digraphs

Theo's Flower Garden Path

Cut out the pictures. Glue the pictures whose names begin with the **/th/** sound on Theo's path.

Try This!

On the back of this paper, write as many words as you can that have /th/ as the middle sound. Use the word wall to help you.

cut

| three | teeth | thermometer |
| thimble | thorn | earth |

Name: _____ Digraphs

Check Out These Sounds

Write the beginning digraph for each word.

1. cheek _____   2. chop _____   3. shovel _____

4. think _____   5. wheel _____   6. thumb _____

Circle the beginning digraph for each picture's name.

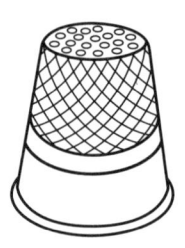

ch   sh   wh   th   sh   ch   th   wh   sh

Write the name of each picture. Circle the beginning digraph.

_____   _____   _____

Try This!
Look around the classroom. On a separate sheet of paper, list all of the things whose names begin with *ch*, *sh*, *th*, or *wh*.

Name: _____

Digraphs

Listen to the Fish

Use the code to color the fish.

ch = yellow **sh** = red **th** = green **wh** = brown

Fish labels: whale, sandwich, trash, teeth, moth, whisk, couch, dish, chair

Try This!

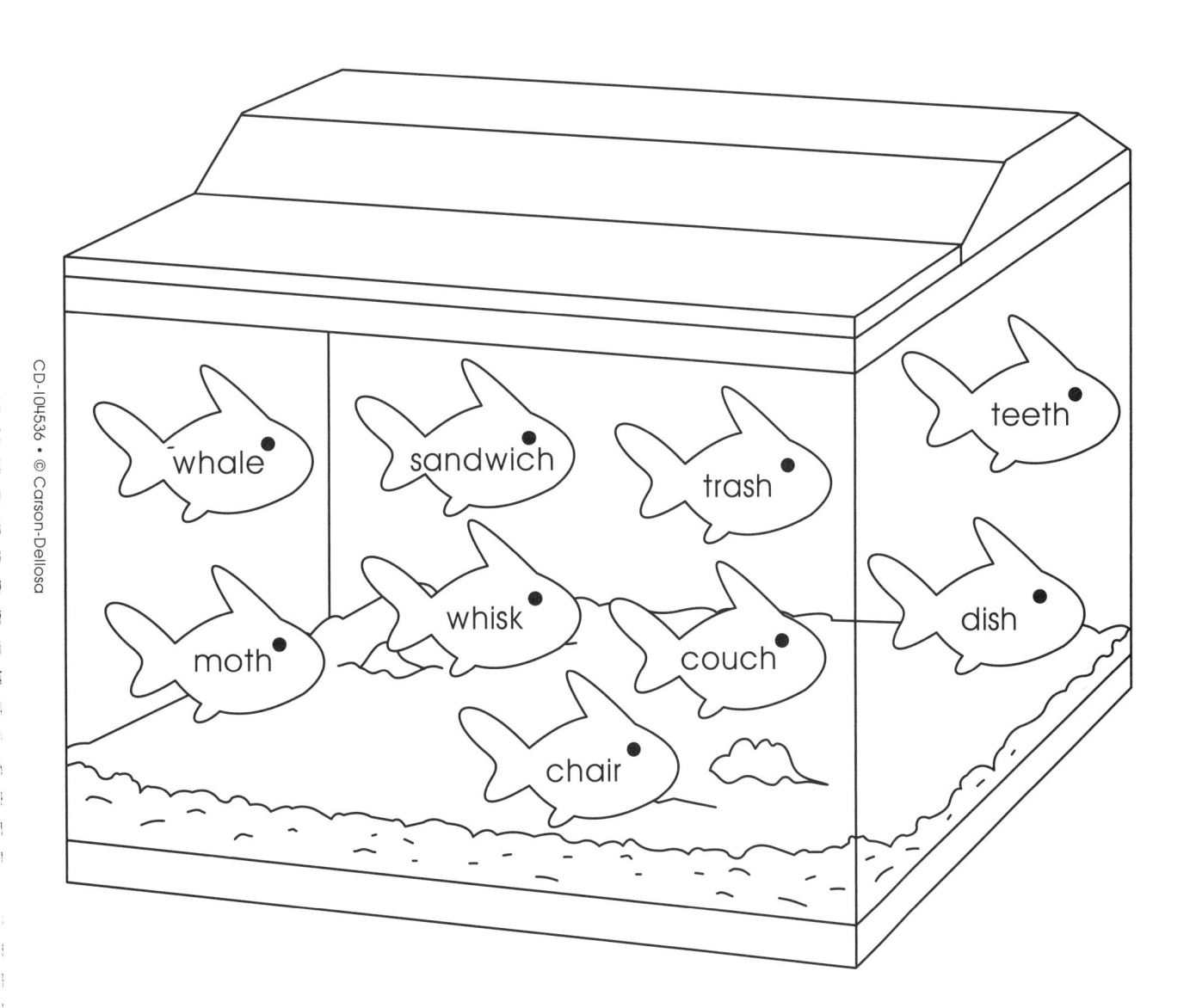

Write three words that each end with a different digraph: *ch*, *sh*, and *th*.

Name: _____

Digraphs

Ring and Sing

Write the letters **ng** to complete each word. Find and circle the words in the word search.

1. wro _____
2. bri _____
3. ra _____

4. stro _____
5. stu _____
6. wi _____

```
w  r  o  n  g  r
i  l  i  o  s  s
n  r  a  n  g  t
g  d  y  e  w  u
b  r  i  n  g  n
s  t  r  o  n  g
```

Try This!
Use construction paper to make a book of *ng* words. Cut the paper in half and staple the pages to make a book. On each page, draw and color a picture of a word that ends with *ng*.

Name: _____   Digraphs

It All Ends Up Here

Fill in the circle for each word that has the digraph **ch**, **sh**, **th**, **wh**, or **ng**.

○ whisk   ○ wheat   ○ moth   ○ thumb

○ strong   ○ hat   ○ bee   ○ dish

Say the name of each picture. Circle the correct digraph.

 sh ch	 ng wh	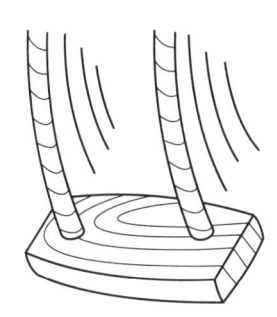 wh ng
 ch th	 th sh	 wh th

Try This!
On a separate sheet of paper, write a story that contains at least 10 words that end with a digraph. Ask a friend to read your story and circle the digraphs.

Name: _____

Digraphs

Picking Out Sounds

Cut out the apples. Glue each apple on the correct picture. Use the code to color the apples.

apples that have the /sh/ sound = red
apples that have the /th/ sound = green
apples that have the /ch/ sound = yellow
apples that have the /ng/ sound = pink

Digraph at the Beginning   Digraph at the End

Try This!
On the back of this paper, write three facts about apples.

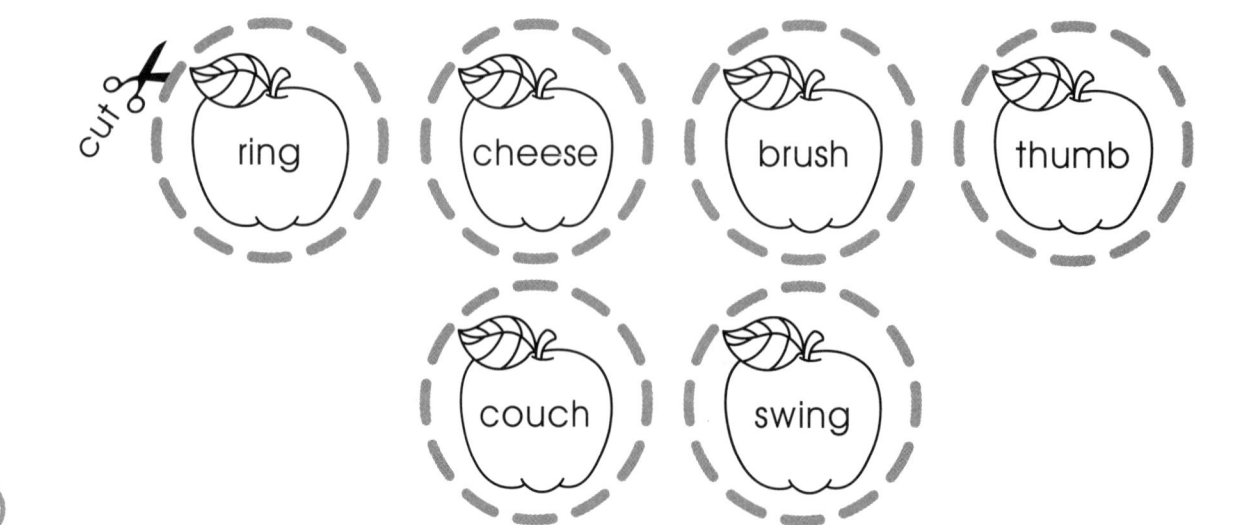

cut

ring   cheese   brush   thumb

couch   swing

64

Name: _____   ow

Do Cows Throw Snowballs?

Sort the words into the correct columns.

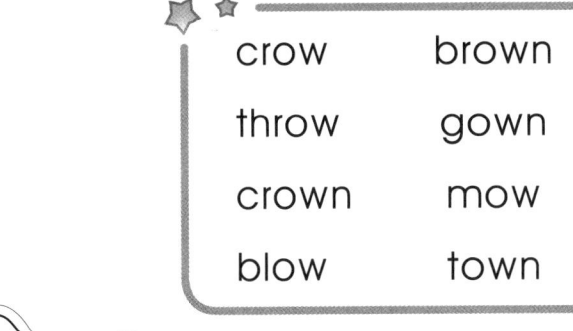

crow	brown
throw	gown
crown	mow
blow	town

/ow/ as in cow

/ow/ as in snow

_____ _____
_____ _____
_____ _____
_____ _____

Write a sentence that uses one word from each column.

_____
_____

Try This! On a separate sheet of paper, write a tongue twister using *ow* words. Challenge a friend to say it as quickly as possible.

Name: _____

oo

Raccoon's Balloon

Help the raccoon find his balloon. Color the stepping-stones if the words have the /oo/ sound, as in **moon**.

- igloo
- spoon
- moon
- baboon
- pool
- school
- hook
- broom
- spool
- look
- took
- tool
- brook
- cook
- snoop
- wood
- good
- boot
- moose
- stool
- goose

Try This!
On a separate sheet of paper, write a story about the raccoon and his balloon. Use at least five of the /oo/ sound words above.

66

Name: _____

Vowel Patterns

Cool Sounds in an Igloo

Underline the correct spelling of each word. Circle the correct vowel pattern.

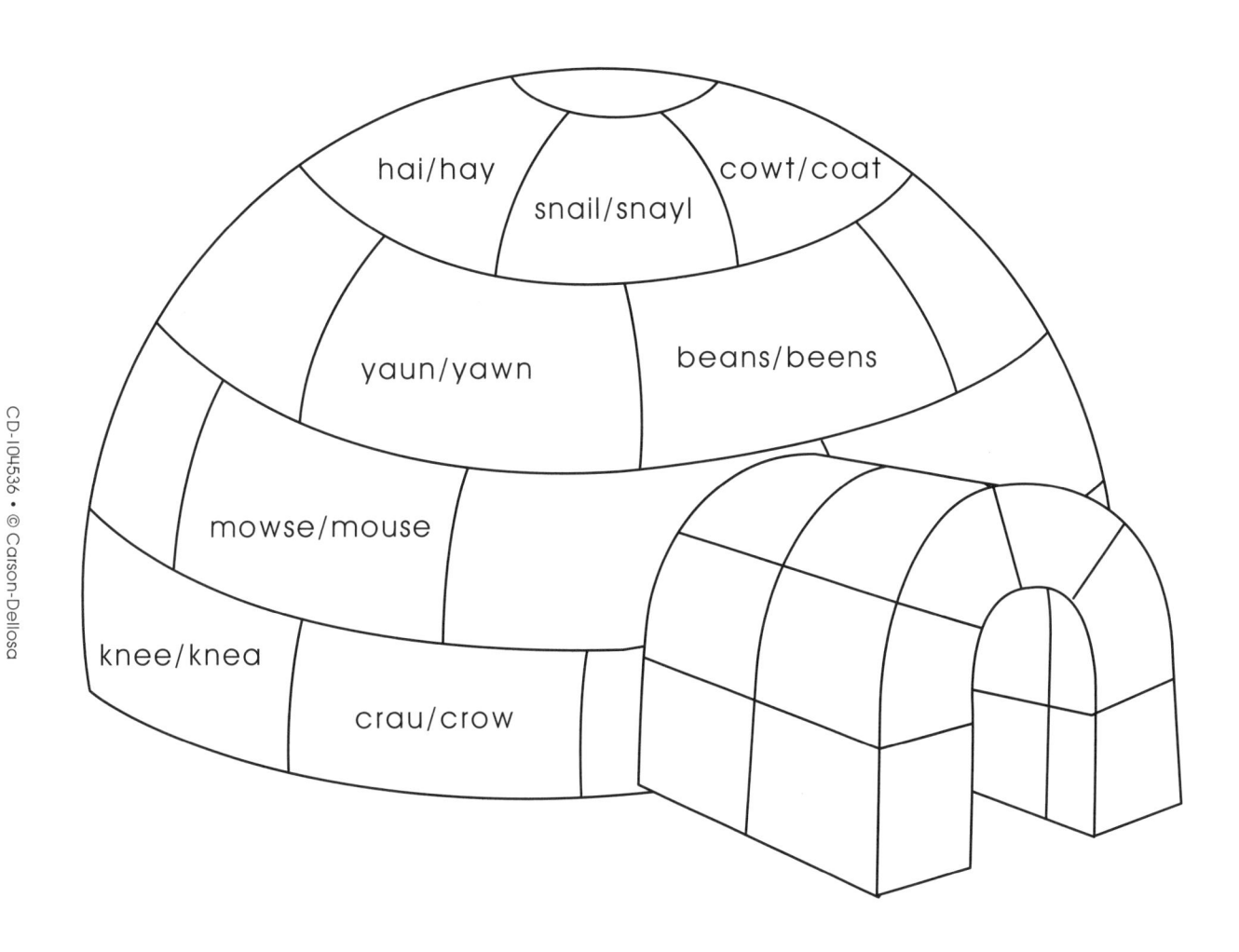

- hai/hay
- snail/snayl
- cowt/coat
- yaun/yawn
- beans/beens
- mowse/mouse
- knee/knea
- crau/crow

Write three words that have the **/oo/** sound, as in **cool**.

_____   _____   _____

Try This!
On a separate sheet of paper, write a story about igloos that includes at least three of the words above.

R-controlled Vowels

Name: _____

Stirring Up Vowels

Write the letters **ir** to complete each word.

sk __ __ t

sh __ __ t

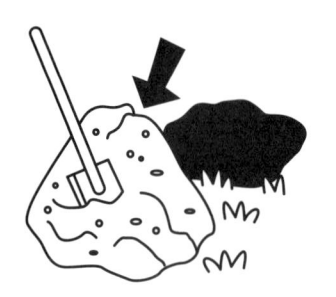

d __ __ t

ha __ __

Draw a circle around each picture whose name has the same sound as **stir**.

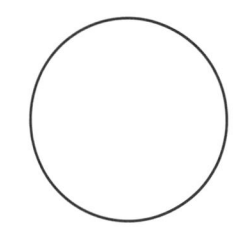

Try This!

For each picture not circled, write the r-controlled vowel sound you hear. Then, write at least two more r-controlled vowel sound words.

Name: _____   R-controlled Vowels

Ready for More

Circle the letters **or** in each word. Draw a line to match each word to the correct picture.

porch

acorn

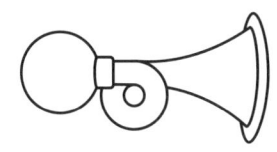

storm

cord

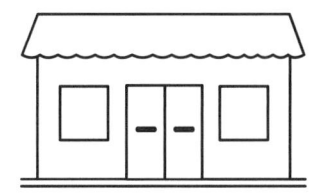

stork

store

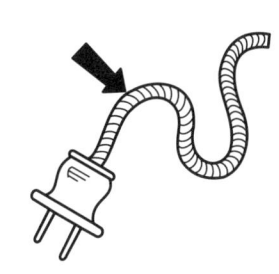

corn

horn

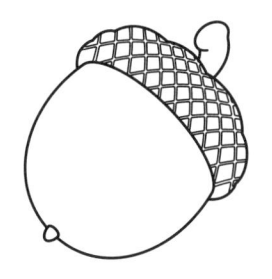

Try This!
On a separate sheet of paper, write the above words in ABC order.

Name: _____   R-controlled Vowels

It's My Turn

Write the word from the word bank that names each picture.

nurse   purse   turnip   turtle

_____   _____

_____   _____

Read each sentence. Circle the **ur** word in each sentence.

1. We had turkey for dinner.

2. The school nurse treated me.

3. Please return the books to Tim.

4. I hurt my leg when I fell.

5. Will you please turn on the radio?

Try This!
On a separate sheet of paper, draw a picture to illustrate one of the above sentences. Circle the sentence that you illustrated.

Name: _____

R-controlled Vowels

All About Turtle

Use the code to color the turtle shell.

ar word = brown **ir** word = green
or word = yellow **ur** word = purple

- nurse
- skirt
- corn
- purse
- yarn
- car
- barn
- fork
- turkey
- bird
- curtain
- star
- horn

Try This!
On a separate sheet of paper, draw a comic strip about a turtle. Include at least five r-controlled words in the speech bubbles.

Name: _____

Color Words

A Colorful World

Write the color word for each picture. Color each picture the correct color.

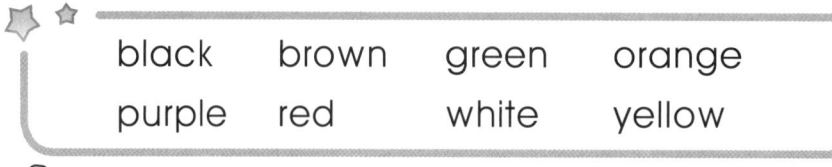

black	brown	green	orange
purple	red	white	yellow

1.  [cherry]

_____

2.  [banana]

_____

3.  [pumpkin]

_____

4.  [grapes]

_____

5. 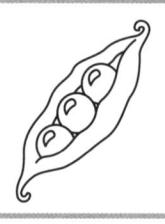 [peas in pod]

_____

6.  [log]

_____

7.  [polar bear]

_____

8.  [tire]

_____

Try This!

What color is made when blue and yellow are mixed? On a separate sheet of paper, mix different paints to create all of the color combinations that you know.

Name: _____

Directional Words

On Mother's Day

Circle the correct word to complete each sentence. Write the words on the lines.

Mother's Day is celebrated _____ the month of May.

up **on** **in**

I give my mom a kiss _____ her cheek.

up **on** **in**

We put flowers _____ a vase.

up **on** **in**

We hold _____ our sign.

up **on** **in**

Try This!

Use construction paper to make a Mother's Day card. Write a message that includes all three directional words above.

Name: _____ Synonyms

Wonderful and Great Crossword Puzzle

Use the synonyms from the word bank to complete the puzzle.

| friend | kind | near | noisy |
| plate | small | smile | tidy |

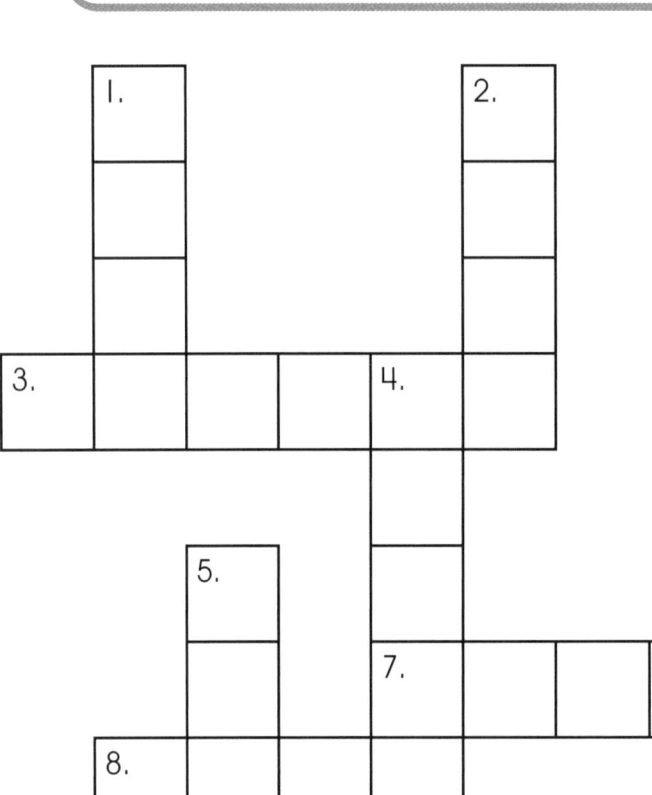

Across
3. pal
7. little
8. neat

Down
1. close
2. nice
4. loud
5. grin
6. dish

Try This!
On a separate sheet of paper, create and decorate a synonym bookmark. On your bookmark, write as many words as you can think of that mean the same as the word *good*.

Name: _____

Synonyms

Study and Learn with Synonyms

Draw lines to match the synonyms.

loud   sloppy

neat   laugh

giggle   noisy

messy   tidy

Cut out the pictures. Glue to match the synonyms.

happy	ill
angry	below

Try This!

On the back of this paper, write five synonyms for the word *nice*. Then, rewrite the following sentence using one of your words.
I had a **nice** piece of cake after dinner.

✂ cut

under   glad    mad    sick

75

Name: _____   Antonyms

Opposites Attract

Unscramble the words. Draw lines to match the antonyms.

tlef _____   yda   _____

ghnti _____   rghti _____

rdy   _____   asd   _____

hyapp _____   etw   _____

Draw a picture to show each word.

left	day
night	right
dry	sad
happy	wet

Try This!

On a separate sheet of paper, draw or write opposites for the words *mean*, *up*, and *hot*.

Name: _____   Antonyms

Antonyms Are All Around

Cut and glue to match the antonyms.

in    little    hard

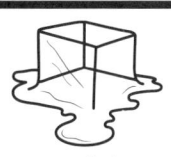

cold    back 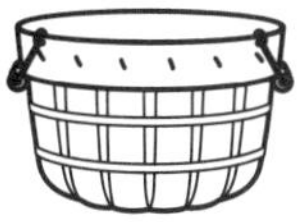   empty

Try This!
On the back of this paper, draw a picture of your favorite food. Write five words that describe the food. Then, write an antonym for each word.

cut

front    out    full

big    hot 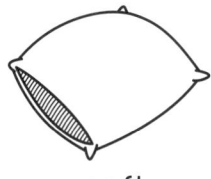   soft

Name: _____

Synonyms and Antonyms

Same or Different

Use the code to color the balloons.

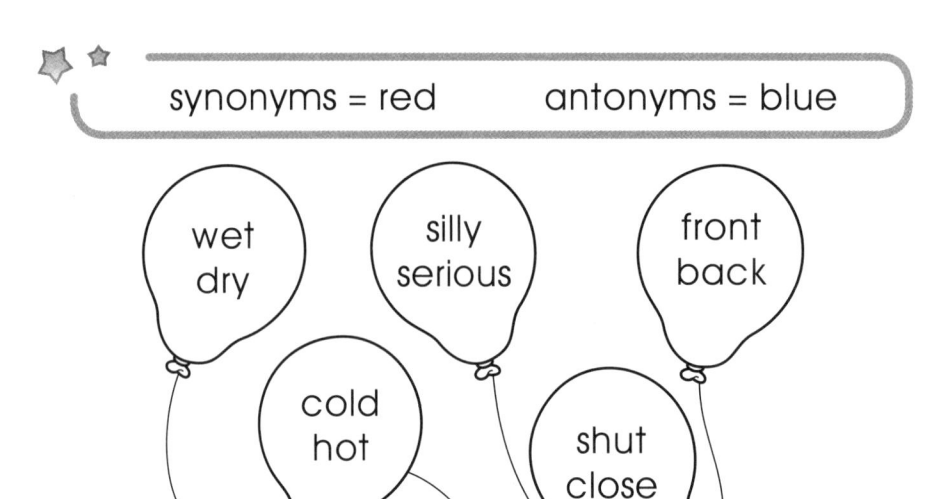

synonyms = red   antonyms = blue

- wet / dry
- silly / serious
- front / back
- cold / hot
- shut / close
- smart / clever

Complete the table for each word.

Word	Synonym	Antonym
nice		
tidy		

Try This!

Work with a partner to create a new type of shoe. Draw and decorate the shoe on a sheet of construction paper. Write a list of words beside the picture that describe the shoe.

Name: _____ Compound Words

Double Word Fun

Write the two words that make up each compound word.

doghouse _____ + _____

ladybug _____ + _____

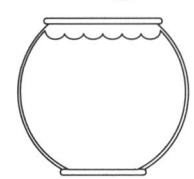

fishbowl _____ + _____

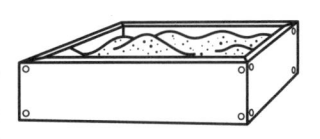

sandbox _____ + _____

rainbow _____ + _____

suitcase _____ + _____

Draw a line to match each word pair that makes up a compound word.

cup	shine
sun	boat
fire	cake
sail	fly

Try This!

On a separate sheet of paper, draw pictures to illustrate the four compound words made in the second part of the activity.

Name: _____

Compound Words

For the Love of Words

Cut out the heart halves. Glue the heart halves next to the words that make compound words. Write the compound words on the lines.

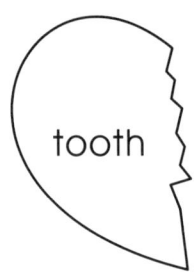

tooth   gold   pan

_____   _____   _____

swim   air   rain

_____   _____   _____

Try This!

Cut out heart shapes from red construction paper. Make your own compound word puzzles and have a friend solve them.

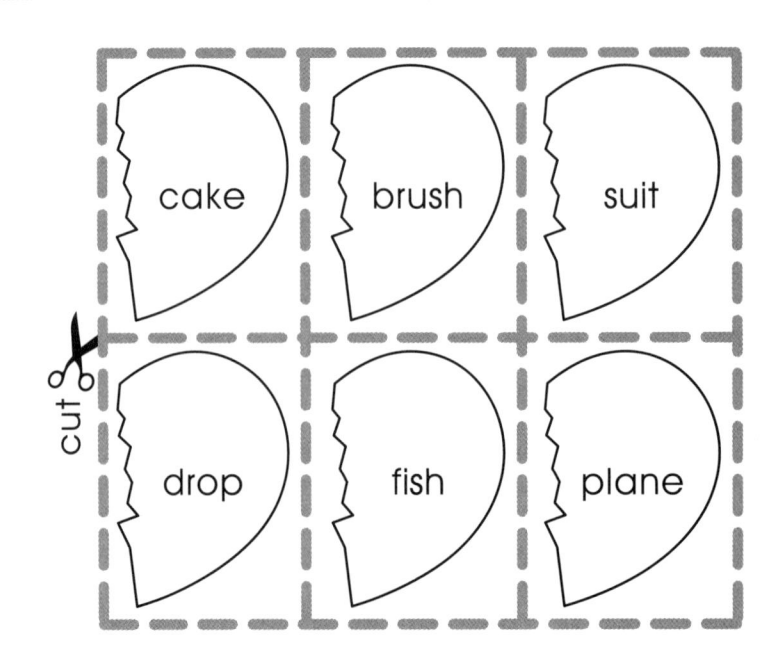

cake   brush   suit

cut

drop   fish   plane

Name: _____

Compound Words

Double Your Word Power

Write words from the word bank to make compound words.

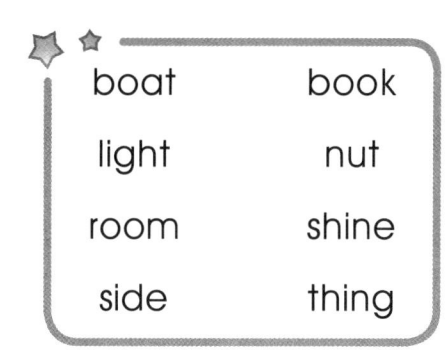

> boat　book
> light　nut
> room　shine
> side　thing

1. bed + _____ = _____

2. note + _____ = _____

3. out + _____ = _____

4. pea + _____ = _____

5. sail + _____ = _____

6. some + _____ = _____

7. stop + _____ = _____

8. sun + _____ = _____

Try This!

Make up your own silly compound word. On a separate sheet of paper, write the word and what it would mean. Then, draw a picture of what it would look like. For example, *cat + flower = catflower*.

Name: _____   Contractions

Clear About Contractions

Write the contraction that means the opposite of each word.

1. should _____   2. can _____

3. will _____   4. did _____

5. is _____   6. do _____

7. could _____   8. does _____

Write the two words that make each contraction.

9. don't   10. haven't   11. wouldn't

_____ _____   _____ _____   _____ _____

Try This!

Read a page of a book and count how many contractions you find. Write the contractions on a separate sheet of paper.

Name: _____   Contractions

I'll Brush My Teeth

Write the contraction from the word bank to complete each sentence.

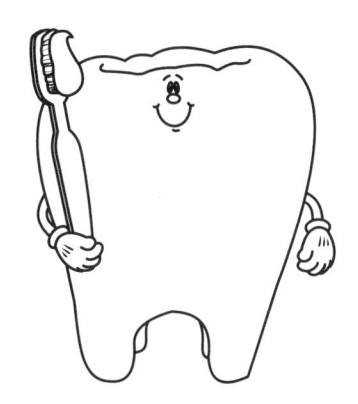

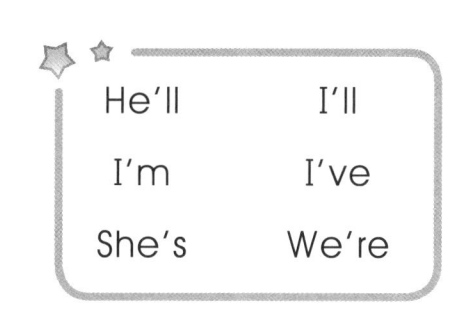

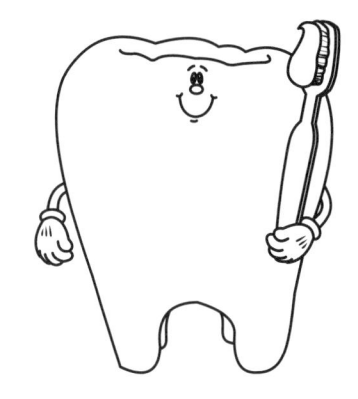

He'll	I'll
I'm	I've
She's	We're

1. (We are) _____ going to the dentist today.

2. (I will) _____ brush my teeth before bed.

3. (She is) _____ going to floss her teeth.

4. (I am) _____ not going to eat too much sugar.

5. (He will) _____ get a cavity if he does not take care of his teeth.

6. (I have) _____ never had a cavity.

Try This! Use construction paper to create your own dental health poster. Use crayons to decorate your poster. Write some things you should do every day to keep your teeth healthy, such as brush and floss.

Name: _____

Contractions

He's Hiding!

Cut out the groundhogs. Glue each groundhog to the hole that matches the contraction. Glue the unused groundhogs to holes 5 and 6. Write the words that make those contractions.

1. I [hole] will
2. you [hole] are
3. he [hole] is
4. we [hole] have
5. ____ [hole] ____
6. ____ [hole] ____

Try This!
On the back of this paper, write three sentences about Groundhog Day. Include at least one contraction in each sentence.

cut

| we've | I'm | he's |
| won't | you're | I'll |

Name: _____   Vocabulary

Way to Grow!

Write each word below the correct picture. Cut out the pictures and glue them in the correct order.

1. seed

2. sprout

3. plant

4. flower

Try This!

Pumpkins are known for their orange color. Look around the classroom. How many objects can you see that are orange? On a separate sheet of paper, write a list of the orange objects.

cut

_____   _____

_____   _____

Name: _____   Vocabulary

Sunglasses or Sleds?

Write each word on the line below the correct picture.

> rainy   cloudy   sunny   foggy   snowy

Write a sentence about your favorite kind of weather.
_____
_____

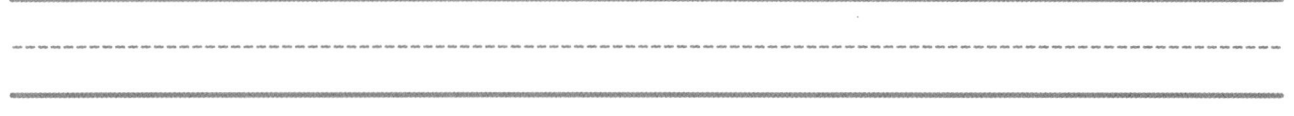

Try This!

How does the weather change from January to October? On a separate sheet of paper, explain your answer.

Name: _____   Sequencing

Busy Birds

Write **1** in front of the picture that comes first. Write **2** in front of the picture that comes next. Write **3** in front of the picture that comes last.

What do you think will happen next? Draw your answer in the box.

Try This!

On a separate sheet of paper, draw and number the steps you go through to get ready for school each day.

Name: _____

Sequencing

Leaves and More Leaves

Color and cut out the pictures. Glue the pictures in order.

1. First

2. Then

3. Next

4. Last

Try This!

On the back of this paper, draw pictures and write sentences about how the weather changes through the seasons. Use the words *First*, *Then*, *Next*, and *Last*.

cut

88

Name: _____

Sequencing

Mixed-Up Story

Cut out the pictures. Glue them on a separate sheet of paper in the right order to tell a story. Write a title for the story.

He rode his bike to the park.

He put his new bike away.

He rode back home.

Logan got a new bike.

Try This!

Work with a partner to draw a map that shows all of the places Logan will ride his bike to. Remember to show the park and his house.

Name: _____

Sequencing

Time for Art

Write **first**, **then**, **next**, or **last** under each picture. Cut out the pictures. On a separate sheet of paper, glue the pictures in the correct order.

Try This!

On a separate sheet of paper, draw and number the steps you go through to get ready for bed each night.

Name: _____

Sequencing

Rainy Day

Write **1**, **2**, **3**, and **4** to order the sentences. Draw pictures to illustrate the story in the empty box.

_____ A few raindrops fell on the dry road.

_____ The road was all wet.

_____ More and more rain came down.

_____ Clouds began to fill the sky.

Try This!

On a separate sheet of paper, draw and label a picture of the water cycle. Remember to include *evaporation*, *condensation*, and *precipitation*.

Name: _____

Sequencing

Some Winter Fun

Cut out the sentences. Glue the sentences in order on a separate sheet of paper. Draw a picture to illustrate each sentence.

The snowman melted.

Dark clouds covered the blue sky.

The warm sun came out.

We built a snowman.

Our lawn had a new coat of white snow.

Big, fat flakes of snow came down.

Try This!

On a separate sheet of paper, write and number the steps for building a snowman.

Name: _____

Following Directions

Life on the Farm

Follow the directions.

1. Color the dog brown.
2. Draw a fish in the pond.
3. Draw a box around the cow.
4. Circle the barn.
5. Color the hen yellow.
6. Draw an apple in the tree.

Try This!

Label everything in the picture.

Name: _____

Following Directions

Wish You Were Here

Follow the directions.

1. Draw a fish in the lake.
2. Draw a whale in the ocean.
3. Draw a dog beside the river.
4. Draw a goat on the mountain.
5. Draw a bird on the island.
6. Color the picture.

Try This!

On a separate sheet of paper, draw and label a picture that includes a hill, a valley, a stream, and a pond.

Name: _____

Following Directions

Welcome Home!

Follow the directions.

1. Color the roof brown.
2. Color the chimney red.
3. Color the bushes green.
4. Draw a picture of your family inside the house.
5. Write your address at the bottom of the page.

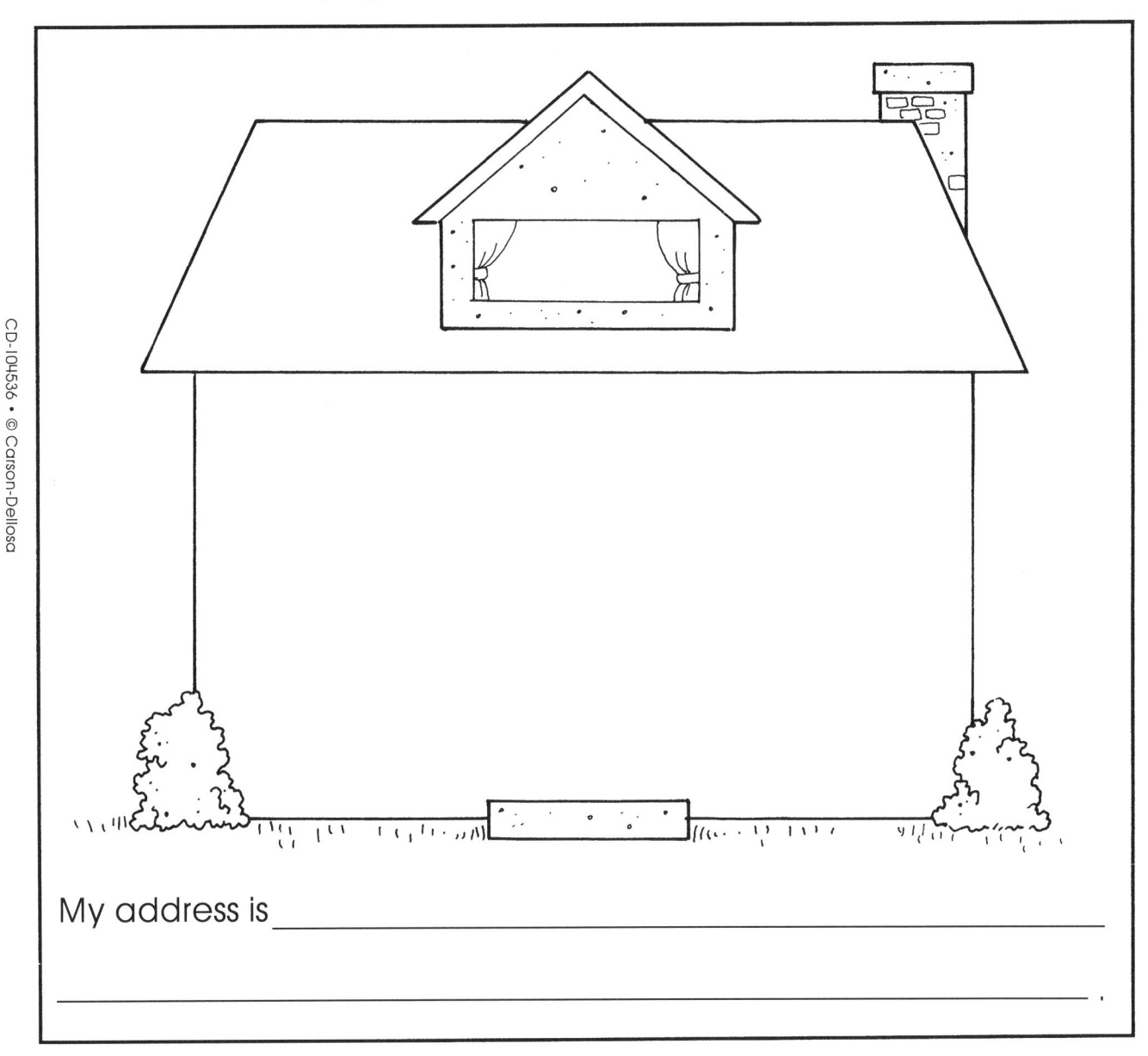

My address is _____
_____

Try This!
On a separate sheet of paper, write a paragraph about your family. Use describing words to tell about each person.

Name: _____

Following Directions

Dress the Snowman

Follow the directions.

1. Draw a hat on the snowman. Color the hat purple and orange.
2. Draw a coat on the snowman. Color the coat blue.
3. Draw boots on the snowman. Color the boots yellow.
4. Draw mittens on the snowman. Color the mittens green.

Try This!
On a separate sheet of paper, write five rules for staying safe when playing in the snow. Draw a picture to illustrate each rule.

Name: _____

Following Directions

My Robot

Follow the directions.

1. Color the hands and the arms yellow.
2. Write your name on the biggest rectangle.
3. Draw a red smile on the face.
4. Draw green dots on the body.
5. Color the feet purple.
6. Color all of the triangles orange.

Try This!
On a separate sheet of paper, explain what you would use the robot for.

Name: _____   Following Directions

To the Moon!

Follow the directions.

1. If the moon is made of snow, write an **s**. _____

   If it is made of rock, write an **r**. _____

2. If men have walked on the moon, write an **o**. _____

   If an old man lives on the moon, write a **b**. _____

3. If the moon always looks round, write an **s**. _____

   If it does not, write a **w**. _____

Write your letters on the lines to spell a word. The same word will fit in all of the blanks.

_____ _____ _____
      1   2   3

Pretty maids all in a _____.

_____, _____, _____ your boat.

Try This!

On a separate sheet of paper, list three things you would find in space other than the moon.

Name: _____

Understanding Text

B Is for Blueberry

Cut out the pictures. Glue each picture where it belongs. Write the numbers **1** to **4** in the boxes to show the order that the blueberries grow.

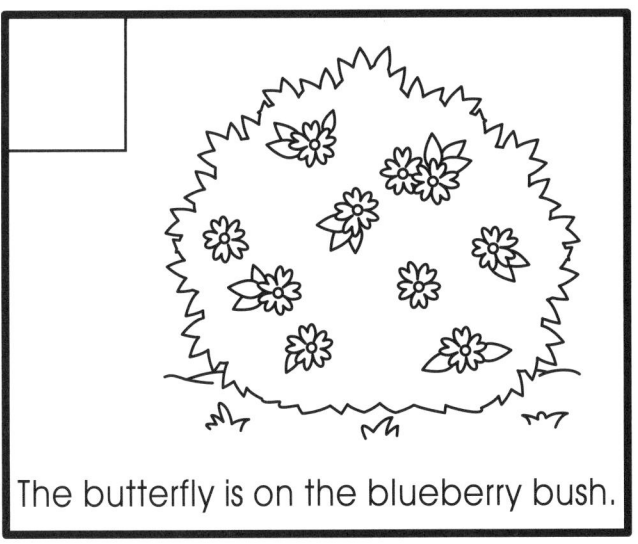

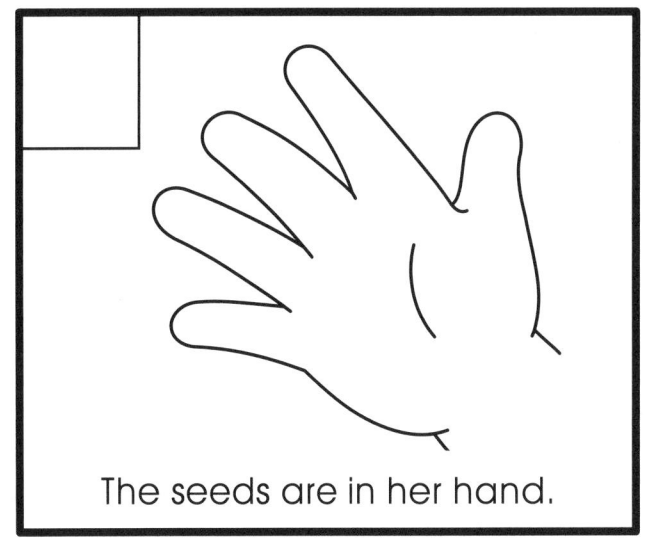

The blueberries are in the basket.	The ladybug is on the sprout.
The butterfly is on the blueberry bush.	The seeds are in her hand.

Try This!

On the back of this paper, draw and label the life cycle of a blueberry. Write a sentence telling about whether you like to eat blueberries.

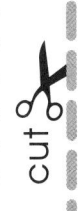

cut

Name: _____

Understanding Text

Web Spinners

Read the paragraph. Answer the questions.

There are many kinds of spiders. Spiders have eight legs. They like to eat insects. Many spiders spin webs. The web is the spider's home. Have you ever seen a spiderweb?

eight   four

Spiders have _____ legs.

web   week

A spider spins a _____.

home   kite

The web is a spider's _____.

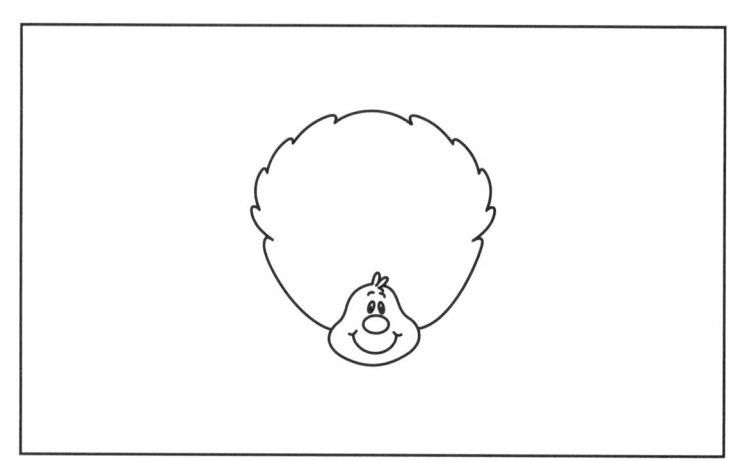

What do spiders eat? ☐ insects   ☐ jelly

Draw eight legs on this spider.
Draw a web for this spider.

Try This!
Where have you seen a spider build a web? Draw a picture of a spiderweb you have seen.

Name: _____

Understanding Text

Feelings Matter

Read the paragraph. Answer the questions.

People can have many feelings. They can feel happy. They can feel sad. People can feel angry. Everyone has feelings. Faces show feelings. How do you feel today?

five   feelings

People have many _____.

Write the emotion for each person.

happy
angry
sad

_____

_____

_____

Draw a face for each emotion.

happy   sad   angry

Try This!
On a separate sheet of paper, draw and color a picture of how you feel today. Share your picture with a friend.

Name: _____   Understanding Text

Is It So?

Circle **yes** if the sentence tells about the picture. Circle **no** if it does not.

yes no	yes no
The running shoe is very old.	The tree has lost its leaves.

yes no	yes no
The soup smells good.	Two butterflies sit on flowers.

Draw a picture that shows this sentence.

The snake is lying on a rock.

★ **Try This!** ★
Play "Is It So?" with a partner. Each person draws a picture on a separate sheet of paper. Swap papers and ask each other questions about the pictures.

Name: _____   Main Idea

We Like to Play

Read the stories. Write the main idea of each story.

Joe went to the park. He went down the slide. He had lunch on a picnic table. He went on the swings after lunch.

_____

Tara wore a princess dress. She put on a crown. She looked in the mirror. Tara loves to play dress-up.

_____

Try This!
Choose one of the stories above and continue the story on a separate sheet of paper.

Name: _____

True/False

Bear Is Busy

Circle **true** if the sentence tells about the picture. Circle **false** if it does not.

true   false

1. It is a very hot day.

true   false

2. The hat is too small.

true   false

3. The bear walks to school.

true   false

4. The bear washed three shirts.

Try This!

Work with a partner to practice finding the main idea. Each person draws a picture on a separate sheet of paper. Swap papers. Above the picture, write the main idea of the picture.

Name: _____   Fiction/Nonfiction

Can You Believe It?

Read each sentence. If the sentence tells something that could really happen, check **nonfiction**. If the sentence tells something that is make-believe, check **fiction**.

	Fiction	Nonfiction
1. A bear can live in a forest.	○	○
2. A bear can search in a store for a lost button.	○	○
3. A bear can sew a button on a shirt.	○	○
4. A bear can catch a fish.	○	○
5. A bear can talk to a girl.	○	○
6. A bear can have a cub.	○	○
7. A bear can climb a tree.	○	○
8. A bear and a puppy can be friends.	○	○
9. A bear sleeps in a bed.	○	○

Try This!
Write the titles of five books. Sort the titles into fiction and nonfiction books. Ask a friend to check your work.

Name: _____   Context Clues

Be Earth's Friend

Write the word from the word bank to complete each sentence.

> cans   clothes   groceries
> off   running

1. I bring my _____ home in reusable cloth bags.

2. We put our empty soft drink _____ in the recycling bin.

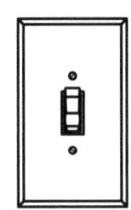

3. You should turn _____ the lights when you leave the room.

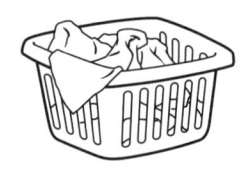

4. My mom gives my _____ to charity when they are too small.

5. Don't leave the water _____ when brushing your teeth.

Try This!
Sort the above sentences: Draw a circle around the number if the sentence tells about recycling. Draw a square around the number if the sentence tells about reusing. Draw a triangle around the number if the sentence tells about reducing.

Name: _____ Context Clues

A Dog's Life

Circle the word that correctly completes each sentence.

1. Dogs have been around for a _____ time.

   men   long   him

2. _____ are more than 400 kinds of dogs.

   There   From   This

3. Dogs _____ us in many ways.

   word   that   help

4. Dogs _____ work.

   be   more   can

Reorder the words to make a sentence.

play   will   Some   fetch.   dogs

_____

Try This!

Work with a partner to make a dog care poster. On construction paper, draw or write five things that people can do to take care of dogs.

Name: _____   Context Clues

Caterpillar Clues

Write the word that correctly completes each sentence.

The butterfly lays one _____ on a milkweed leaf. friend cent egg	The egg hatches into a _____. leaf caterpillar bird
The hungry caterpillar eats the _____. leaf pizza butterfly	The caterpillar grows and is soon ready to _____. shop swim change
It forms a _____ chrysalis. green apple car	The caterpillar is now a _____. rabbit butterfly fish

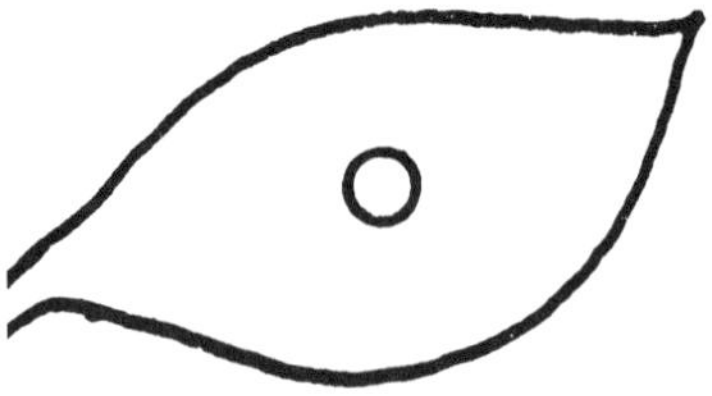

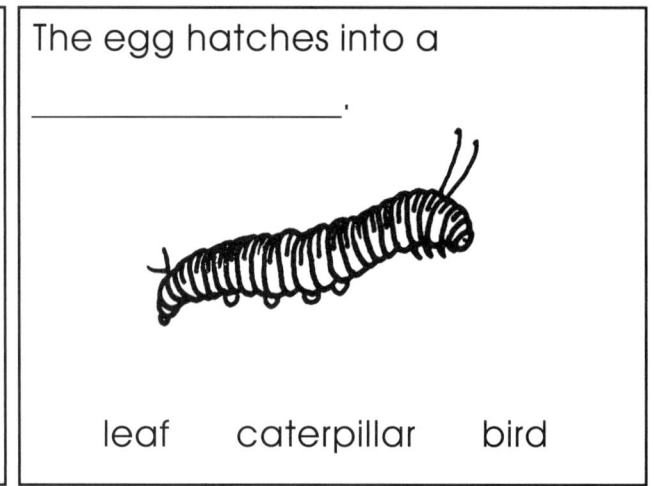

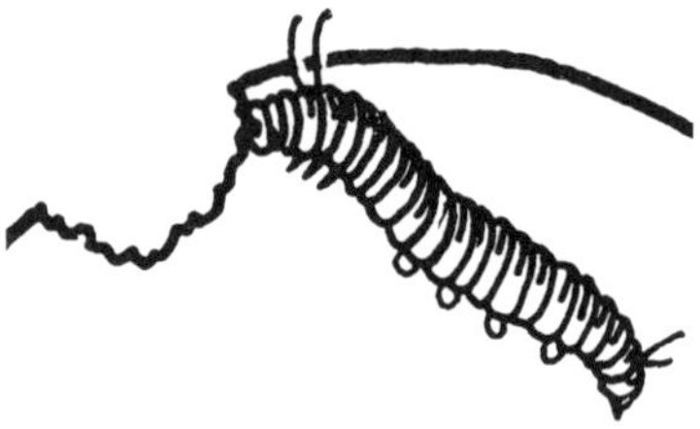

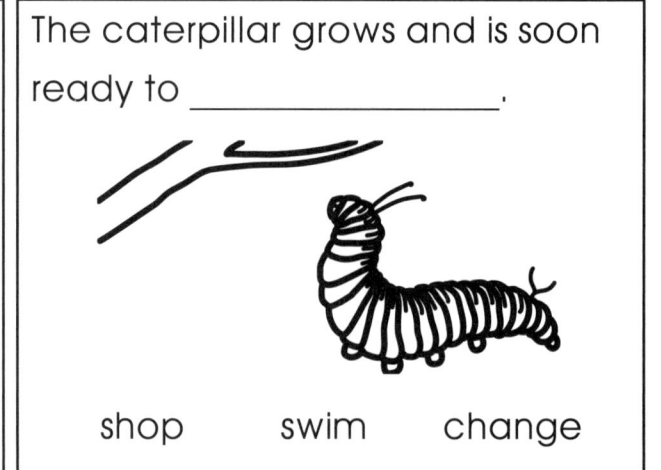

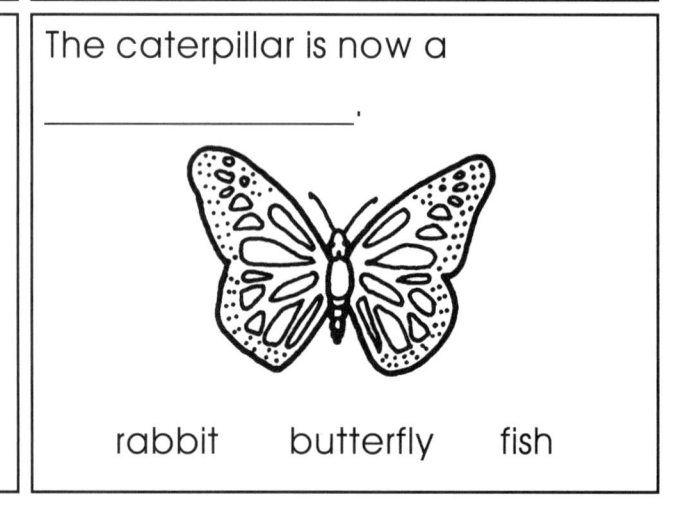

Try This!
Cut out the boxes and staple them into a booklet. Add a page at the end that illustrates the butterfly life cycle.

Name: _____   Context Clues

Animal Puzzlers

Use the words from the word bank to solve the puzzle.

> held   keep   kind
> live   make   under

Across

3. Bees _____ in hives.
4. A cat is one _____ of pet.
5. Ants live _____ the ground.

Down

1. Some birds _____ nests.
2. The dog _____ the bone in his mouth.
4. Hens sit on eggs to _____ them warm.

Try This!
On a separate sheet of paper, write each word in the word bank in a new sentence.

Name: _____   Reading for Details

Fun Fox Facts

Read the paragraph. Answer the questions.

> A fox can live in the woods, near a farm, or in the desert. Foxes can even live in the city. They run fast. They hunt for what they eat. They can have red, gray, or white fur. A baby fox is called a kit. A fox's home is called a den.

1. Name two places a fox can live.

   _____   _____

2. What colors of fur can foxes have?

   _____   _____   _____

3. How does a fox get food? _____

4. What is a fox home called? _____

Try This!
Use a sheet of construction paper to make a fox information poster. Draw a picture of a fox and write four to five facts on the poster.

Name: _____

Reading for Details

Packing Day for David

Read the story. Answer the questions.

> David has to move. His family found a new home in the city. David has to pack all of his toys. He will give away the old toys. He will place the newer toys in a big box.

1. Where did David's family find a new home?

   _____

   _____

2. What will he do with his newer toys?

   _____

   _____

3. What will he do with his old toys?

   _____

   _____

Try This!

On a separate sheet of paper, tell about a time you gave away a toy.

Name: _____   Compare and Contrast

Which Pet?

Read each sentence. If the sentence tells how dogs and cats are the same, write **S** on the line. If the sentence tells how dogs and cats are different, write **D** on the line.

1. Dogs and cats are animals. _____

2. Dogs bark, and cats meow. _____

3. Dogs and cats have four feet. _____

4. Dogs like to chew, and cats like to scratch. _____

5. Dogs and cats can be good pets. _____

Write your own sentence about how dogs and cats are different.

_____

_____

Try This!

Think of a friend or a family member. On a separate sheet of paper, write two ways you are the same and two ways you are different.

Name: _____   Cause and Effect

Out in the Cold

Write **C** in front of each sentence that tells about the cause. Write **E** in front of each sentence that tells about the effect. Write and label your own cause-and-effect sentence for number 4.

1. _____ Tom was cold.

   _____ He rubbed his hands together.

2. _____ The rubbing made his hands warm.

   _____ He rubbed his hands harder.

3. _____ He rubbed his hands faster.

   _____ That made his hands hot.

4. _____ Tom _____.

   _____ _____.

Try This!
On a separate sheet of paper, write about a time when you were cold. What caused you to feel cold? What did you do?

Name: _____ Cause and Effect

Tell Me Why

Read each pair of words. Which one is the cause? Which one is the effect? Write the words on the correct lines.

1. rain, wet

   cause _____   effect _____

2. hot, sun

   cause _____   effect _____

3. plant, seed

   cause _____   effect _____

Write a cause-and-effect sentence that uses one set of words from above.

_____

_____

Try This!
On a separate sheet of paper, write three causes and their effects.

Name: _____   Predicting Outcomes

Fun at the Zoo

Circle the ending that makes sense.

1. Jade's class was going on a trip. They were going to the zoo.

   A big bus came to get them.

   They all went home.

   They got on the bus.

   They went out to play.

2. They rode for a long time. Then, the bus came to a stop.

   They were at the zoo!

   They all got off the bus.

   They went to the store.

   They got on top of the bus.

Write an ending that makes sense.

   They went into the zoo. They went to see the lion.
   He had a big mane. He had big teeth.

   _____

   _____

Try This!
On a separate sheet of paper, list 15 animals you would see at the zoo.

Name: _____   Drawing Conclusions

Anna Is on Time!

Cut out the sentences. Glue each sentence under the correct picture.

Anna's alarm clock rings.	Anna picks up her books.

Anna is getting hungry.	Anna hears the school bell ring.

Try This!
Work with a partner to cut out a picture from a magazine or a newspaper. Each person should write a different conclusion for the same picture.

✂ cut

| It is time to get up. | It is time to go to school. |
| It is time to go home from school. | It is time to eat lunch. |

Name: _____   Word Categories

Sort Them Out

Circle the name of the animal that does not belong in each group. Write the letters beside the circled words to solve the riddle.

Birds
1. L   robin
   N   bluebird
   I   cow
   J   crow

Insects
2. L   snake
   A   ladybug
   N   wasp
   T   bee

Dogs
3. B   collie
   I   beagle
   S   shepherd
   L   ox

Reptiles
4. R   snake
   I   horse
   G   turtle
   W   alligator

Farm Animals
5. G   tiger
   K   pig
   O   cow
   Y   hen

Jungle Animals
6. J   lion
   B   cheetah
   U   tiger
   A   rat

Zoo Animals
7. M   bear
   O   giraffe
   T   dog
   F   zebra

Ocean Animals
8. H   octopus
   T   whale
   K   shark
   O   camel

Fish
9. R   raccoon
   I   salmon
   V   catfish
   L   tuna

What do you call a sick crocodile?

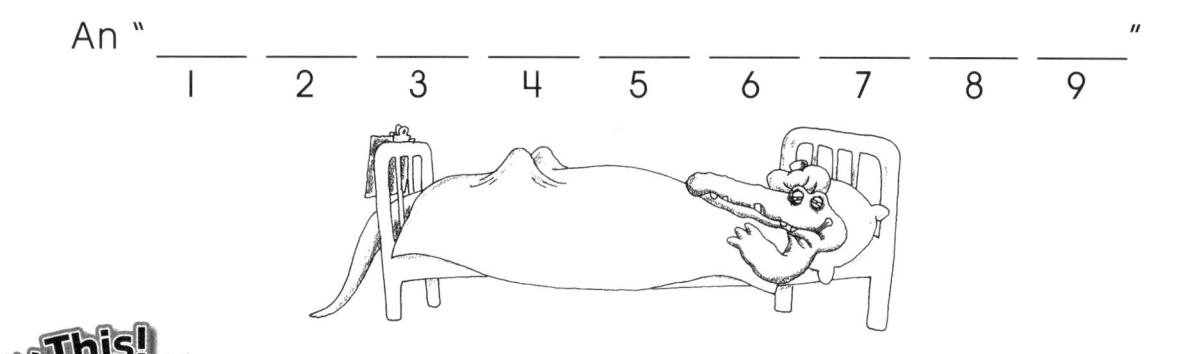

An " ___ ___ ___ ___ ___ ___ ___ ___ ___ "
     1   2   3   4   5   6   7   8   9

Try This!
On a separate sheet of paper, list five kinds of pets. Then, add one animal that is not a pet to your list. Ask a friend to read your list and circle the animal that does not belong.

Name: _____

Word Categories

Where to Wear?

Write each word in the correct column.

head	feet	hands
_____	_____	_____
_____	_____	_____

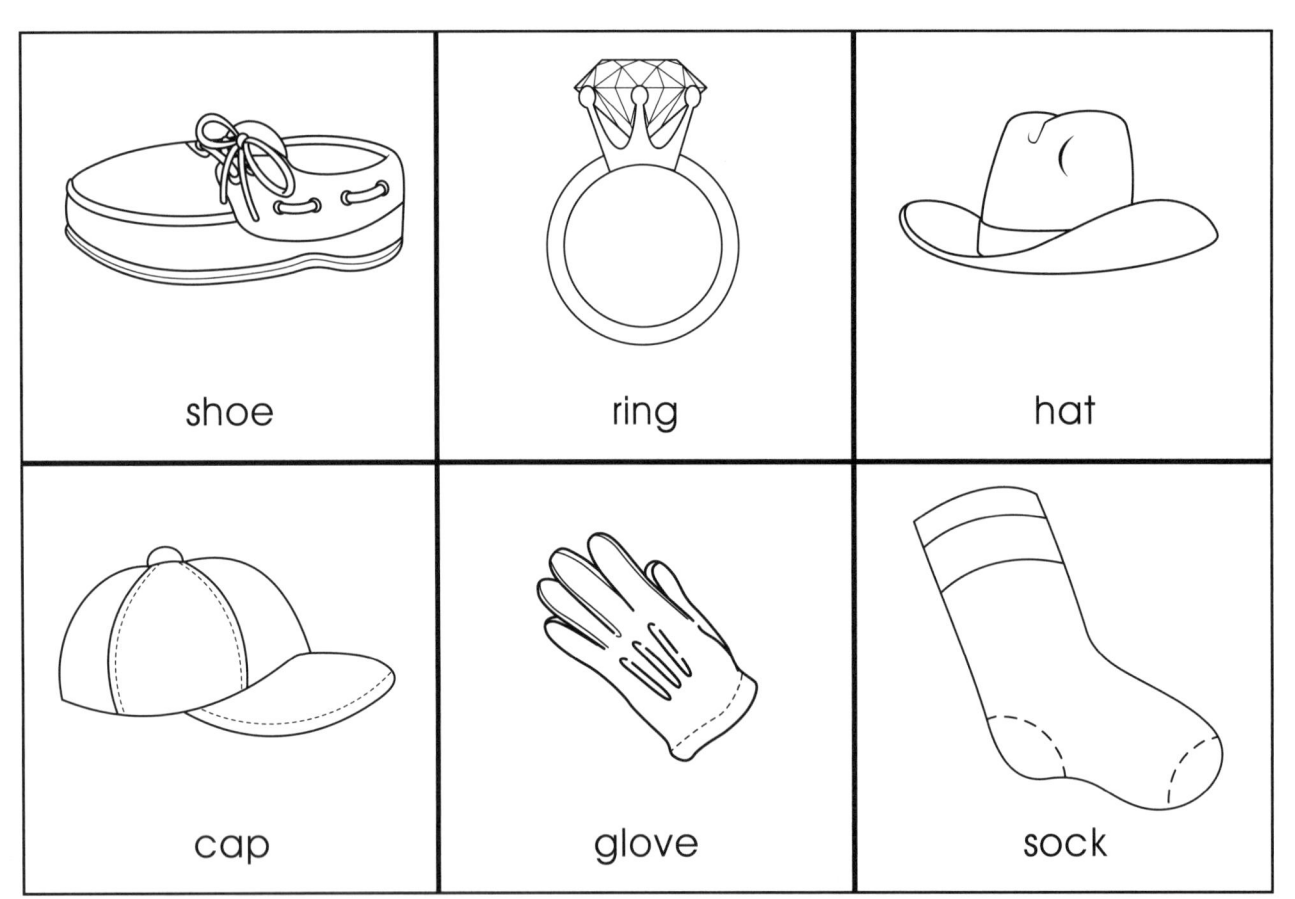

shoe	ring	hat
cap	glove	sock

Try This!
On a separate sheet of paper, make a tally chart that shows the different types of shirts worn by your classmates. Sort the shirts by style (short sleeve, long sleeve, etc.) or color.

Name: _____

Word Categories

How Many Legs?

Cut out the pictures. Glue each picture in the correct column. Draw one more picture in each column.

two legs	four legs	six legs

Try This!

On the back of this paper, draw or list three animals that are born alive and three animals that are hatched from eggs.

Name: _____   Nouns

The Right Name

Cut and glue the picture of each noun where it belongs.

Person

Place

Thing

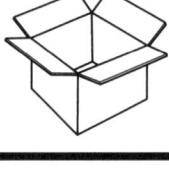

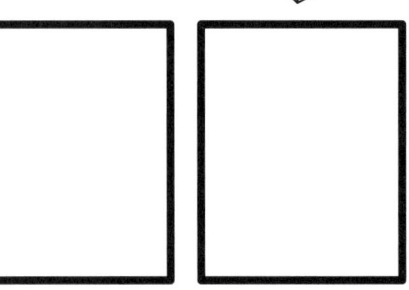

Try This!

Divide a sheet of paper into three sections. Label the sections *person*, *place*, and *thing*. Cut out pictures from newspapers or magazines. Glue the pictures in the correct columns.

cut

| girl | school | firefighter | key | book | farm |

Name: _____   Nouns

Helpful Friends

Circle the nouns in each sentence. Use the pictures as clues.

1. The bus takes me home after school.

2. The chef made a pizza for lunch.

3. The firefighter helped put out the fire.

4. My school librarian helped me find a great book.

5. The nurse checked my temperature when I was sick.

Try This!
On a separate sheet of paper, make a chart to sort the circled nouns into people, places, and things.

Name: _____   Plural Nouns

Add Some More

Write **s** or **es** to make each word plural. Choose three words and draw the plural forms.

horse _____	box _____	shoe _____
dish _____	match _____	pumpkin _____
drum _____	table _____	bear _____

Try This!

Draw pictures to illustrate three plural nouns. Ask a partner to write the plural word for each of your pictures.

Name: _____   Singular and Plural Nouns

One, Two, or Three

Circle the correct plural word to complete each sentence.

1. Put the (boxes   boxs) in the garage.

2. The (dishs   dishes) in the sink are dirty.

Circle the correct word to complete each sentence.

3. The _____ are in a traffic jam.
   car   cars

4. The _____ is pretty tonight.
   moon   moons

Try This!
On a separate sheet of paper, list 10 things you see in your classroom. Ask a friend to make each word plural.

Name: _____

Action Verbs

What Is Happening Today?

Write the verb from the word bank that completes each sentence.

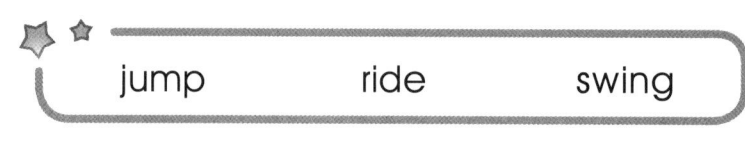

> jump   ride   swing

1. I like to _____ my bike.

2. My sister loves to _____ high.

3. Nick can _____ like a frog.

Circle the verb in each sentence.

4. The baby cries for her bottle.

5. The cat sits in the tree.

6. Dad cooks dinner for me.

Try This!
Use a marker or a crayon to circle all of the verbs you can find on a page from a newspaper or a magazine.

Name: _____   Action Verbs

People on the Go

Write the verb from the word bank that matches each picture.

> cook   drive   sew   swim

1. _____
2. _____ 
3. _____ 
4. _____ 

Write the verb from the word bank that completes each sentence.

> feeds   plants   works

5. Mr. Henry _____ hard on his farm.

6. He _____ all of the hungry animals.

7. He _____ corn and oats.

Try This!
Look around you. On a separate sheet of paper, write five sentences about what people are doing. Circle the verb in each sentence.

Name: _____

Nouns and Verbs

Gumball Fun

Cut out the words. Glue each word on the correct gumball machine.

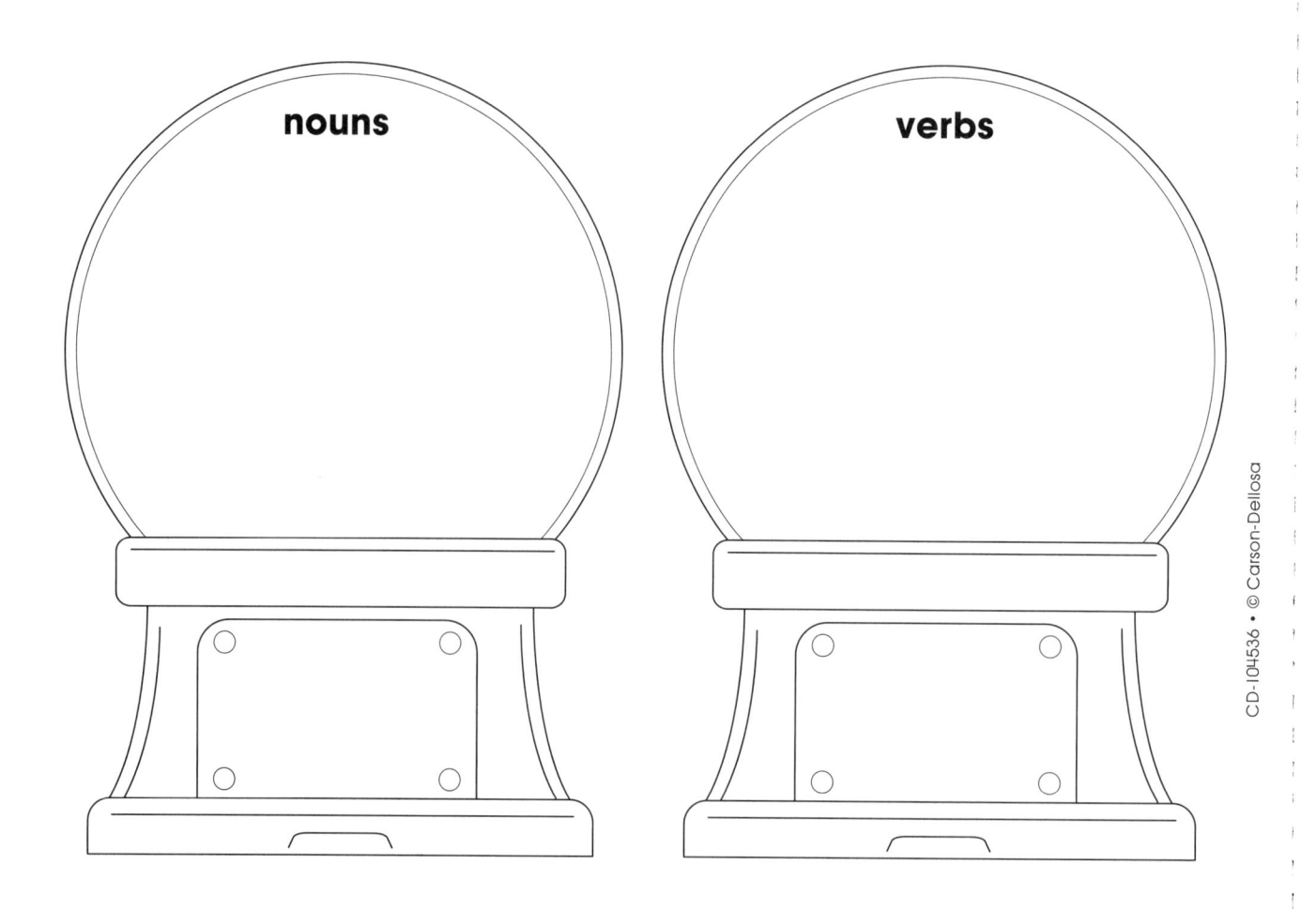

nouns

verbs

Try This!

On the back of this paper, write a sentence that includes one noun and one verb from the gumball machines above.

✂ cut

| swim | drive | apple | cat | run | toy |

Name: _____ Past-Tense Verbs

Baked a Cake

Write the verb that tells what has already happened.

1. Mom _____ the cake pan.
   washes/washed

2. My brother _____ the cake batter.
   stirred/stirs

3. I _____ the milk.
   poured/pour

Write the verb to show what already happened.

4. I (help) wash the dishes. _____

Try This!
On a separate sheet of paper, list five things you do every day. If you have already done any of those things today, use past-tense verbs to explain.

Name: _____

Linking Verbs

No School Today

Write **am**, **is**, or **are** to complete each sentence.

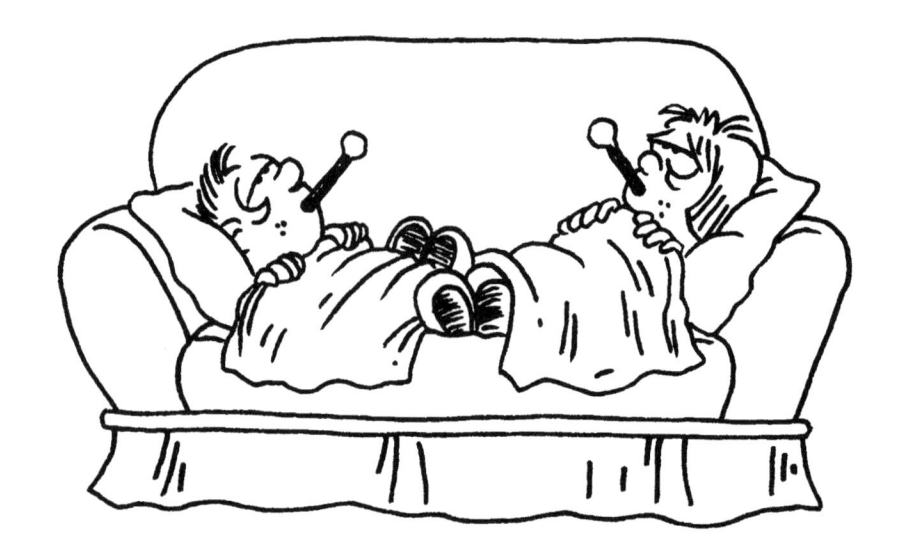

1. Hannah _____ sick today.

2. Carlos _____ sick too.

3. Hannah and Carlos _____ not in school.

4. I _____ at home resting.

Write a sentence that uses the linking verb shown.

5. am

_____

6. is

_____

7. are

_____

Try This!

On a separate sheet of paper, write a sentence about yourself. Use *am*, *is*, or *are*. Circle the linking verb in your sentence.

Name: _____   Linking Verbs

Matt Was the Star

Write **was** or **were** to complete each sentence.

1. Matt and Rachel _____ excited.

2. The school play _____ about to start.

3. The play _____ about a toy maker.

4. I _____ the toy maker in the play.

Which linking verb is correct? Write **was** or **were** beside each noun phrase.

5. the stage _____   6. the show _____

7. the toys _____   8. the actors _____

Try This!
On a separate sheet of paper, finish the story about Matt and the play. Circle each linking verb in your story.

Name: _____   Adjectives

It Looks Like This

Circle the adjectives.

1. big shoe

2. fuzzy puppy

3. tiny pebble

4. three bears

Write an adjective to describe each noun.

5. _____ dog

6. _____ bicycle

7. _____ squirrel

8. _____ cowboy

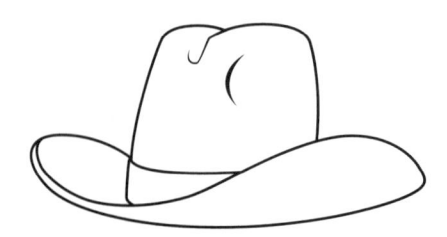

Try This!
On a separate sheet of paper, draw a picture of yourself. Write five adjectives that describe you or your picture.

Name: _____ Pronouns

Toss Around Names

Write the pronoun from the word bank that replaces each noun phrase.

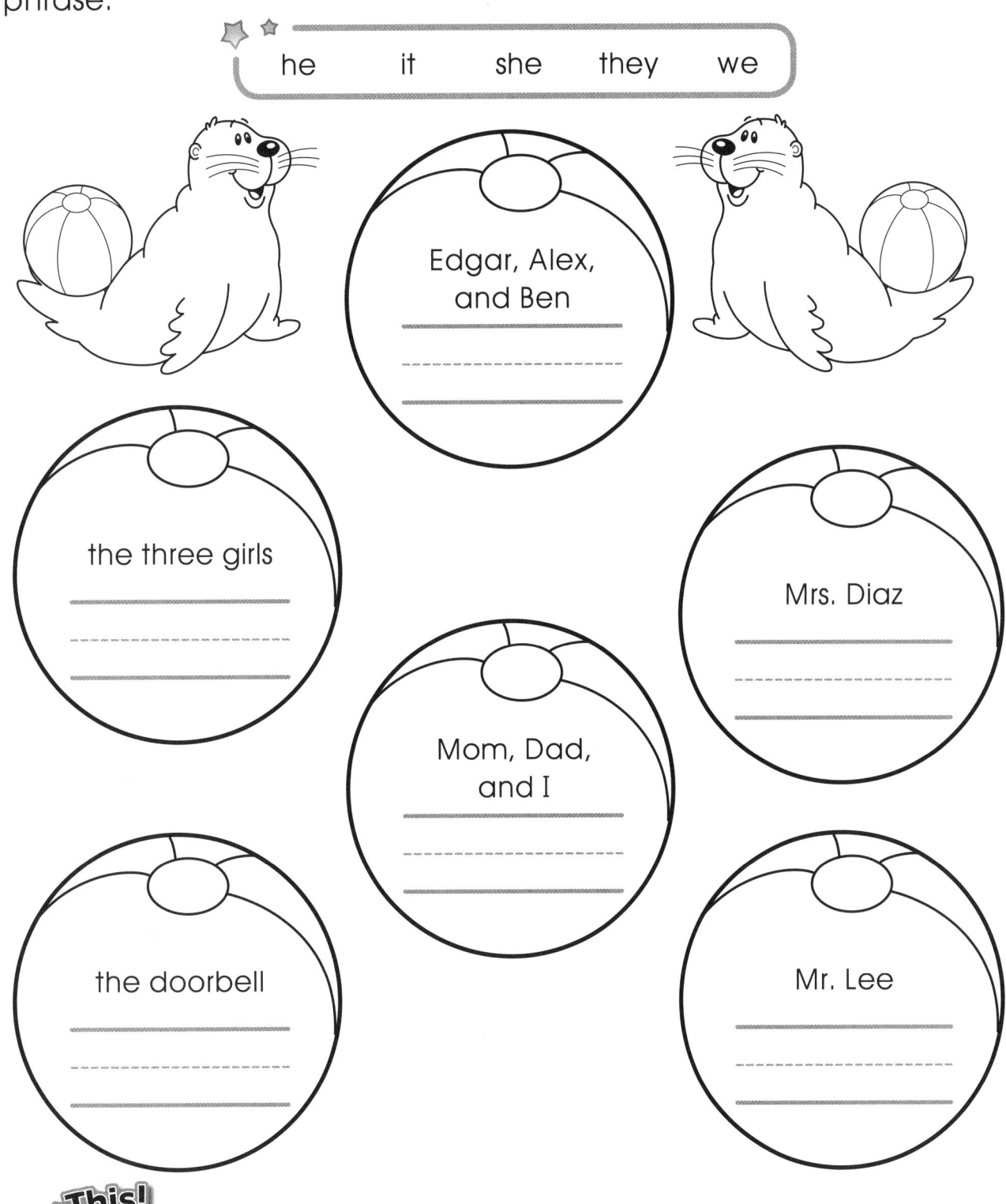

he   it   she   they   we

Edgar, Alex, and Ben
_____

the three girls
_____

Mrs. Diaz
_____

Mom, Dad, and I
_____

the doorbell
_____

Mr. Lee
_____

Try This! On a separate sheet of paper, write a sentence for each pronoun in the word bank.

Name: _____

Capitalization

The Perfect Start

Circle the letters that need to be capitalized. Choose one sentence to rewrite on the lines. Remember to use correct capitalization.

1. she played ball on our team.

2. dr. sharma is our dentist.

3. do you know paul brown?

4. we are going to atlanta in december.

5. may we go to the park on sunday?

6. on tuesday, we can go swimming.

_____

_____

Try This!

On a separate sheet of paper, write all of the words on this month's calendar that are capitalized.

Name: _____   Question Sentences

Fishing for Answers

Write the first word of each question. Remember to begin with a capital letter. End each question with a question mark. On the last line, write your own question about the picture.

1. _____ that your boat _____
   (is)

2. _____ you catch that fish _____
   (did)

3. _____ much does it weigh _____
   (how)

4. _____ you eat it _____
   (will)

5. _____

Try This! _____
Interview a friend or a family member. On a separate sheet of paper, write five questions you would like to ask. Write the answers under the questions.

Name: _____

Punctuation

Pet Fair Punctuation

Write a period or a question mark at the end of each sentence. Write a sentence about the picture. End with the correct punctuation mark.

1. Can the fish jump out of the tank

2. Two snakes are in that cage

3. What is the turtle's name

4. I like the cute dog

5. _____

Try This!

On the back of this paper, write three sentences about adopting a pet. Use a colorful crayon to write your punctuation marks.

Name: _____   Punctuation

For You to Decide

Write the correct punctuation mark at the end of each sentence. Color the boxes with a question mark red.

1. May I play outside ☐

2. What is your name ☐

3. I am moving next week ☐

4. Math is my favorite subject ☐

5. Can you tie your shoes ☐

6. When do we go home ☐

7. I ate soup for lunch today ☐

8. Can we go to the beach ☐

Try This!

On a separate sheet of paper, write three questions. Remember to use correct punctuation.

Name: _____   Punctuation Review

Bat Basics

Write each sentence with a capital letter and end with a period or a question mark. Choose one sentence to illustrate in the box.

bats are the only flying mammals

_____

some bats live in caves

_____

i love to read about bats

_____

do all bats eat insects

_____

some bats eat frogs or small fish

_____

Try This!
On a separate sheet of paper, write a question about bats. Remember to use correct punctuation. Draw a picture to illustrate your question.

Name: _____   Sentence Writing

The Picture Tells the Story

Complete each sentence to match the picture.

1. My friend likes _____.

2. Will you close the _____?

Complete each sentence. Draw a picture to illustrate each sentence.

3. I want _____.

4. She went _____.

Try This!
On a separate sheet of paper, write one sentence that asks a question, one sentence that is a statement, and one sentence that shows excitement. Ask a friend to write the punctuation marks.

Name: _____   Using Direction Words

Little Acorn Grows Up

Write **First**, **Next**, and **Last** beside each picture to put them in order. Write about what happens in each picture.

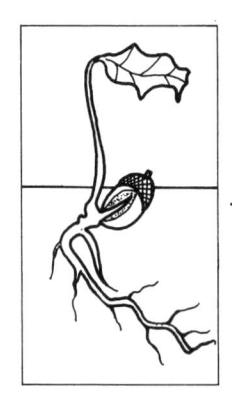

_____ _____
          _____
          _____
          _____

_____ _____
          _____
          _____
          _____

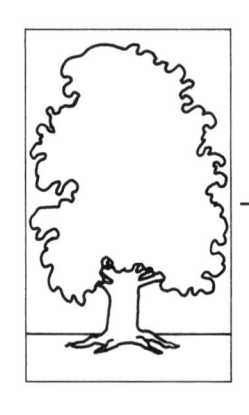

_____ _____
          _____
          _____
          _____

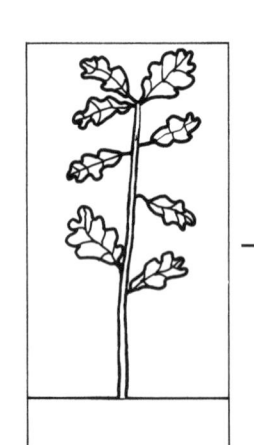

Try This!

On a separate sheet of paper, draw a picture of a leaf pile and write the steps for raking leaves in autumn. Use the words *First*, *Next*, and *Last* in your sentences.

Name: _____ Composition

In the Future

Draw a picture in the oval of what you want to do when you grow up. Finish the story.

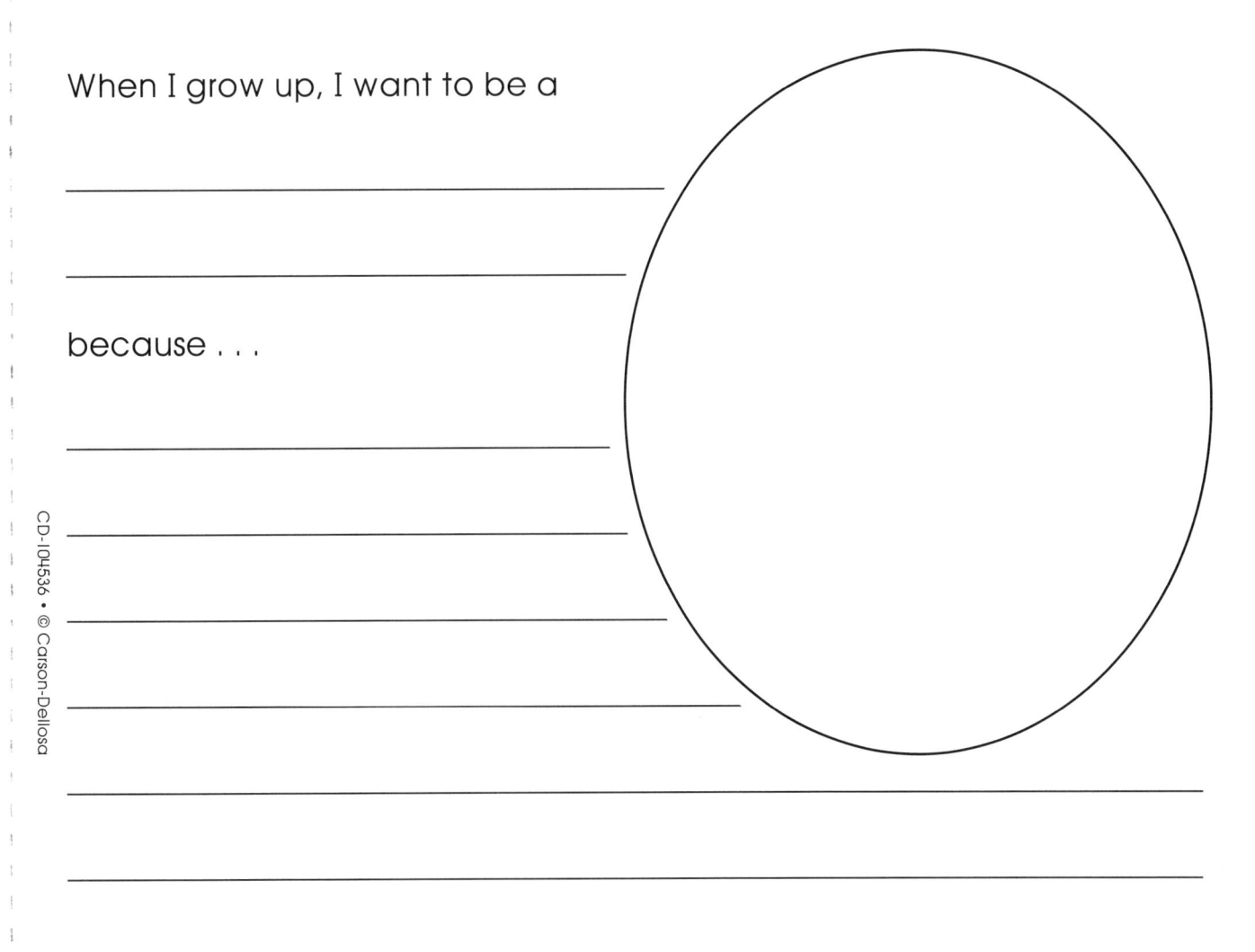

When I grow up, I want to be a

_____

_____

because . . .

_____

_____

_____

_____

_____

_____

_____

_____

_____

Try This!

What questions do you have about your dream job? Write five of them on a separate sheet of paper. Ask your teacher or family to help you find the answers.

Composition

All About Me

Draw and color a picture of yourself.

By _____

Try This!

Write an acrostic poem about yourself. Write the letters of your first name down the left side. Use the letters to write words that describe you.

Composition

Draw some of your favorite things next to the toy box. Color your pictures. Complete the sentences below.

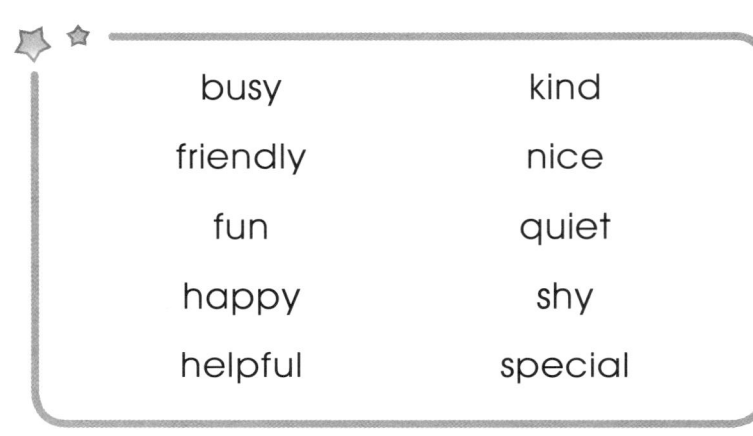

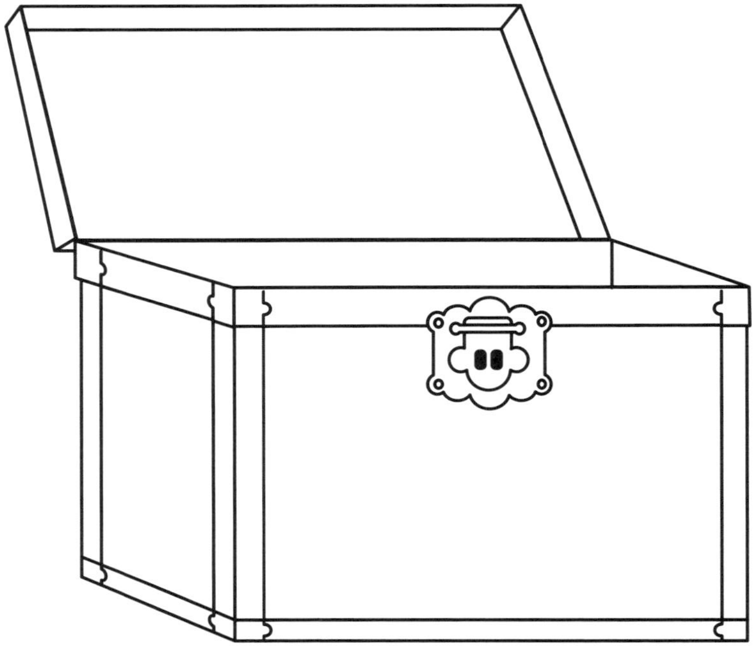

My favorite game is _____

My favorite book is _____

My favorite toy is _____

Complete the sentences. Use the answers to write a story about yourself on a separate sheet of paper.

My name is _____

My favorite color is _____

Write some words that tell about you. Use the words in the word bank.

busy	kind
friendly	nice
fun	quiet
happy	shy
helpful	special

_____

_____

_____

Composition

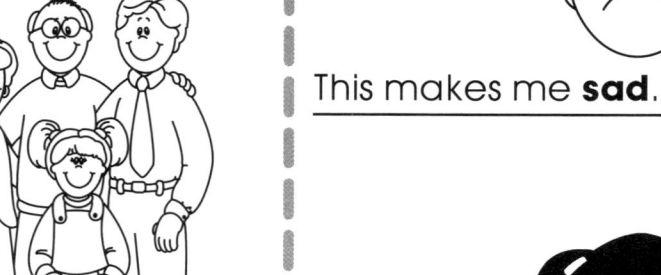

Read the sentences. Draw a picture in each box.

This makes me **happy**.	This makes me **angry**.
This makes me **sad**.	This makes me **laugh**.
This makes me **scared**.	This makes me **proud**.

Tell about your family.

Write the correct numbers.

I have . . .
☐ brother(s)   ☐ sister(s)
☐ uncle(s)   ☐ aunt(s)
☐ cousin(s)

Check one.

I am . . .
☐ the oldest.
☐ in the middle.
☐ the only child.
☐ the youngest.

Composition

Families have different rules to keep everyone safe and happy. Write some of the rules in your family.

Safety rules in my family:
_____
_____

Cleanup rules in my family:
_____
_____

Complete these sentences about yourself.

I feel **happy** when _____

I feel **angry** when _____

I feel **sad** when _____

I **laugh** when _____

I feel **scared** when _____

I feel **proud** when _____

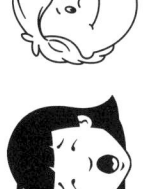

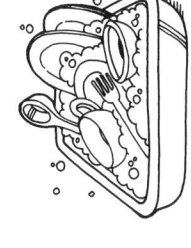

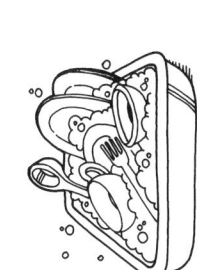

Today, I feel _____

143

Name: _____

Number Recognition

Number Art

Use the code to color the rainbow.

1 = red   2 = blue   3 = yellow
4 = green   5 = orange

How many 2s do you see? _____

Try This!
On a separate sheet of paper, draw a picture of what you might see on a sunny day. Draw more than one of each object. Label the number of each object. For example, draw 3 birds in a tree.

Name: _____   Number Recognition

Colorful Critters

Use the code to color the picture. Write how many of each number on the lines.

1 = yellow ____   2 = pink ____   3 = white ____
4 = purple ____   5 = red ____   6 = brown ____   7 = black ____
8 = blue ____   9 = green ____   10 = orange ____

Try This!

Make your own flash cards by cutting a sheet of construction paper into 10 equal pieces. On one side, write a number from 1 to 10. On the other side, draw a matching number of animals.

Name: _____   Counting to 10

Apple Insides

Count the seeds in each apple. Write that number on the leaf.

Draw the correct number of seeds in each apple.

4   2   7

Try This!
How many seeds are there altogether? _____

Name: _____   Counting to 10

Animal Travels

Count each set of footprints. Match each set to the correct number.

4

8

1

7

2

6

3

9

5

10

Try This!
On a separate sheet of paper, write the number word for each numeral.

Name: _____

Counting to 30

Watermelon Garden

Count the watermelons. Write the number in each watermelon. Circle each group of 10.

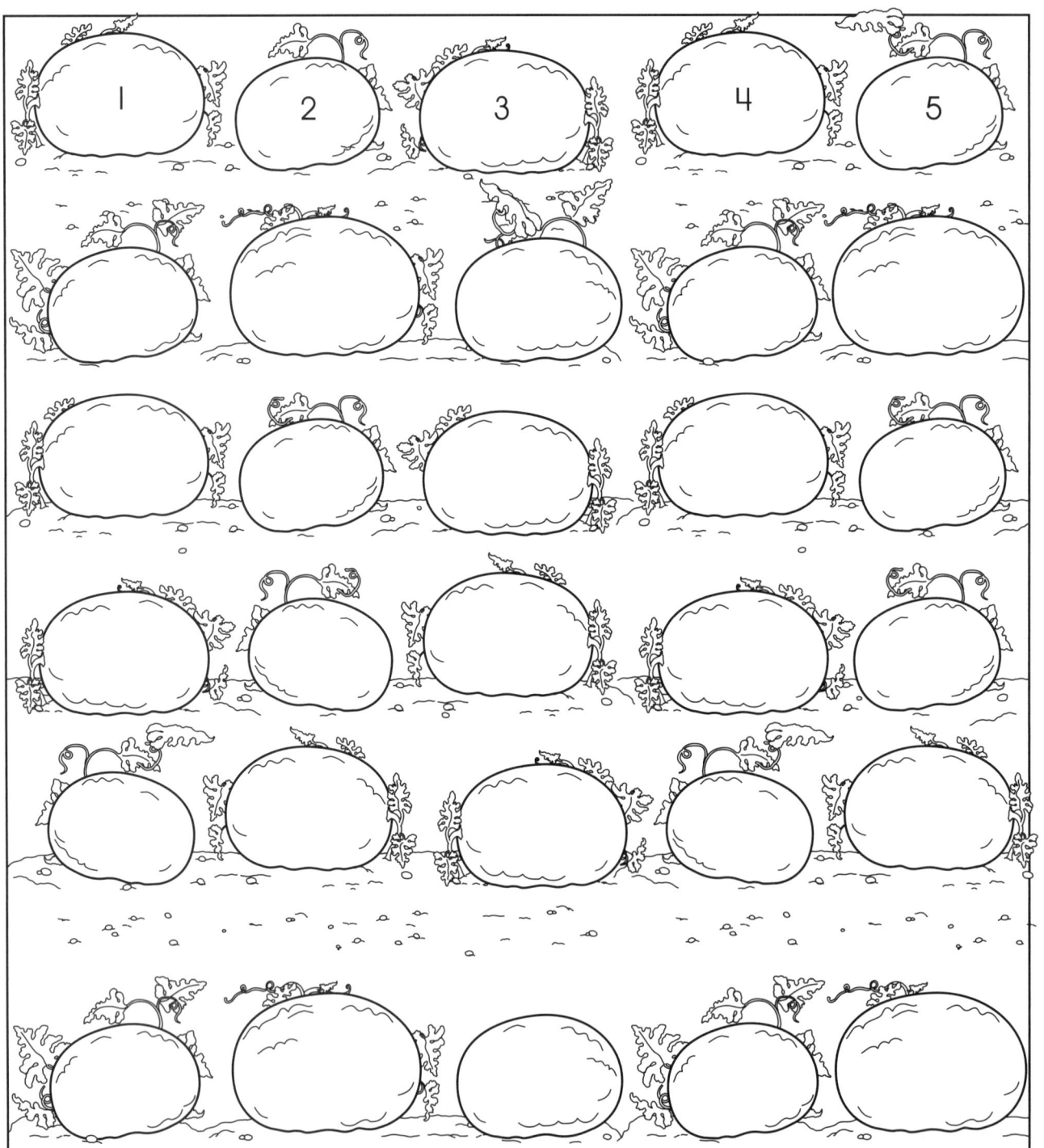

1 2 3 4 5

Try This!

Color odd-numbered watermelons green and even-numbered watermelons yellow.

Name: _____   Counting to 100

One Hundred Places

Write the missing numbers. Circle each number that ends with **0**.

		3							
11									
				25					30
			34						
	42								
51									
			64						70
					76				
				85					
	92								

Try This!
Make a number pattern. Use different colors to shade squares in the number chart. For example, color square number 1 blue, square number 2 red, and square number 3 blue to make the ABA pattern.

Name: _____

Number Before

Take a Step Back

Count each set of objects. Write the number that comes before.

1. _____

2. _____

3. _____

4. _____

Draw a set of objects that shows the number that comes before.

3

5

Try This!

Count backward from 20. Write the numbers on a separate sheet of paper.

Name: _____   Number in the Middle

Right in the Middle of Things

Count each set of objects. Write the number that comes between.

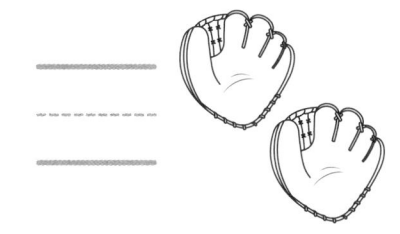

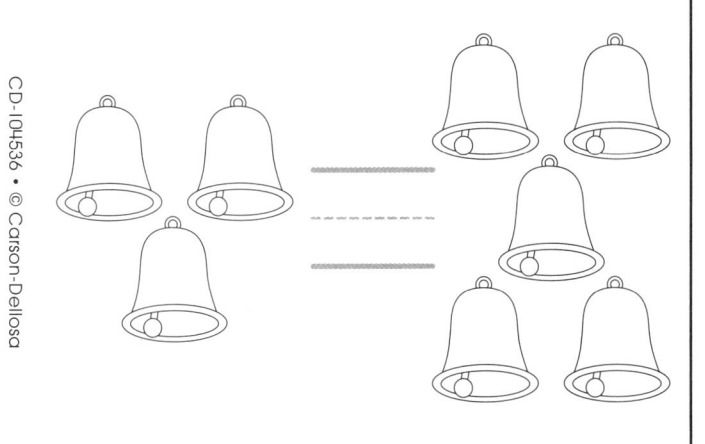

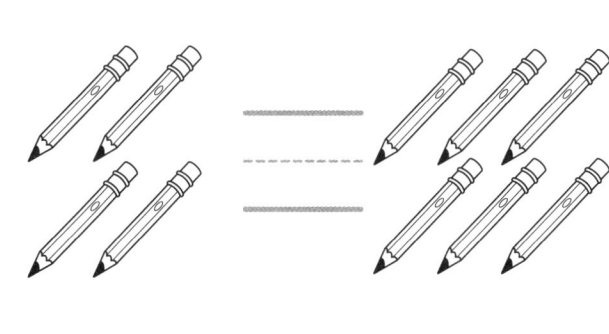

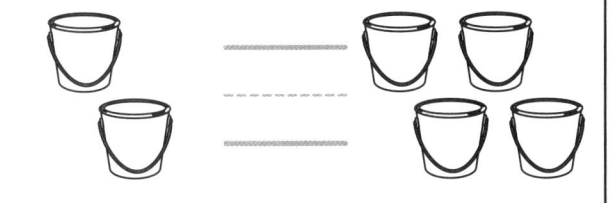

Try This!

What day comes between Friday and Sunday? On a separate sheet of paper, write a sentence telling what you like to do on that day.

Name: _____   Number After

What Comes Next?

Count each set of objects. Write the number that comes after.

1. _____

2. _____

3. _____

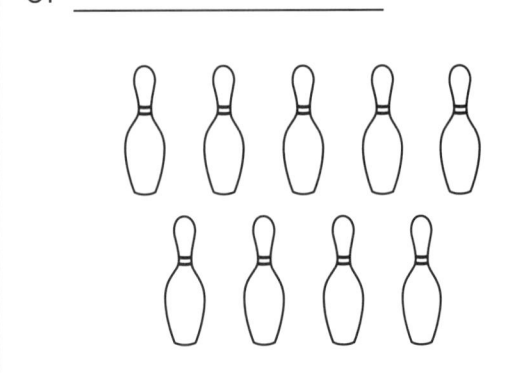

4. _____

Draw a set of objects that shows the number that comes after.

2

6

Try This!

Find 10 small objects. Put them in order by size. Then, try putting them into ABC order.

Name: _____   Least and Greatest

A Little Less or a Little More

Circle the smallest number in each shape. Draw an X on the greatest number in each shape.

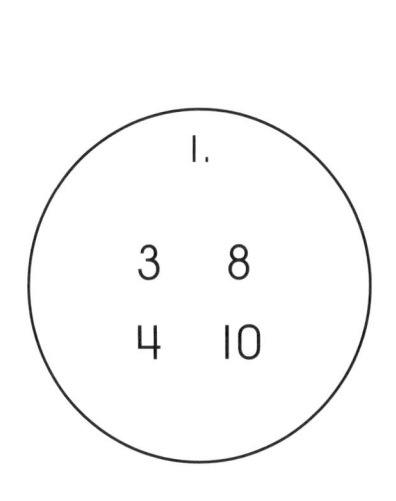

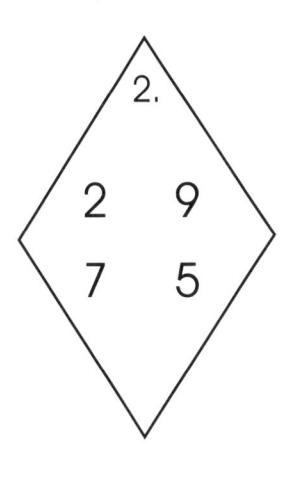

1. 3, 8, 4, 10

2. 2, 9, 7, 5

3. 7, 12, 20, 5, 3, 16, 6

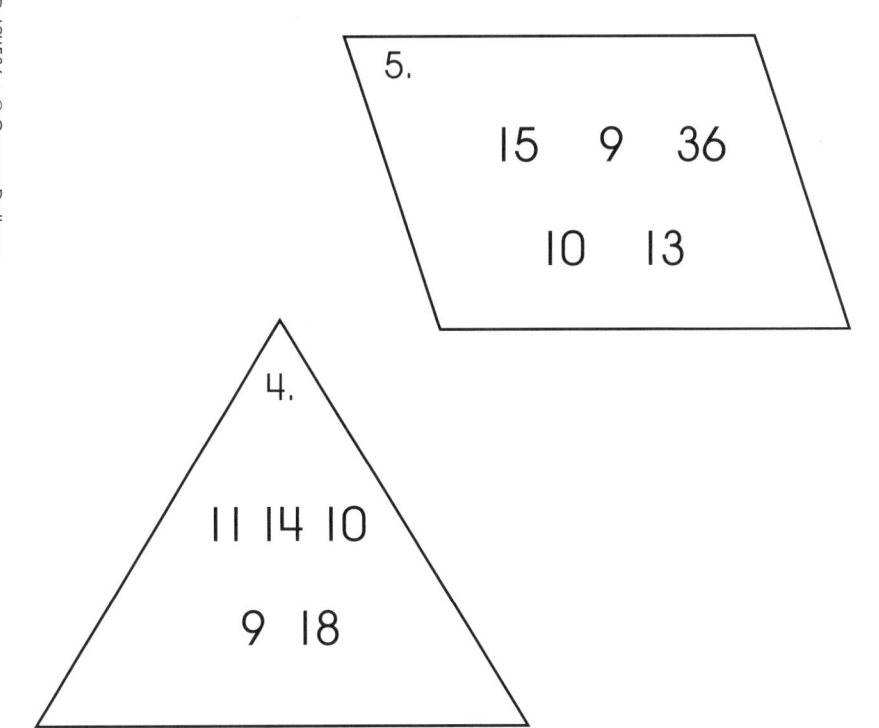

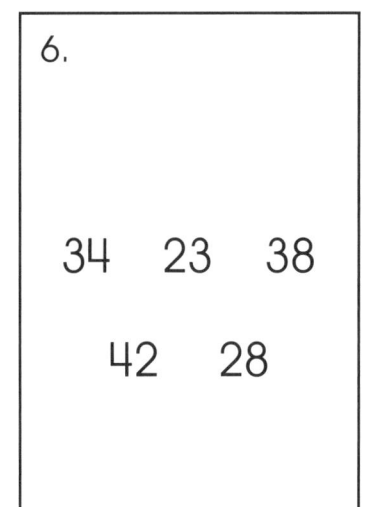

5. 15, 9, 36, 10, 13

4. 11, 14, 10, 9, 18

6. 34, 23, 38, 42, 28

Try This!
On a separate sheet of paper, write each set of numbers in order from least to greatest.

Name: _____   Inequalities

One Has Fewer

Circle the amount that is less in each box.

1.	2.
3.	4.
5.	6.

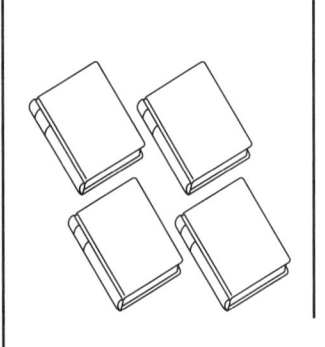

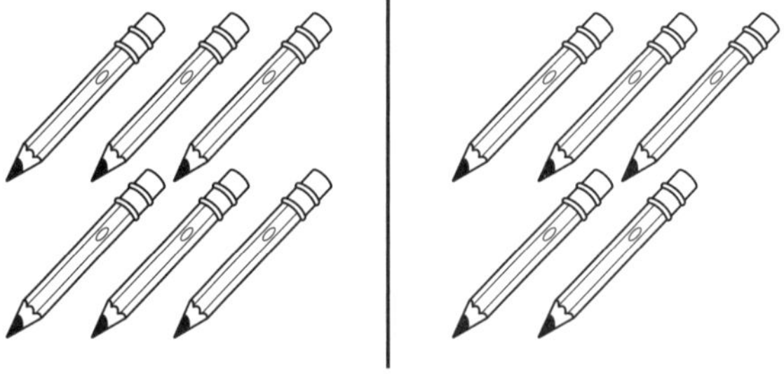

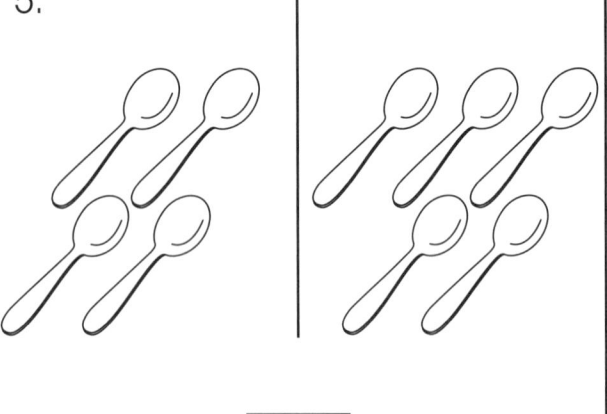

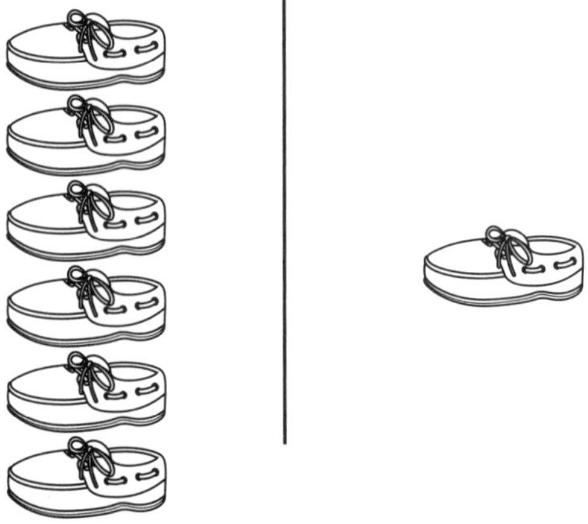

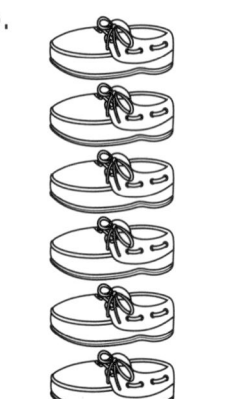

Try This!

Write > or < on each line to show greater than or less than for each box.

Name: _____   Inequalities

One Has More

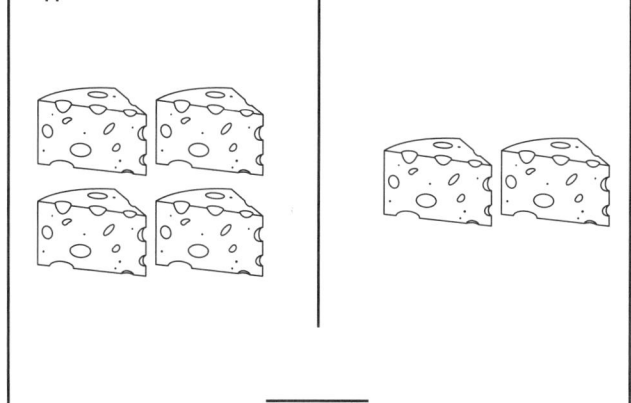

Circle the amount that is more in each box.

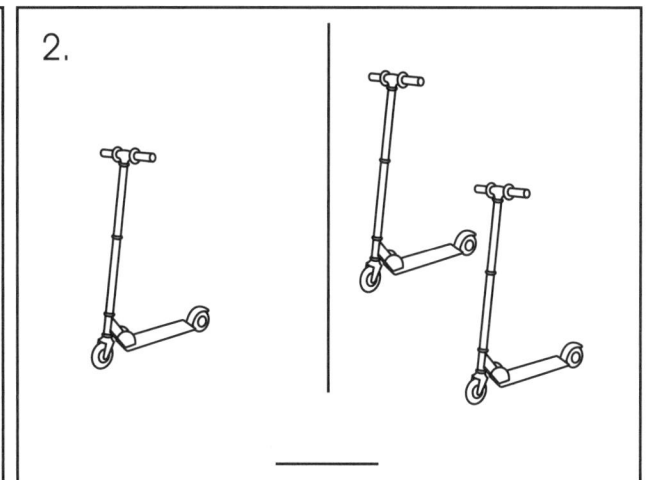

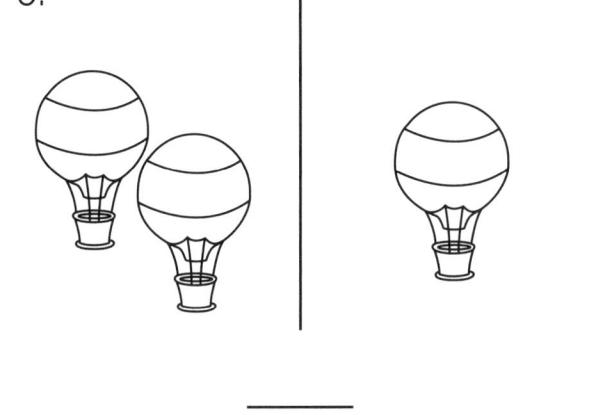

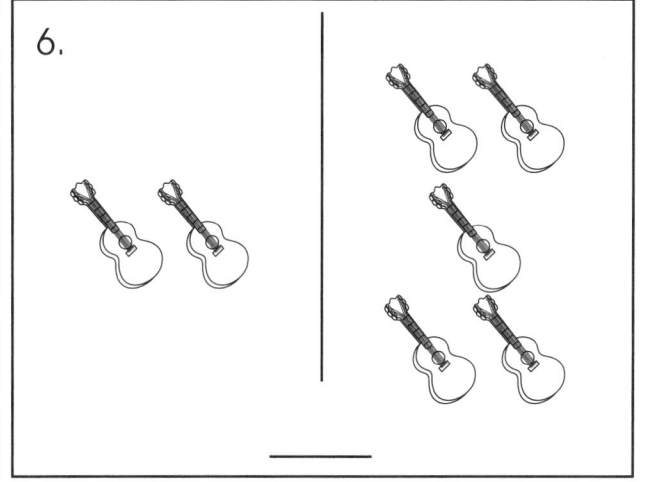

1.	2.
3.	4.
5.	6.

Try This!

Write > or < on each line to show greater than or less than for each box.

155

Name: _____   Inequalities

Could Be More or Less

Fill in the number line.

| 1 | 2 | | | 6 | | | |

5 > 3
5 is greater than **3**.

3 < 5
3 is less than **5**.

Write > or < to show greater than or less than. Use the number line to help you.

1. 5 ____ 2
2. 1 ____ 7
3. 1 ____ 9
4. 8 ____ 5

5. 3 ____ 4
6. 9 ____ 3
7. 8 ____ 7
8. 2 ____ 4

9. 6 ____ 5
10. 5 ____ 3
11. 5 ____ 7
12. 3 ____ 5

Try This!
On a separate sheet of paper, draw a tree with apples on it. Ask one friend to draw an apple tree that shows fewer apples and another friend to draw a tree that shows more apples.

Name: _____

Number Words

Number Train

Number the train.

Draw a line from the number word to the number.

seven	1
two	8
five	3
nine	4
six	7
four	5
one	6
three	2
eight	9

Try This!

Use the code to color the train cars.

one = red   two = blue   three = green
four = yellow   five = orange   six = brown

Name: _____   Number Words

Words for Numbers

Count the dots above each line. Write the correct number word.

1. 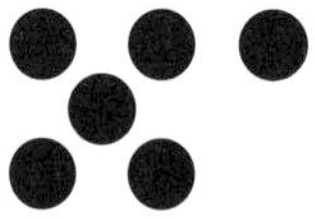 _____   2.  _____   3. _____

4. _____   5.  _____   6. _____

Draw the correct number of dots.

| seven | two | nine |

Try This!
On a separate sheet of paper, write the number words used above in order from least to greatest.

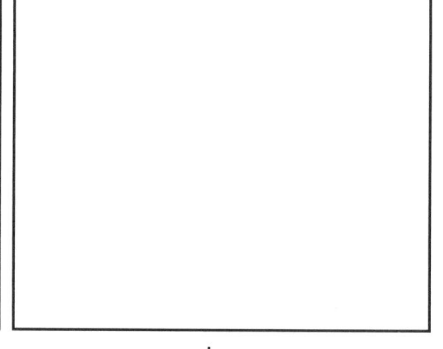

Name: _____   Ordinal Numbers

First in Fire Safety

Draw lines to match the pictures to the correct order words.

third first second fifth fourth

Write the order word for each of the fire hydrants.

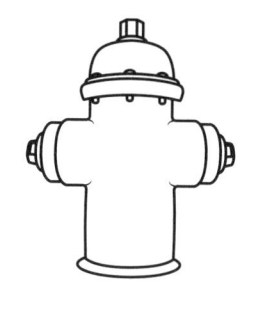

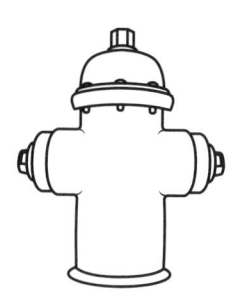

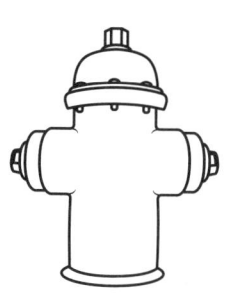

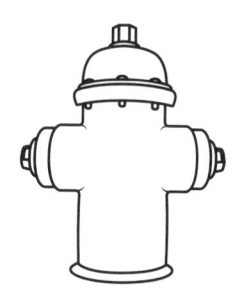

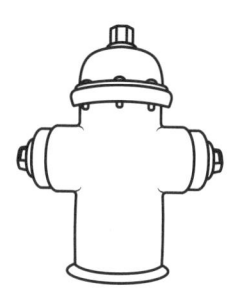

_____   _____   _____   _____   _____

Try This!

Pretend you are in line for lunch. Four children are in front of you, and two children are behind you. What position in line are you? Draw a picture to show where you are in line.

Name: _____

Ordinal Numbers

Ducks on Parade

1. Color the **ninth** flag red.
2. Write **O** on the **second** flag.
3. Color the **eighth** flag blue.
4. Write **D** on the **fourth** flag.
5. Color the **sixth** flag yellow.
6. Write **G** on the **first** flag.
7. Color the **tenth** flag purple.
8. Write **O** on the **third** flag.
9. Color the **seventh** flag green.
10. Color the **fifth** flag orange.

Try This!

On a separate sheet of paper, write a story that tells about the picture. Your story should have at least five sentences. Use ordinal number words in your story.

Name: _____

Counting by Twos

Leaping Lily Pads!

Count by 2s to lead the frog to the log. Color the lily pads that show the number path.

5, 2, 4, 6, 8, 10, 15, 11, 9, 12, 22, 20, 18, 16, 14, 24, 17, 34, 25, 26, 32, 36, 28, 30, 38, 45, 31, 35, 40, 47, 44, 42, 46, 43, 49, 48, 50

Try This!
If you could have 50 of something, what would it be? Explain your answer on a separate sheet of paper.

Name: _____

Counting by Twos

Drop by Twos

Count by 2s to 50 in the water drops. Start at the top of the slide and write the numbers.

Try This!

On a separate sheet of paper, continue counting by 2s to 100. Write number words for five of the numbers.

Name: _____

Counting by Fives

Does the Trash Count?

Count by 5s to 50. Write the numbers on the lines.

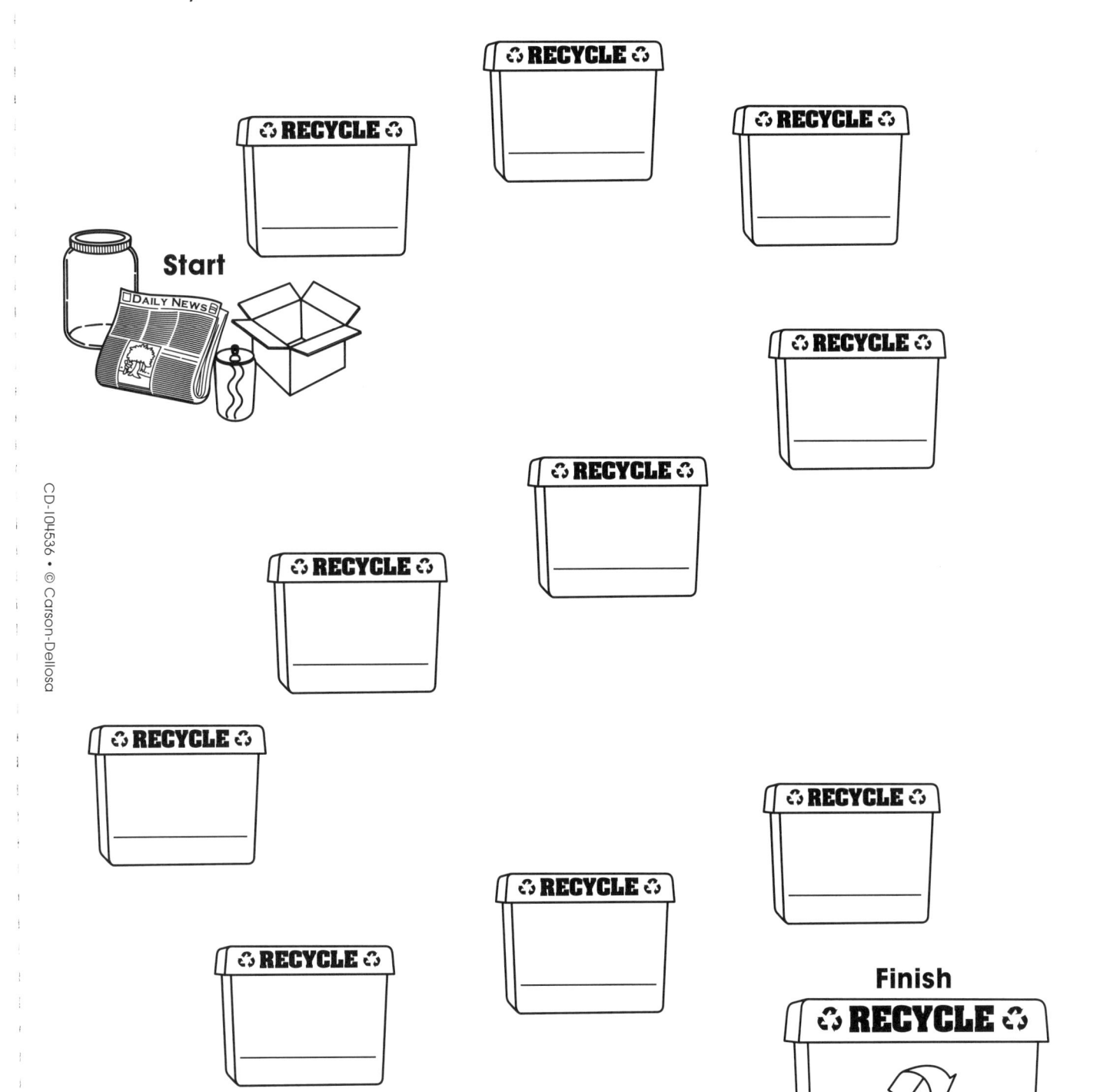

Start

Finish

Try This!

Work with a partner to make a recycling poster. Show five things from school and five things from home that can be recycled.

Name: _____

Counting by Fives

Five Feather Fun

Count by 5s to 50. Write the numbers in the feathers. Color odd-numbered feathers red and even-numbered feathers orange.

5

★ Try This! ★
Trace your hand on a sheet of white paper to make a handprint turkey. Color your turkey. Under your turkey, write five things you are thankful for.

164

Name: _____   Counting by Tens

Letters in the Mail

Cut out the mailboxes. Glue each mailbox on the correct post.

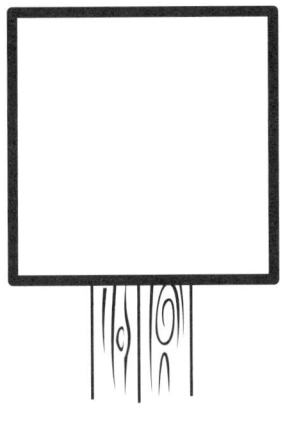

ten

twenty

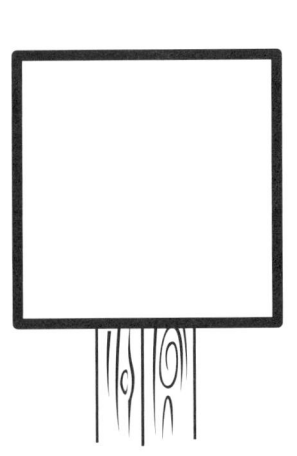

thirty

forty

fifty

Try This!

If each mailbox has 10 letters, how many letters are there in all?

cut

| 50 | 30 | 10 | 20 | 40 |

Name: _____   Count On

Learning to Count On

Draw the number of objects that comes next. Circle that number.

1.   1   2   3

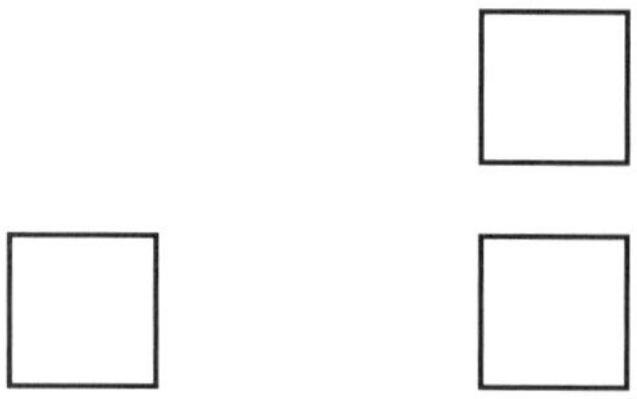

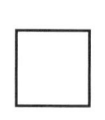

2.   2   3   4

3.   2   3   4

4.   3   4   5

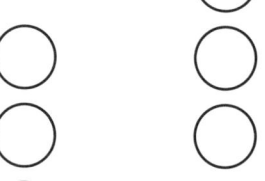

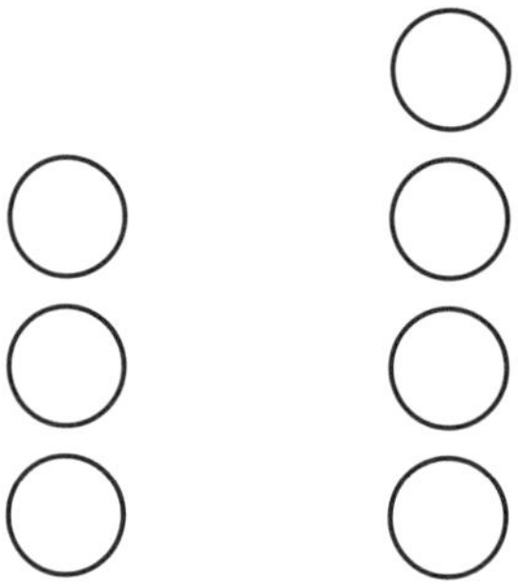

5.   1   2   3

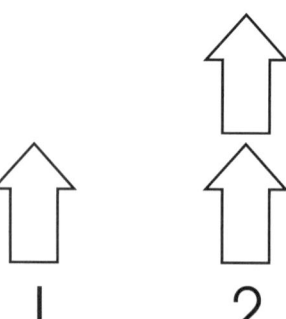

6.   4   5   6

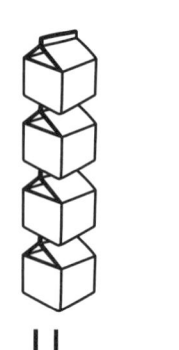

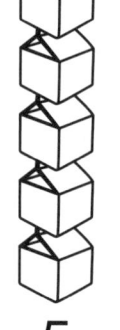

Try This!
Work with a partner to practice counting on from 10 to 50. Say the numbers aloud. Use a number line if you need help.

Name: _____

Making Tens

Making 10

Complete each picture to show 10. How many did you draw to make 10? Write that number.

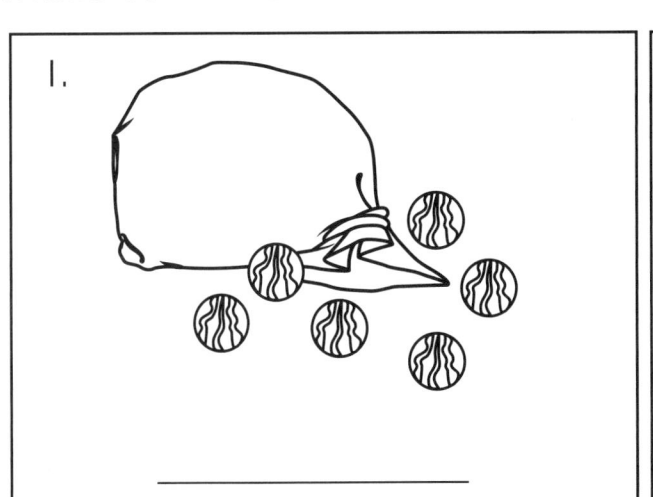

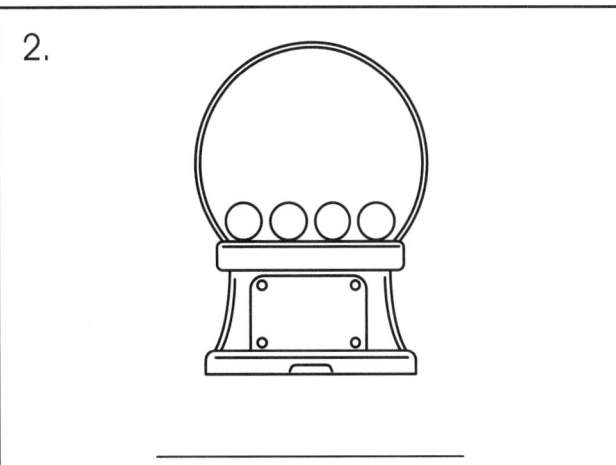

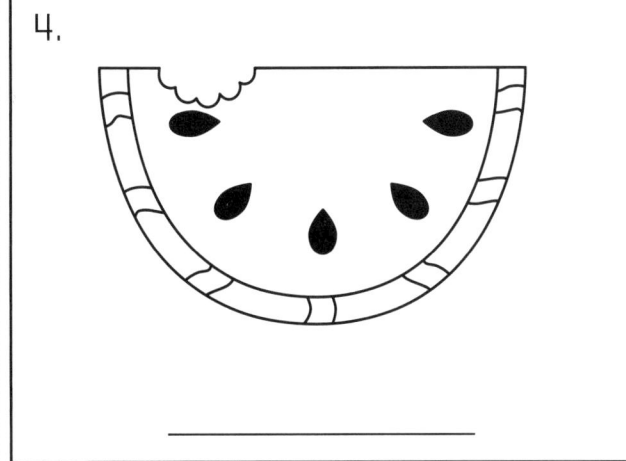

1.

2.

3.

4.

5.

6.

Try This!

Write an addition sentence for each picture problem.

Name: _____

Fractions

Half as Much Fun

Color $\frac{1}{2}$ of each shape or object.

Try This!

On a separate sheet of paper, draw four new shapes or objects. Color $\frac{1}{2}$ of each shape or object red and $\frac{1}{2}$ of each shape or object blue.

Name: _____   Fractions

It Shows This Much

Circle the fraction shown in each picture.

1.

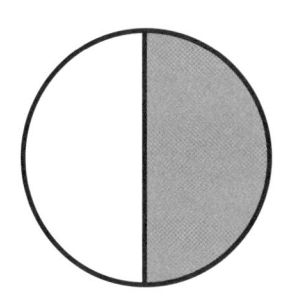

$\frac{1}{3}$ $\frac{1}{4}$ $\frac{1}{2}$

2.

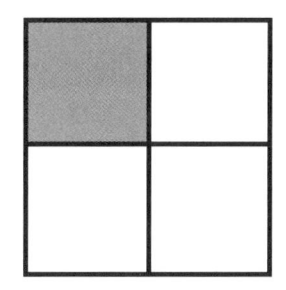

$\frac{1}{3}$ $\frac{1}{4}$ $\frac{2}{4}$

3.

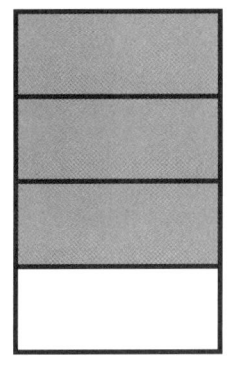

$\frac{2}{3}$ $\frac{3}{4}$ $\frac{2}{4}$

4.

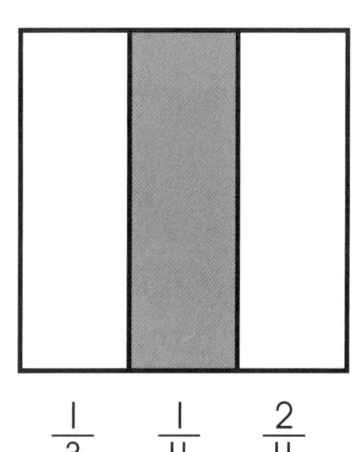

$\frac{1}{3}$ $\frac{1}{4}$ $\frac{2}{4}$

Color each picture to show the fraction.

5.

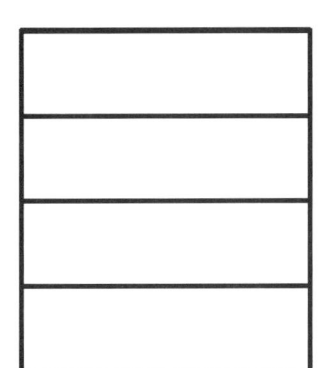

$\frac{2}{4}$

6.

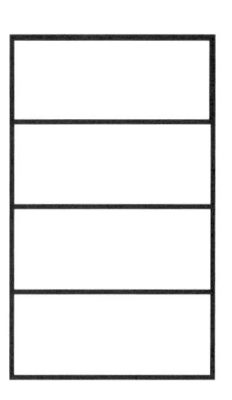

$\frac{1}{4}$

Try This!

Write these fractions in order from least to greatest: $\frac{1}{4}$ $\frac{3}{4}$ $\frac{2}{4}$

Name: _____   Fractions

Equal Parts Make a Whole

Write the number of equal parts.

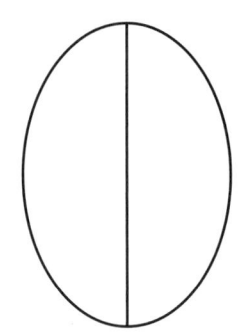

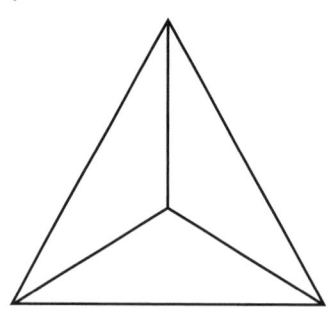

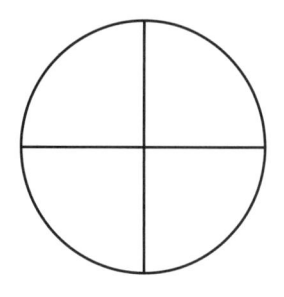

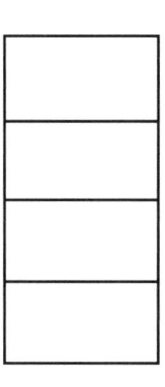

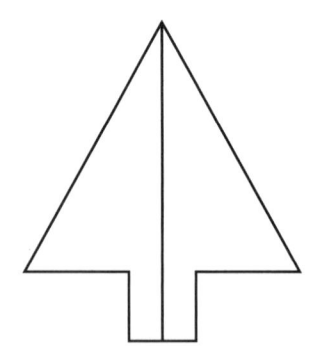

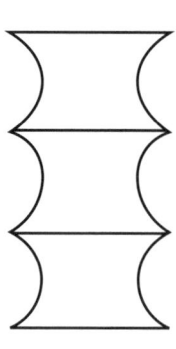

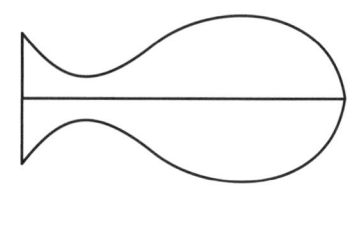

_____   _____   _____

_____   _____

_____   _____   _____

Try This!
Cut a square out of construction paper. Fold it into four equal parts. Label each part with the correct fraction.

Name: _____

Basic Addition Facts

Sums of Shells

Add. Write the sums. Go through the tunnels to connect each matching sum.

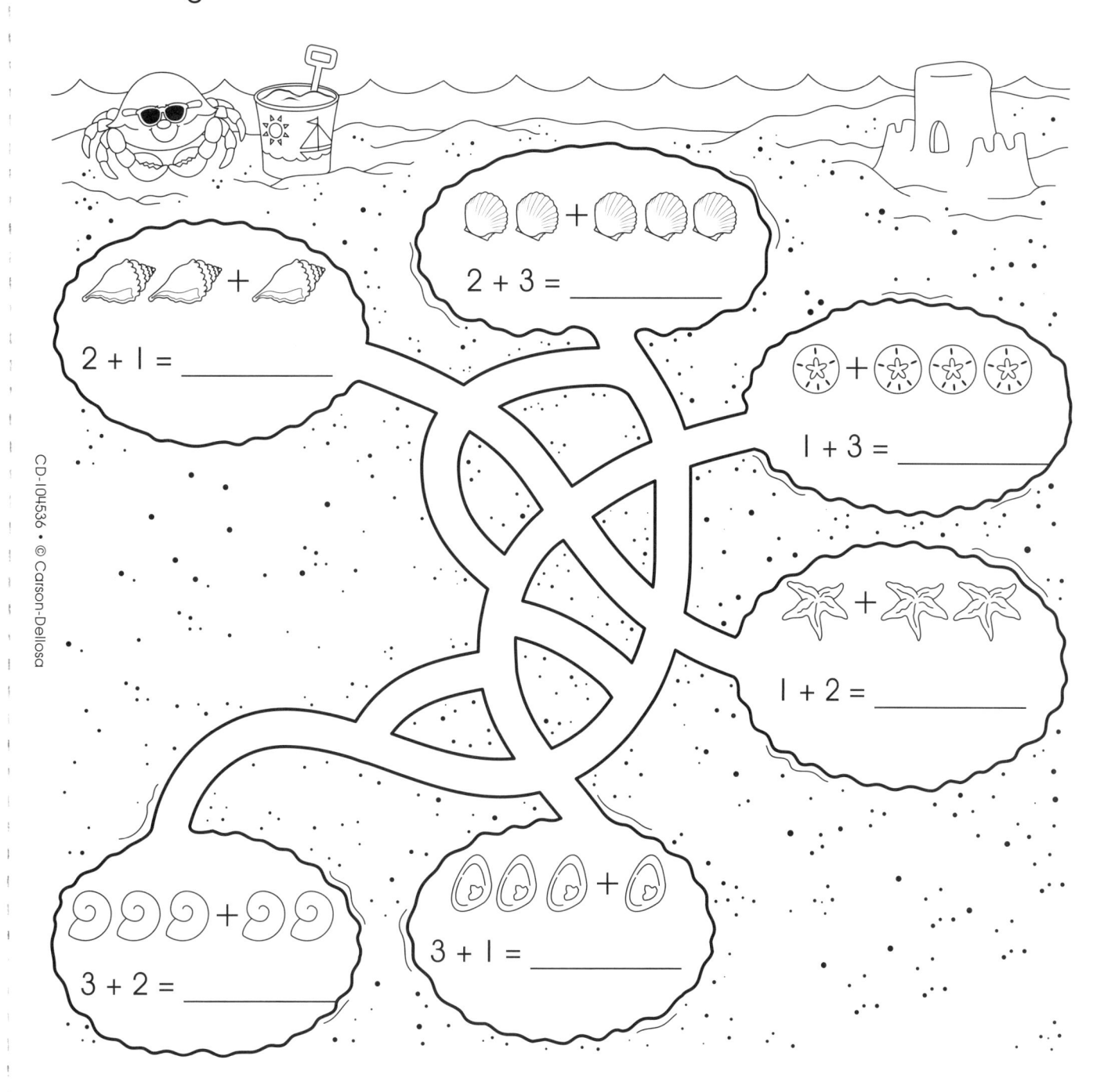

2 + 1 = _____

2 + 3 = _____

1 + 3 = _____

1 + 2 = _____

3 + 2 = _____

3 + 1 = _____

Try This!

On a separate sheet of paper, write five addition problems that all have a sum of 10.

Name: _____

Basic Addition Facts

Double Up

Add. Color all of the spaces with doubles problems orange. Color the rest of the spaces blue.

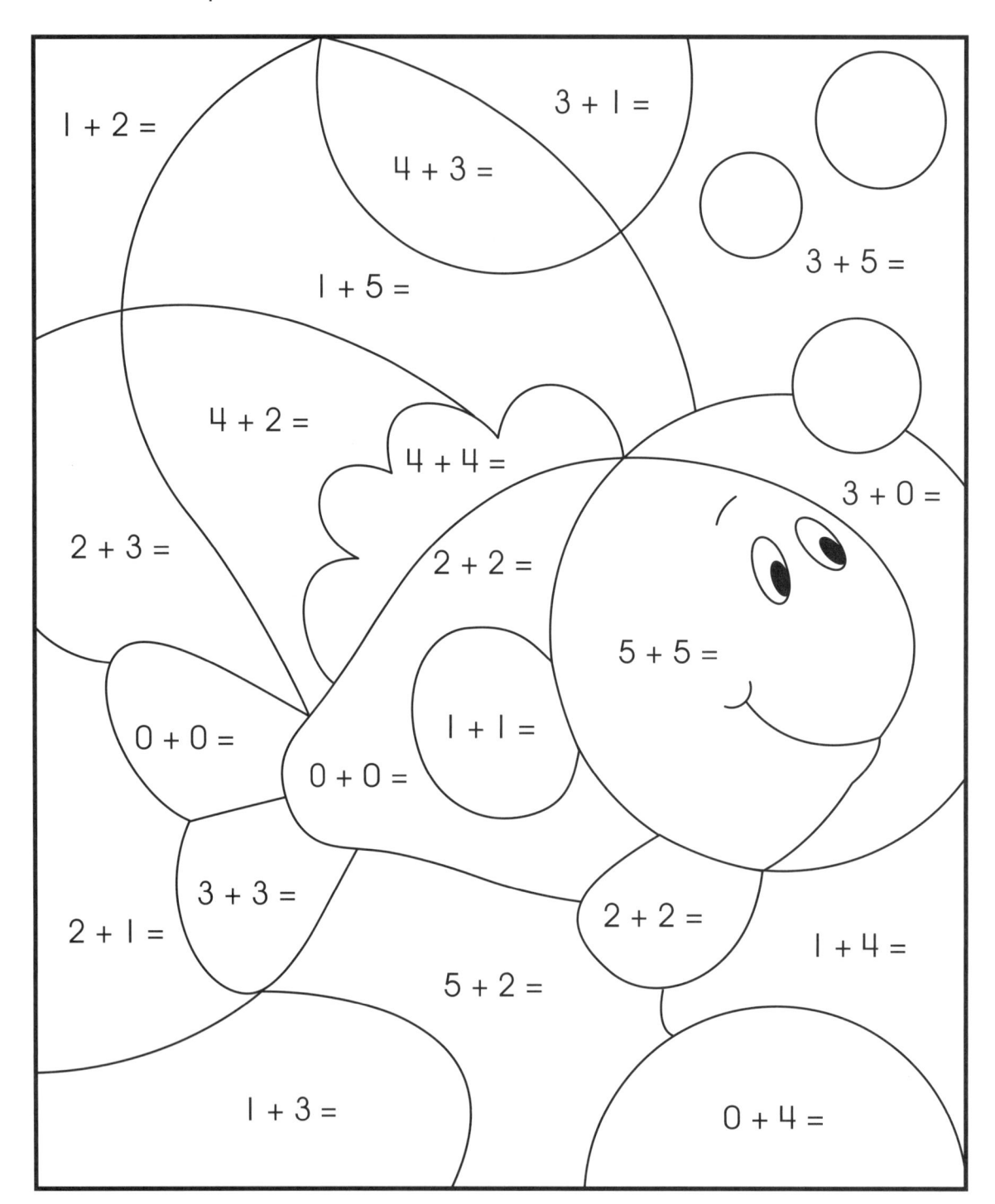

1 + 2 =
3 + 1 =
4 + 3 =
1 + 5 =
3 + 5 =
4 + 2 =
4 + 4 =
3 + 0 =
2 + 3 =
2 + 2 =
5 + 5 =
0 + 0 =
1 + 1 =
0 + 0 =
3 + 3 =
2 + 2 =
2 + 1 =
1 + 4 =
5 + 2 =
1 + 3 =
0 + 4 =

Try This!

On a separate sheet of paper, write and solve addition of doubles from 0 to 10. For example, 0 + 0 = , 1 + 1 = , etc.

Name: _____

Basic Addition Facts

Under-the-Sea Addition

Solve the problems. Use the code to color the picture.

0 and 1 = yellow   2 and 3 = blue
4 and 5 = orange   6 and 7 = purple

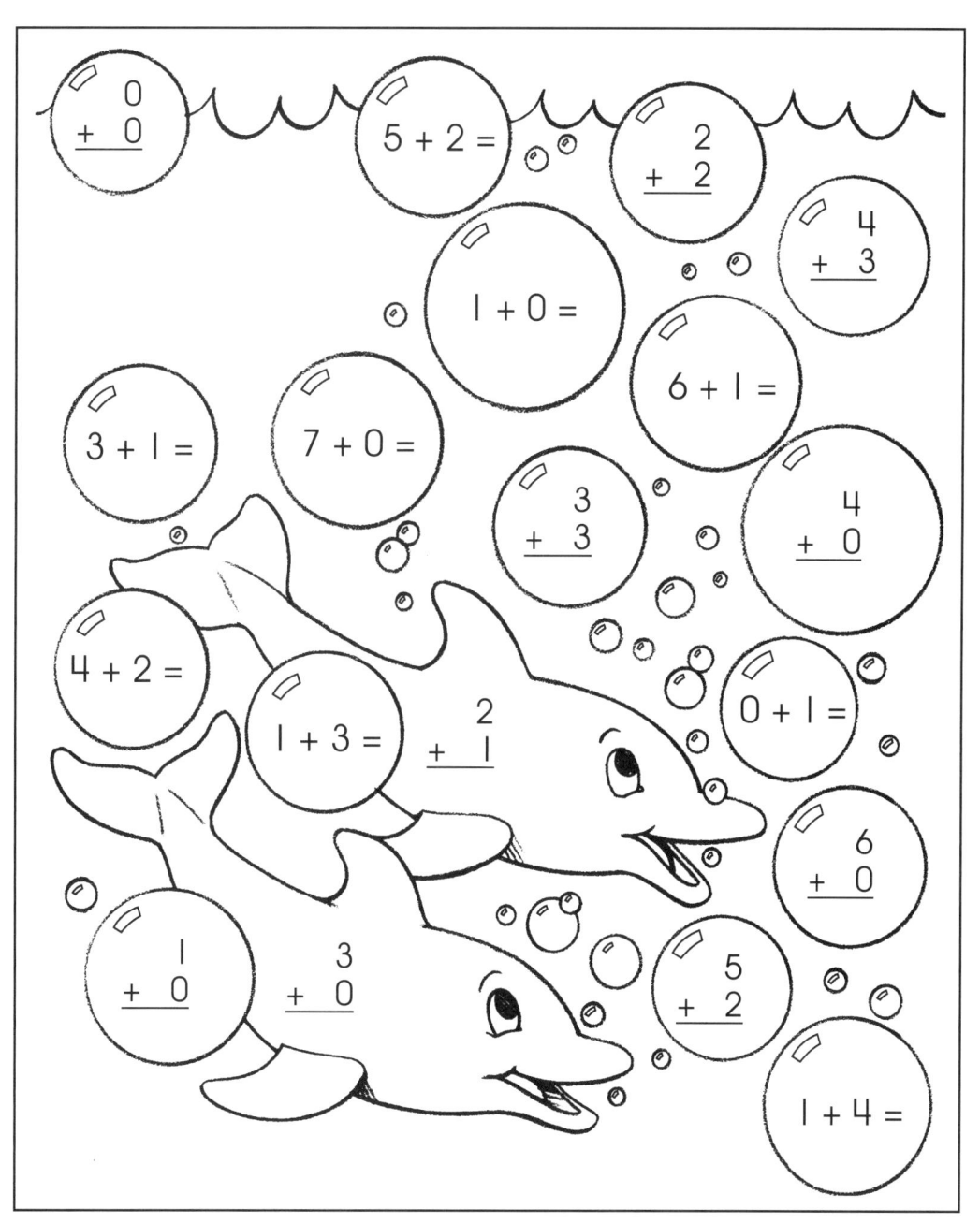

0 + 0
5 + 2 =
2 + 2
4 + 3
1 + 0 =
6 + 1 =
3 + 1 =
7 + 0 =
3 + 3
4 + 0
4 + 2 =
1 + 3 =
2 + 1
0 + 1 =
6 + 0
1 + 0
3 + 0
5 + 2
1 + 4 =

Try This!

On a separate sheet of paper, write an addition word problem about the dolphins in the picture. Write the matching number sentence under the problem.

Name: _____ Sums to 15

Apples in All

Solve the problems. Draw a line to match each problem to the correct answer.

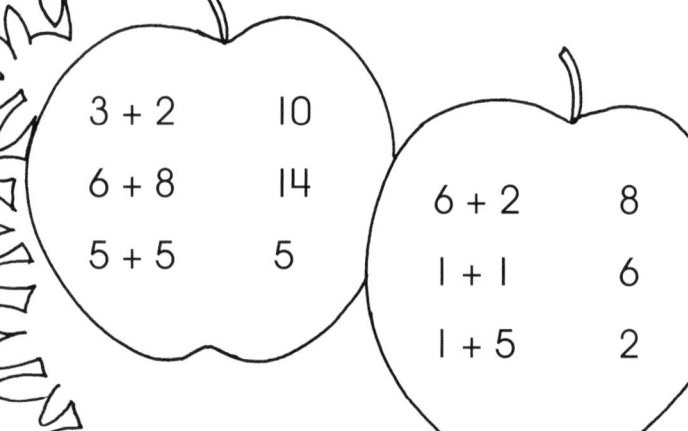

8 + 2	15
9 + 6	4
2 + 2	10

1 + 2	11
6 + 7	3
5 + 6	13

6 + 6	12
6 + 3	9
3 + 4	7

3 + 2	10
6 + 8	14
5 + 5	5

6 + 2	8
1 + 1	6
1 + 5	2

Try This!
Do more of your classmates like red or green apples? Ask seven classmates their favorite flavors and write an addition sentence using the numbers.

Name: _____   Sums to 18

Bats Are Everywhere!

Solve the problems. Color each bat with a sum greater than 10 black. Color each bat with a sum less than 10 brown.

$7 + 4$

$3 + 3$

$6 + 6$

$8 + 4$

$5 + 4$

$2 + 7$

$9 + 9$

$4 + 1$

$7 + 6$

$6 + 2$

Try This!

Write two new math problems in the activity above. Use the same color code to draw a black or brown circle around each problem.

Name: _____   Three Addend Sums

Add All Three

Solve the problems. Write the sums in order from least to greatest on the lines below.

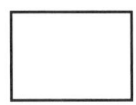

```
    7          6          4          4
    4          5          4          3
  + 2        + 3        + 3        + 6
  ---        ---        ---        ---
  [ ]        [ ]        [ ]        [ ]

    4          4          7          8
    2          6          2          8
  + 5        + 2        + 4        + 1
  ---        ---        ---        ---
  [ ]        [ ]        [ ]        [ ]
```

___ ___ ___ ___ ___ ___ ___ ___

Try This!

On a separate sheet of paper, write two addition problems that each have three addends and a sum of 12.

Name: _____

Two-Digit Sums

Double-Digit Sums

Solve the problems. Color the spaces with sums greater than 50 red. Color the spaces with sums less than 50 blue.

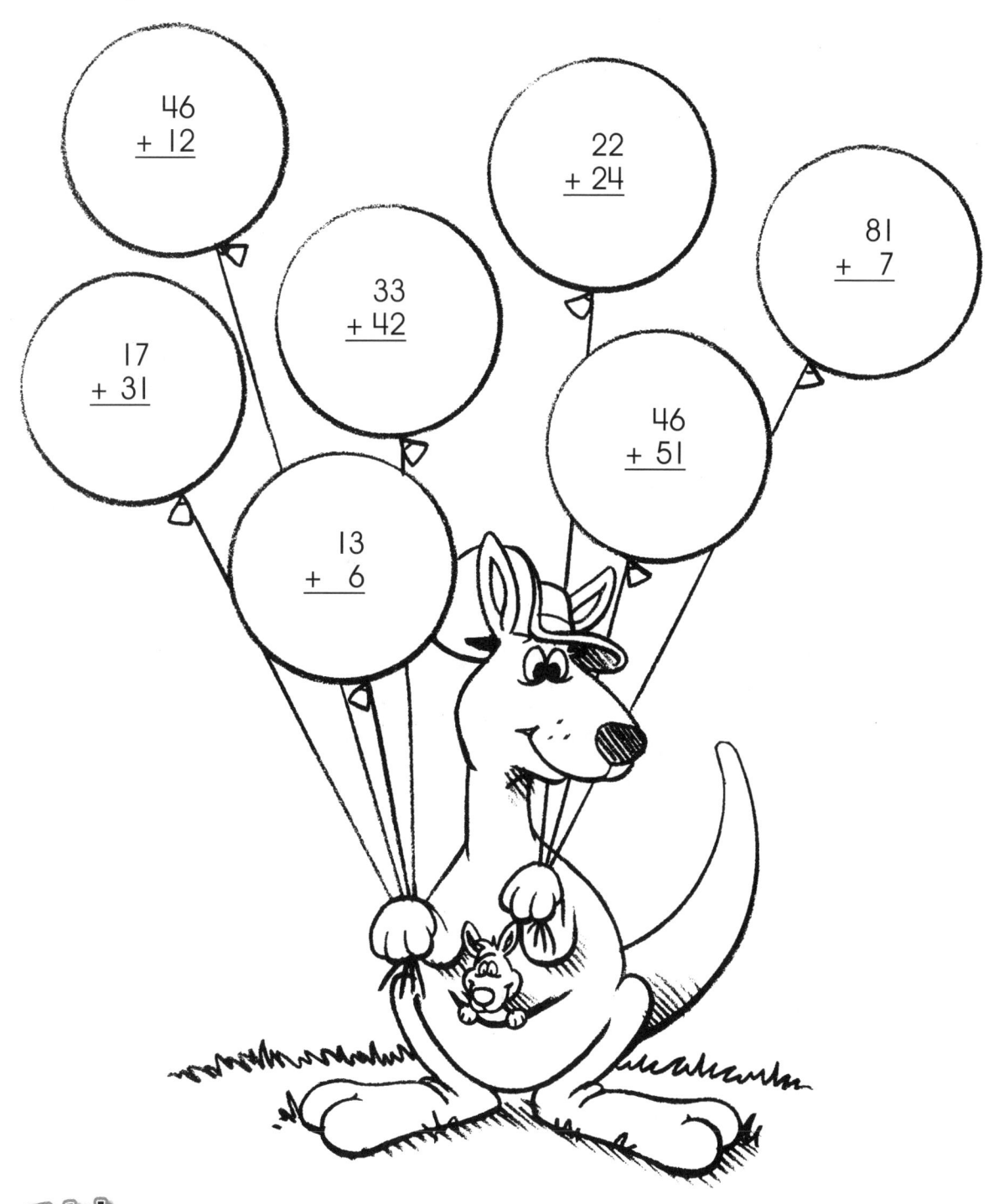

- 46 + 12
- 22 + 24
- 81 + 7
- 33 + 42
- 17 + 31
- 46 + 51
- 13 + 6

Try This!

Draw two empty balloons. Inside the empty balloons, write one addition problem that has a sum greater than 50 and one addition problem that has a sum less than 50. Color the balloons the correct color.

Name: _____   Two-Digit Sums

In Outer Space

Solve the problems. Color the problems with odd answers red. Color the problems with even answers yellow.

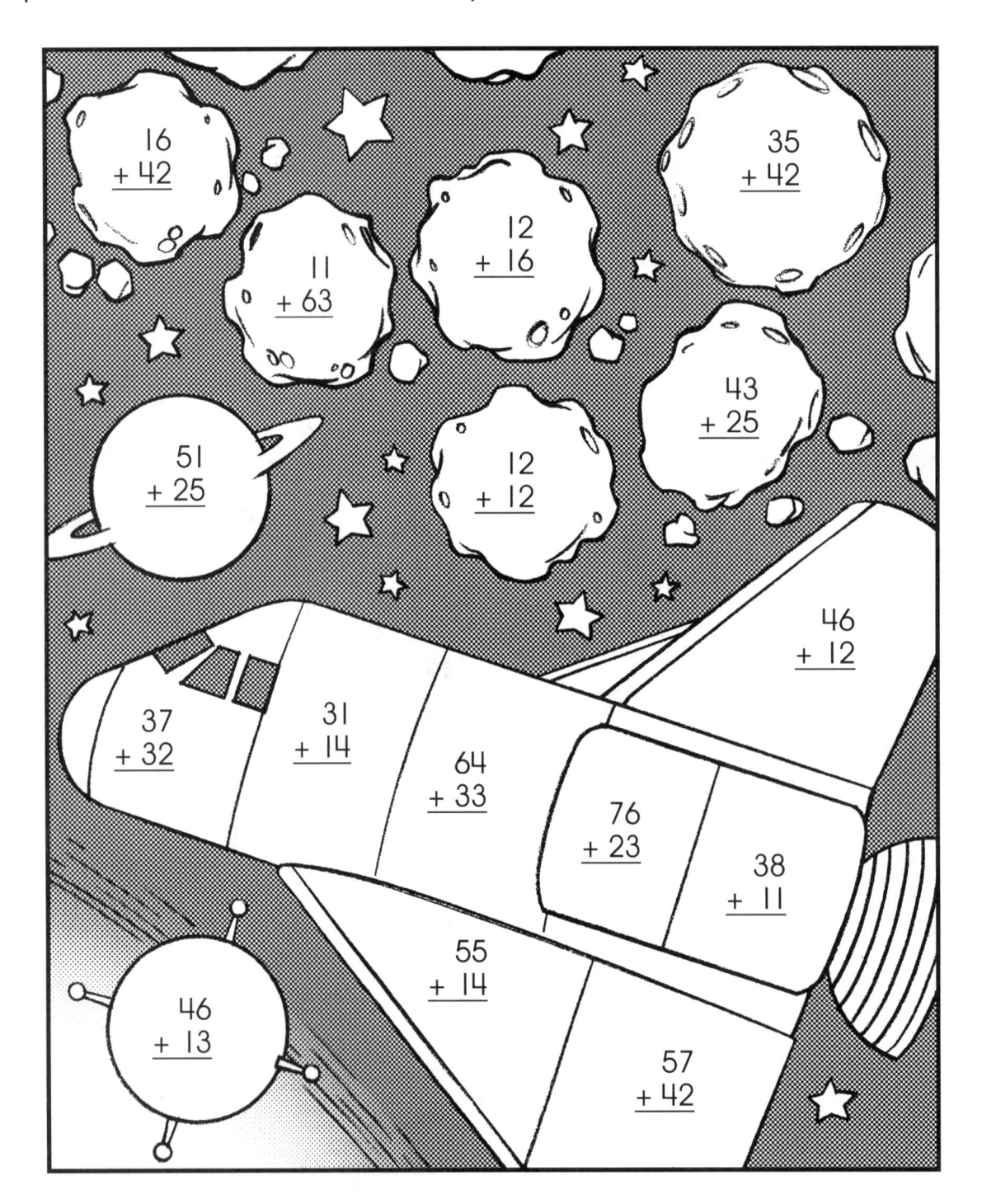

16 + 42

35 + 42

11 + 63

12 + 16

43 + 25

51 + 25

12 + 12

46 + 12

37 + 32

31 + 14

64 + 33

76 + 23

38 + 11

55 + 14

46 + 13

57 + 42

Try This!

On a separate sheet of paper, name five objects that are in space. Write a word problem about two of the space objects.

Name: _____

Addition with Regrouping

Presidential Addition

Solve the problems. Use the answers to solve the riddle.

N	A	O	S
14 + 17	26 + 47	35 + 25	17 + 29

T	H	B	E
16 + 36	53 + 18	19 + 21	29 + 29

What is a nickname for the 16th president of the United States?

$\overline{71}$ $\overline{60}$ $\overline{31}$ $\overline{58}$ $\overline{46}$ $\overline{52}$ $\overline{73}$ $\overline{40}$ $\overline{58}$

Try This!

With an adult, use the Internet to find a picture of the 16th U.S. president. Write three facts and three opinions about this president.

Name: _____ Differences to 10

Solving Problems in the Stars

Subtract. Write the differences. Color each space with a difference of 2 or 3 yellow. Color the rest of the spaces purple.

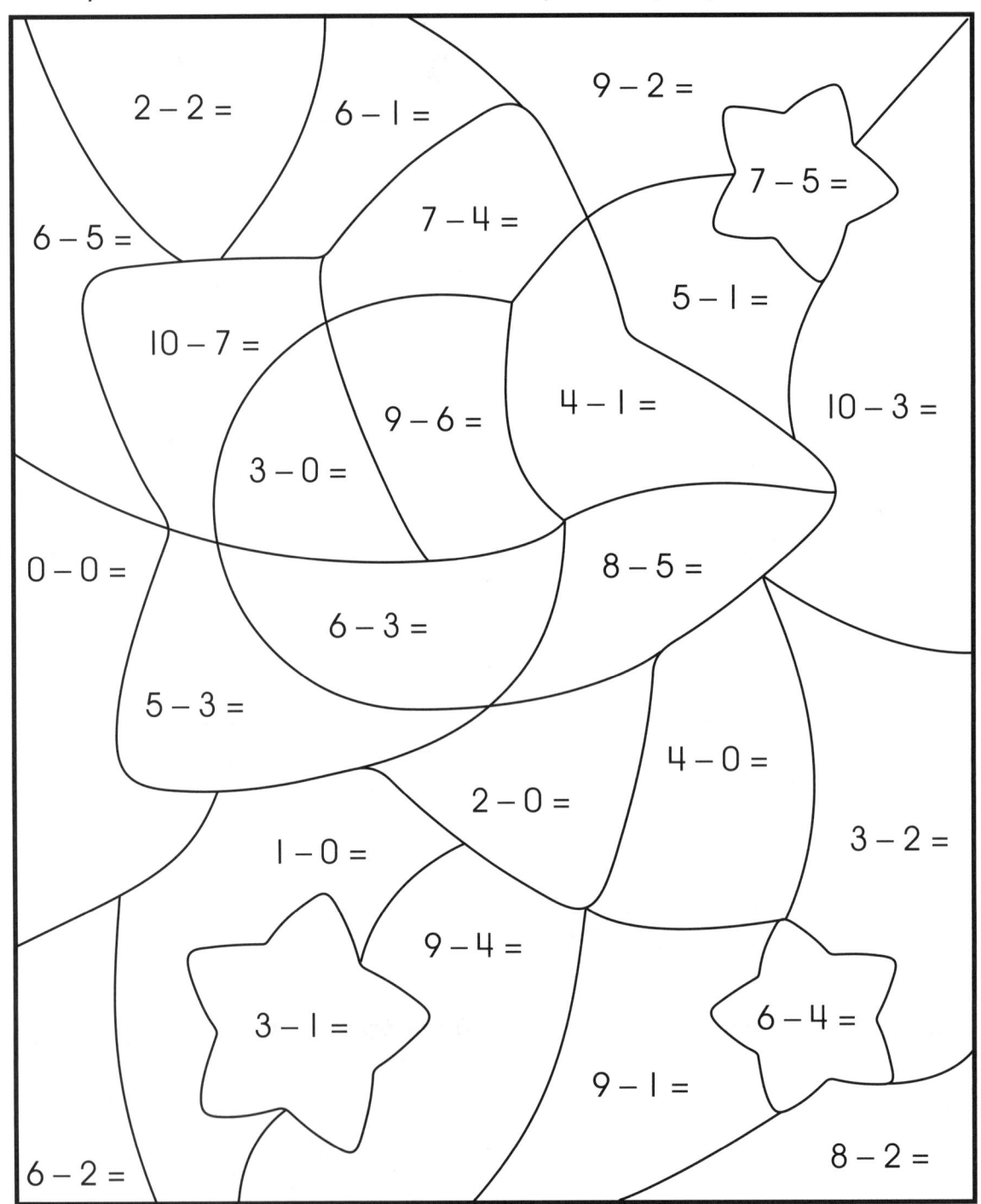

2 − 2 =

6 − 1 =

9 − 2 =

7 − 5 =

6 − 5 =

7 − 4 =

5 − 1 =

10 − 7 =

9 − 6 =

4 − 1 =

10 − 3 =

3 − 0 =

0 − 0 =

8 − 5 =

6 − 3 =

5 − 3 =

4 − 0 =

2 − 0 =

1 − 0 =

3 − 2 =

9 − 4 =

3 − 1 =

6 − 4 =

9 − 1 =

6 − 2 =

8 − 2 =

Try This!

Jay saw 9 shooting stars. He made wishes on 6 of them. How many stars did he not wish on? On a separate sheet of paper, write a subtraction sentence that shows the problem. Then, subtract to find the answer.

Name: _____   Differences to Five

Springtime Subtraction

Subtract. Use the code to color the worms.

1 = red   3 = yellow
2 = orange   4 = brown

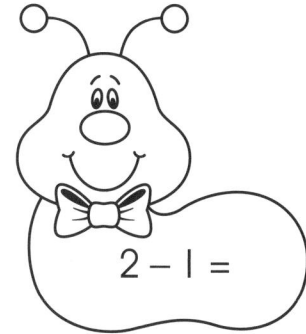

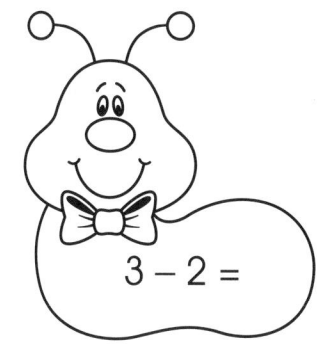

5 − 1 =   4 − 2 =   5 − 2 =

3 − 1 =   4 − 3 =   5 − 3 =

2 − 1 =   4 − 1 =   3 − 2 =

Try This!
A total of 8 birds were in a tree. Some flew away, and 3 birds were left in the tree. How many birds flew away? On a separate sheet of paper, write a subtraction sentence that shows the problem. Then, subtract to find the answer.

Name: _____   Differences to 20

Crayons in a Box

Count the crayons. Write the number on the line. Circle all of the problems that have a difference equal to that number.

1. _____

13 − 2 =   15 − 4 =

15 − 5 =   12 − 1 =

   13   14
 − 2   − 3

2. _____

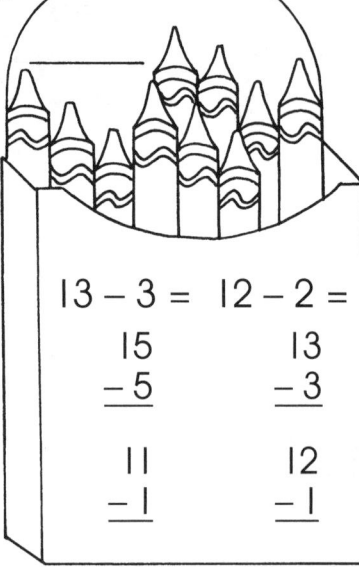

13 − 3 =   12 − 2 =

   15   13
 − 5   − 3

   11   12
 − 1   − 1

3. _____

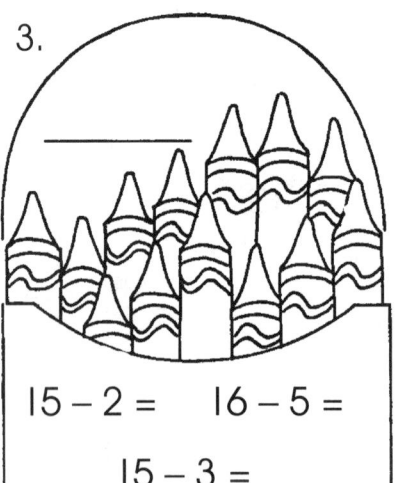

15 − 2 =   16 − 5 =

15 − 3 =

   18   19
 − 5   − 6

   14
 − 1

4. _____

18 − 6 =   20 − 8 =

14 − 4 =

   13
 − 1

   17   15
 − 9   − 3

5. _____

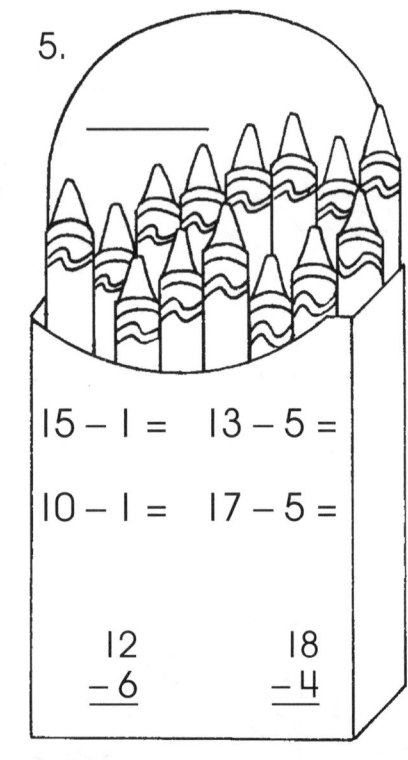

15 − 1 =   13 − 5 =

10 − 1 =   17 − 5 =

   12   18
 − 6   − 4

Try This!

Make a collage with your favorite color. Cut 20 pictures out of magazines that show things in your favorite color. Glue them on a sheet of construction paper.

Name: _____   Differences to 20

Exploring Differences

Solve the problems. Use the answers to solve the riddle.

P	T	I	N
19 − 4	14 − 2	5 − 1	9 − 6

M	A	S	R
9 − 0	15 − 4	19 − 1	7 − 0

What three "friends" did Columbus sail with?

__ __ __ __ , __ __ __ __ __ , and
 3 4 3 11   15 4 3 12 11

__ __ __ __ __   __ __ __ __ __
18 11 3 12 11   9 11 7 4 11

Try This!

If you could explore a new land, where would it be, and how would you get there? Explain your answer on a separate sheet of paper.

Name: _____   Differences to 20

See the Simple Machine

Solve the problems. Use the answers to solve the riddle.

S	O	C	A
18 − 4	17 − 4	6 − 4	8 − 2

R	I	P	F
9 − 1	13 − 3	20 − 1	7 − 6

What simple machine looks like an *X* when open and a *Y* when closed?

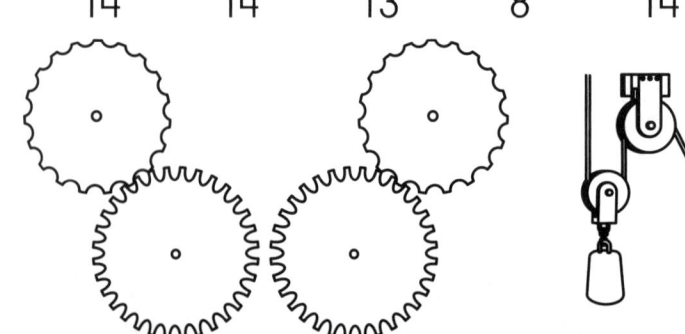

___ ___ ___ ___ ___   ___ ___
 6   19 6 10 8   13 1

___ ___ ___ ___ ___ ___ ___ ___
14   2 10 14 14 13 8 14

Try This!
On a separate sheet of paper, draw a picture of the simple machine and write three things it is used for.

184

Name: _____   Two-Digit Differences

Bees and Flower Favorites

Subtract the numbers to find the differences. Cut out and glue the differences next to the flowers.

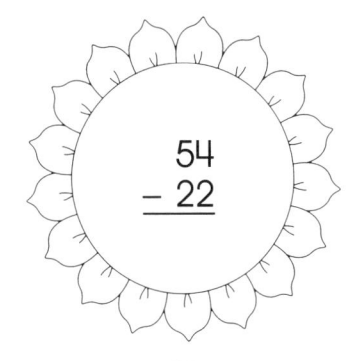

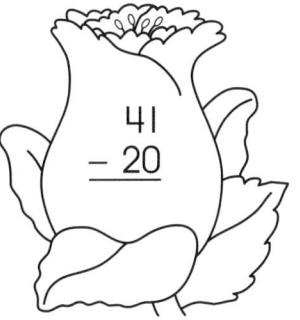

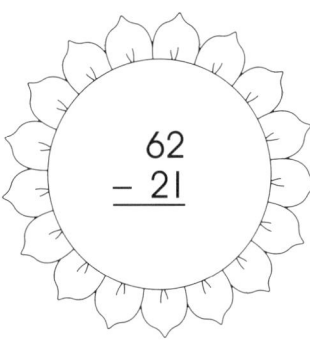

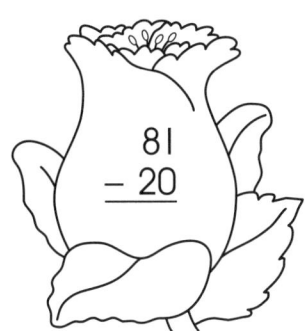

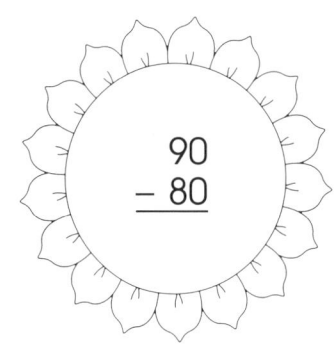

54
− 22

62
− 10

27
− 14

41
− 20

62
− 21

39
− 17

75
− 52

81
− 20

90
− 80

Try This!

On a separate sheet of paper, draw a picture of your favorite flower. Label the parts of the flower.

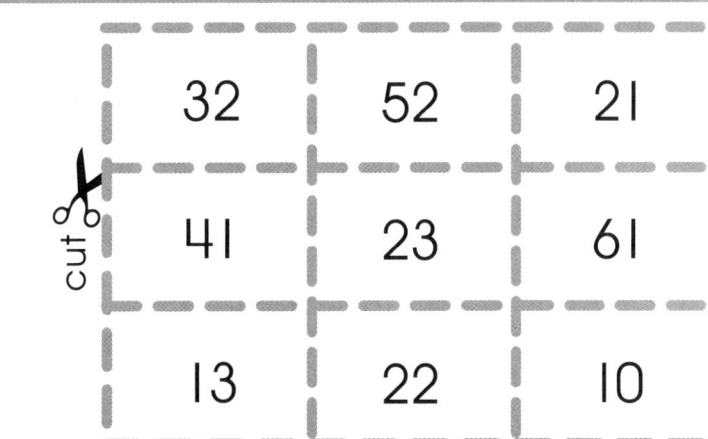

32	52	21
41	23	61
13	22	10

cut

Name: _____

Two-Digit Differences

Find the Matching Difference

Subtract the numbers to find the differences. Draw lines to match the answers that are the same.

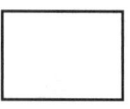

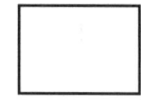

```
  29              45
- 12            - 23
```

```
  99              87
- 65            - 36
```

```
  87              39
- 65            - 22
```

```
  76              67
- 25            - 33
```

Try This!

On a separate sheet of paper, write an addition problem for each difference.

Name: _____

Subtraction with Regrouping

Lucky in Subtraction

Subtract. Cut out and glue the pot of gold with the matching answer on each rainbow.

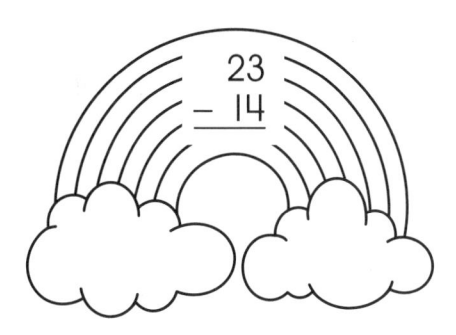

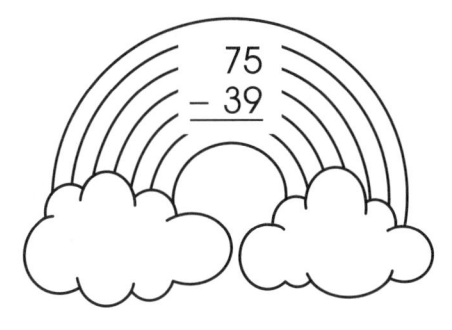

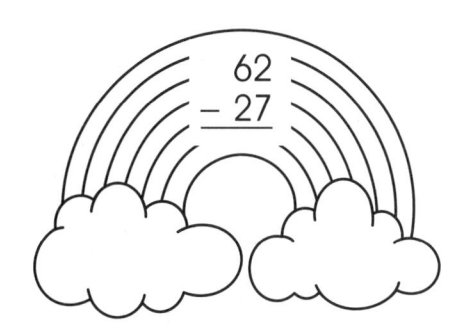

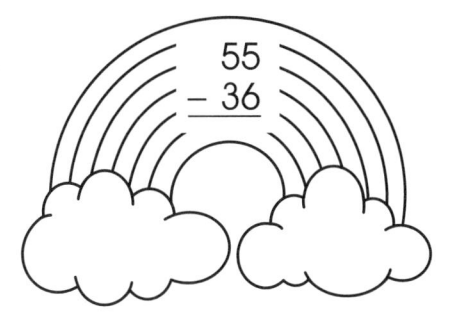

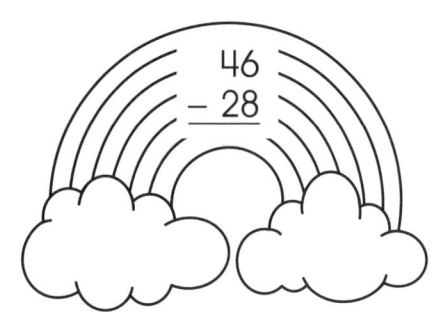

71 − 19

23 − 14

75 − 39

62 − 27

55 − 36

46 − 28

Try This!
On the back of this paper, write what you would do if you found a pot of gold.

9   35   52   19   36   18

Name: _____   Mixed Practice Sums and Differences

Pet Problems

Look at the pictures. Finish the number sentences.

1. 
   5 ⊕ 6 = 11

2. 
   11 ◯ 4 = _____

3. 
   12 ◯ 7 = _____

4. 
   7 ◯ 6 = _____

5. 
   5 ◯ 5 = _____

6. 
   8 ◯ 6 = _____

Try This!

Find a magazine or catalog picture with several animals in it. On a separate sheet of paper, write one addition and one subtraction sentence about the picture.

Name: _____   Mixed Practice Sums and Differences

Bananas over Math

Write **+** or **−** to make each problem correct. Trace a path to connect each monkey to the correct banana. For Marcus, connect all of the addition problems. For Mona, connect all of the subtraction problems.

Marcus  (+)   **Mona** (−)

3 ◯ 2 = 5

5 ◯ 5 = 10

3 ◯ 3 = 0

9 ◯ 1 = 10

9 ◯ 4 = 5

2 ◯ 6 = 8

10 ◯ 8 = 2

5 ◯ 4 = 9

10 ◯ 3 = 7

6 ◯ 4 = 10

8 ◯ 2 = 6

5 ◯ 2 = 7

7 ◯ 3 = 4

5 ◯ 3 = 8

6 ◯ 3 = 3

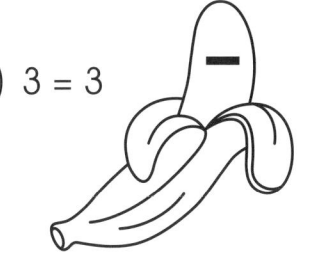

2 ◯ 7 = 9

Try This!

What animals live in a rain forest with monkeys? On a separate sheet of paper, draw a picture of a rain forest that shows at least five animals that live in it. Write three to four sentences telling about your picture.

Name: _____   Related Facts

Number Sentences

Solve the problems. Write an addition sentence and a subtraction sentence for each problem.

1. [8]

___ + ___ = ___
___ − ___ = ___

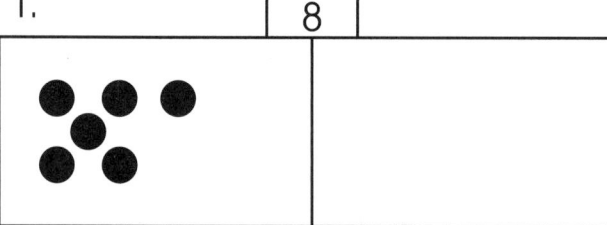

2. [12]

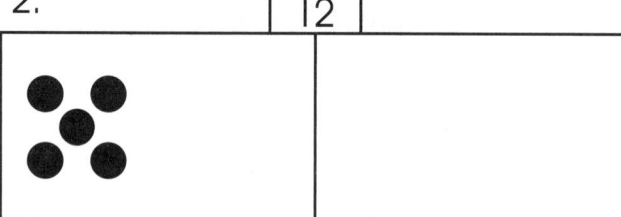

___ + ___ = ___
___ − ___ = ___

3. [3]

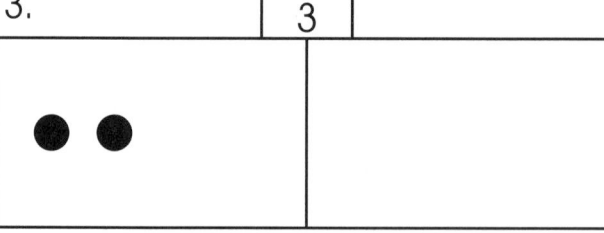

___ + ___ = ___
___ − ___ = ___

4. [6]

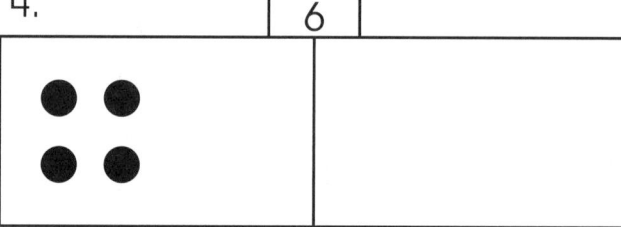

___ + ___ = ___
___ − ___ = ___

5. [11]

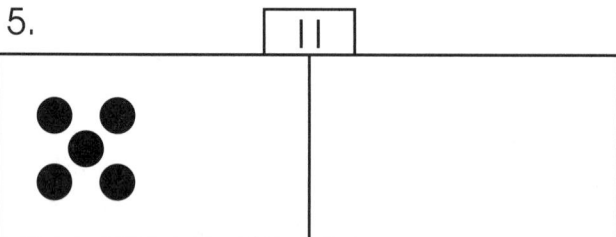

___ + ___ = ___
___ − ___ = ___

6. [7]

___ + ___ = ___
___ − ___ = ___

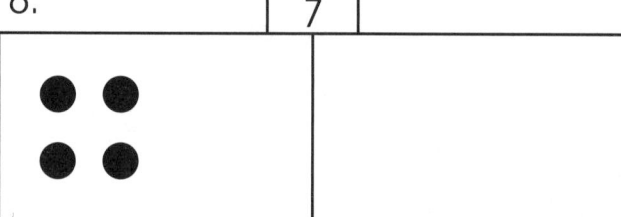

Try This!
How many math facts can you think of that have a whole of 10? Write your answers on a separate sheet of paper.

Magnet Math

Solve the problems. Use the answers to solve the riddle.

N	T	H	R	P	L
5 + 5	14 − 12	19 − 6	4 + 7	3 + 1	15 + 4

O	E	S	U	A	D
7 − 2	7 + 8	12 − 6	10 − 7	17 − 9	9 + 8

What do magnets have in common with the earth?

Answer: They both have . . .

__A__ __N__ __O__ __R__ __T__ __H__
  8   10   5   11   2   13

__P__ __O__ __L__ __E__   __A__ __N__ __D__ __A__
  4   5   19   15   8   10   17   8

__S__ __O__ __U__ __T__ __H__   __P__ __O__ __L__ __E__.
  6   5   3   2   13   4   5   19   15

Try This!

On a separate sheet of paper, list five things that are attracted to magnets and five things that are not attracted to magnets.

Name: _____   Mixed Practice Sums and Differences

Gift of Math

Solve the problems. Color the gifts with answers greater than 20 red. Color the gifts with answers less than 20 blue.

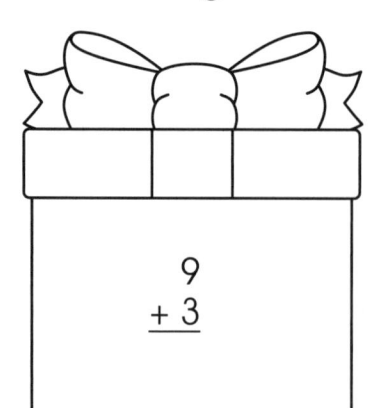

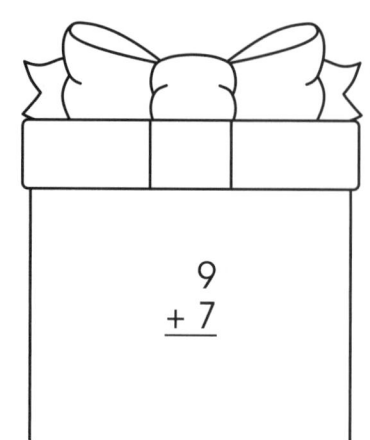

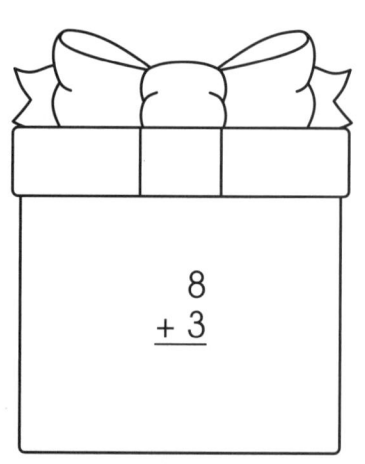

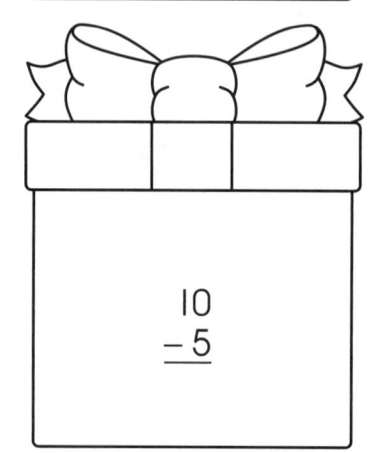

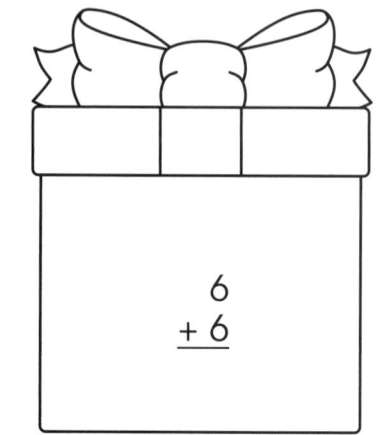

$9 + 3$

$10 + 5$

$9 + 7$

$6 + 6$

$16 - 6$

$8 + 3$

$19 - 9$

$10 - 5$

$6 + 6$

Try This!

If you had 10 gifts and wanted to share some with one other person, how many would you give away, and whom would you give them to? Explain your answer on a separate sheet of paper. Write a subtraction sentence that shows your answer.

192

Name: _____   Mixed Practice Sums and Differences

Make the Connection

Solve the problems. Draw lines to match the answers that are the same. Color the picture.

```
  12              49
+ 13            − 24

  69              16
− 30            + 23

  32              84
+ 10            − 42

  99              35
− 41            + 23

  26              99
+ 43            − 30

  99              62
− 12            + 25
```

Try This!
On a separate sheet of paper, write one two-digit addition problem and one two-digit subtraction problem that have the same answer.

Name: _____   Mixed Practice Sums and Differences

Staying Healthy

Solve the problems. Circle the healthful foods. Draw a box around each food that you should only eat once in a while.

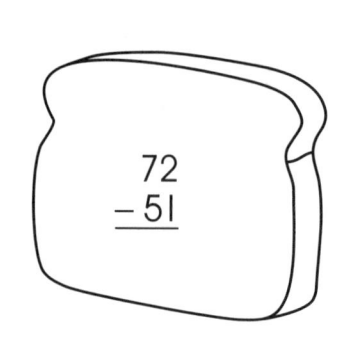

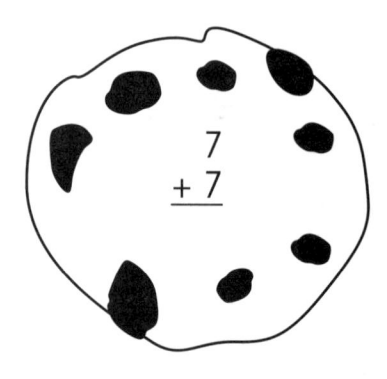

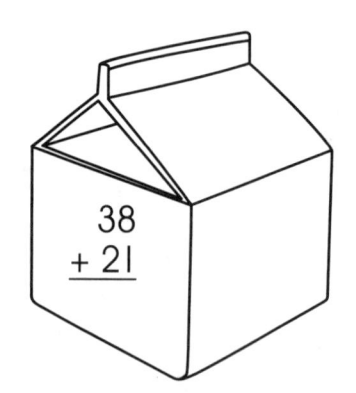

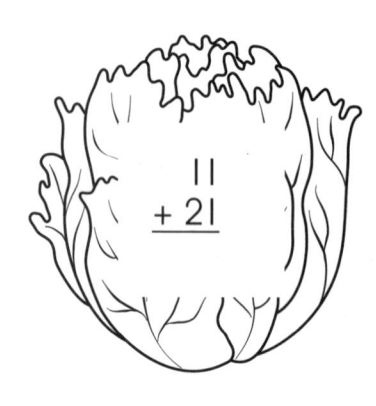

Apple: 14 + 11

Bread: 72 − 51

Strawberry: 8 − 5

Cookie: 7 + 7

Milk carton: 38 + 21

Soda can: 19 − 9

Lettuce: 11 + 21

Yogurt: 9 − 3

Ice cream cone: 14 + 13

Try This! On a separate sheet of paper, write or draw a shopping list for 10 healthful snacks.

Name: _____

Repeating Patterns

Garden Patterns

Continue the patterns. Make your own pattern on the empty vine.

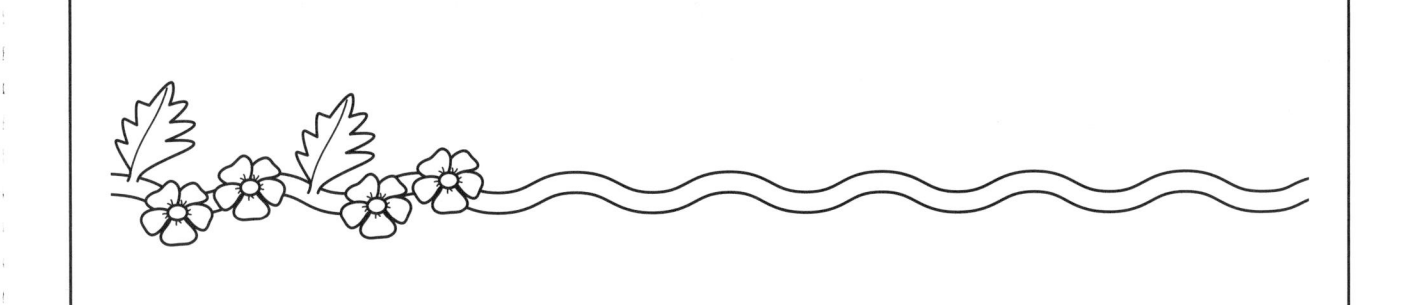

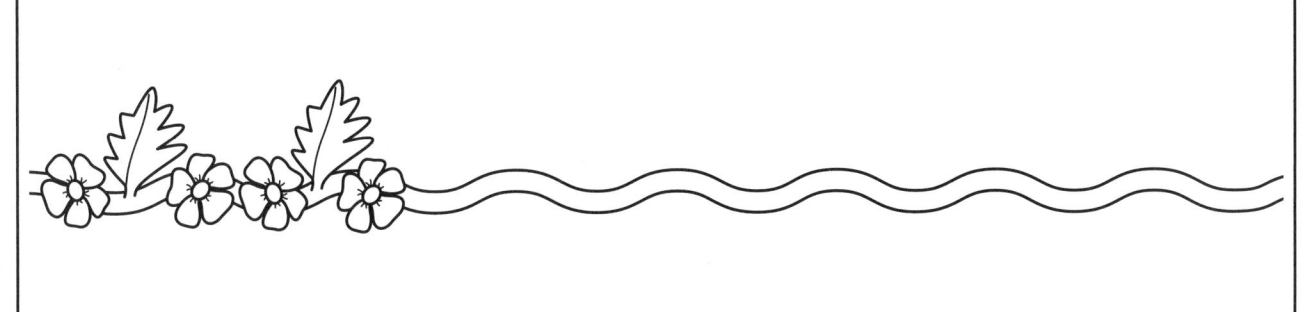

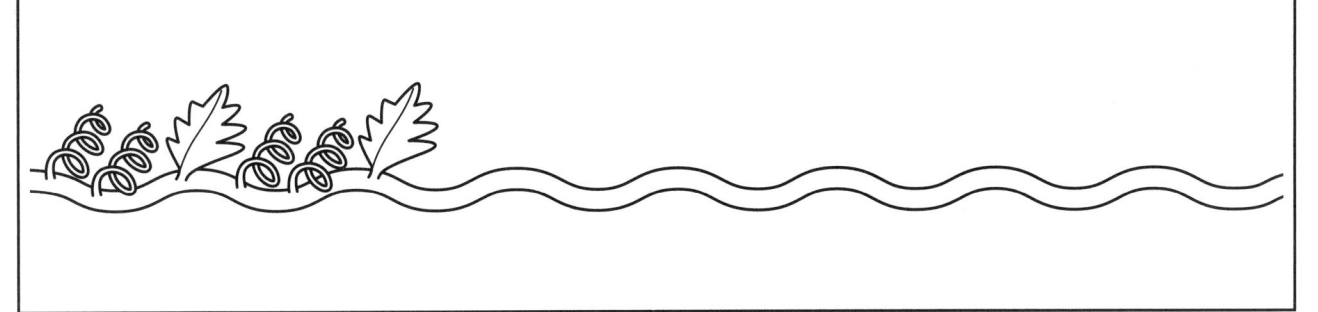

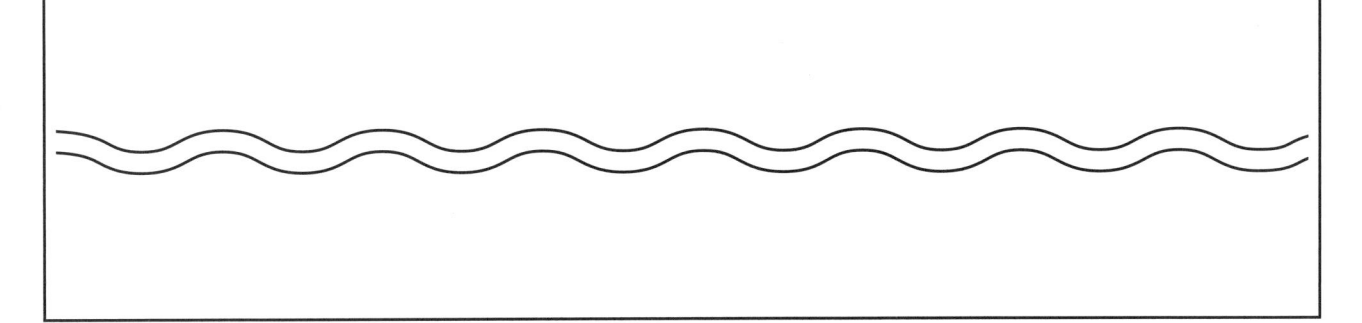

Try This!
Below each picture, use letters or numbers to name the pattern.

Name: _____

Repeating Patterns

Hearts in a Row

Continue the patterns. Color the large hearts red and the small hearts pink.

Try This!

Draw hearts on a sentence strip. Color the hearts to show a pattern. Tape the sentence strip together to make a hat.

Name: _____

Repeating Patterns

Let's Have a Ball!

Continue the patterns.

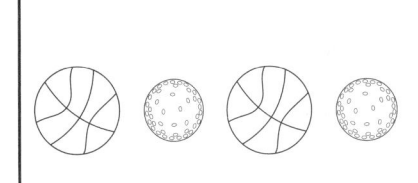

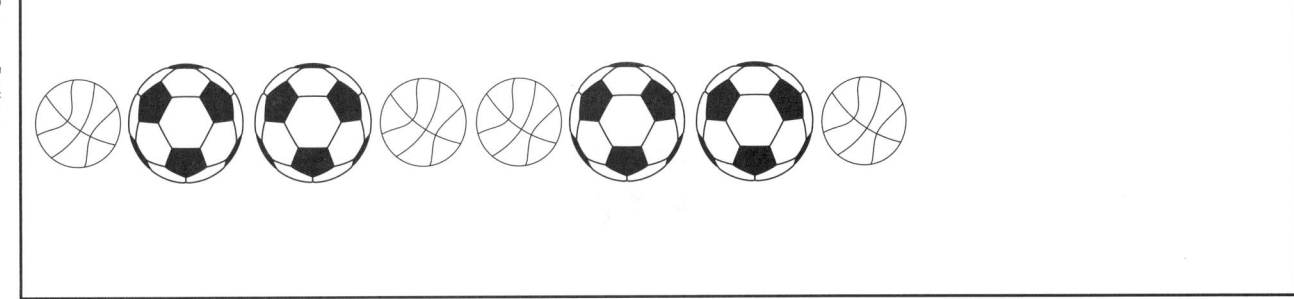

Make your own pattern.

Try This! Which sport is the best? Explain your answer on a separate sheet of paper. Write at least three sentences that support your answer.

197

Name: _____

Growing Patterns

Berries in Baskets

Draw the correct number of strawberries in the baskets to continue each pattern.

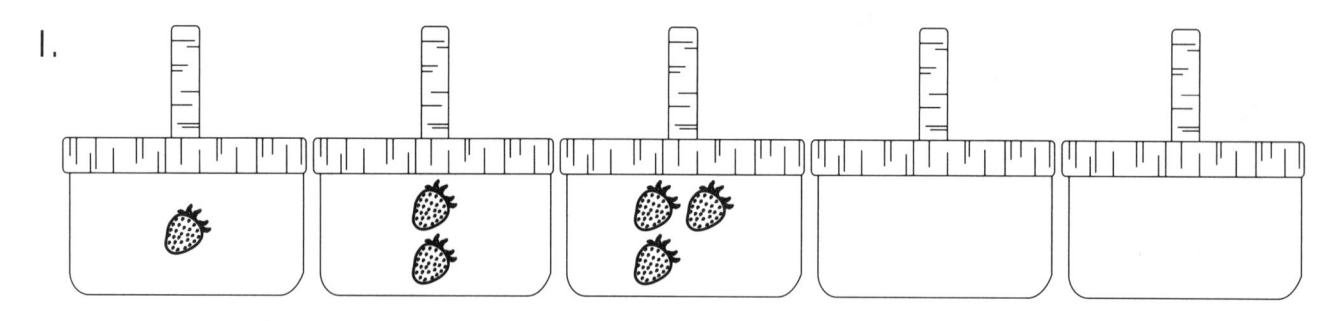

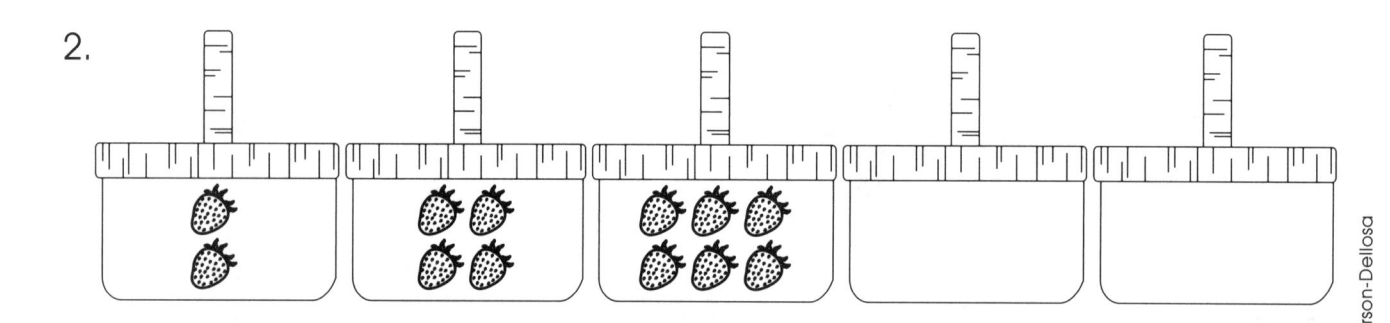

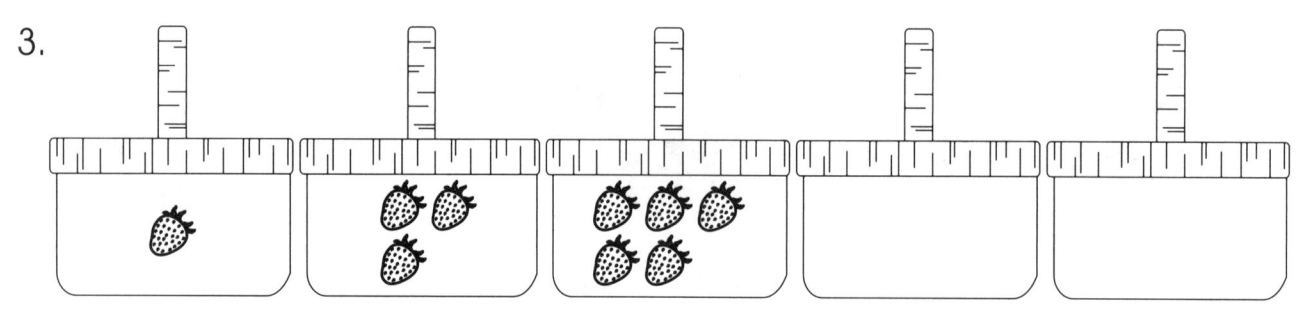

1.

2.

3.

Make your own pattern.

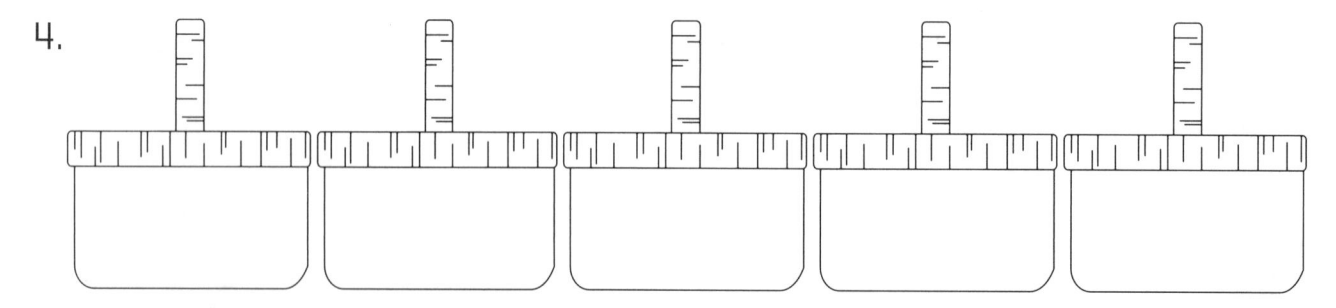

4.

Try This!

What grows on a farm besides strawberries? On a separate sheet of paper, draw a picture of a farm that includes at least five types of crops. Label the crops.

Name: _____

Growing Patterns

Growing with Seeds and Petals

Continue the patterns.

1.

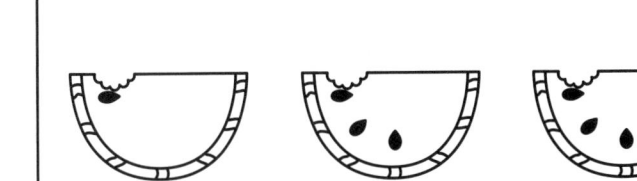

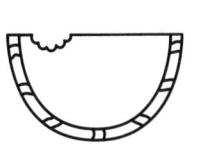

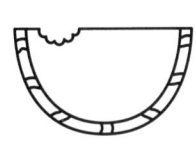

2.

3.

5   10   15   ___   ___

Make your own growing pattern.

4.

Try This!

Show two ways that this growing pattern can be continued.
1.   1, 2, 4, . . .
2.   1, 2, 4, . . .

Name: _____   Related Facts

All in the Family

Use the numbers on each house to complete the fact family number sentences.

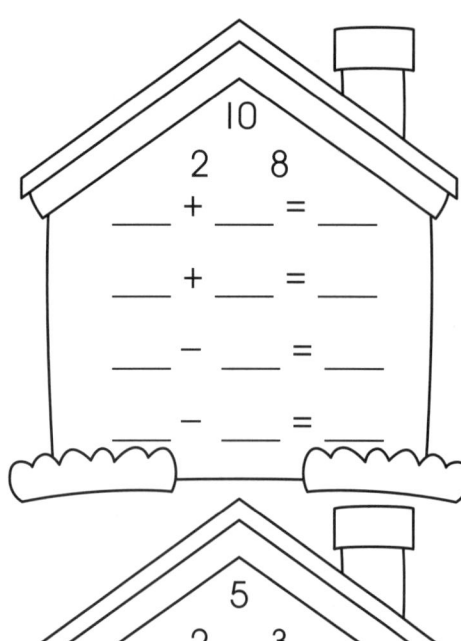

House 1: 10, 2, 8
___ + ___ = ___
___ + ___ = ___
___ − ___ = ___
___ − ___ = ___

House 2: 7, 3, 4
___ + ___ = ___
___ + ___ = ___
___ − ___ = ___
___ − ___ = ___

House 3: 5, 2, 3
___ + ___ = ___
___ + ___ = ___
___ − ___ = ___
___ − ___ = ___

House 4: 8, 5, 3
___ + ___ = ___
___ + ___ = ___
___ − ___ = ___
___ − ___ = ___

Write your own fact family.

___ + ___ = ___
___ + ___ = ___
___ − ___ = ___
___ − ___ = ___

Try This!
How many different fact families have 10 as the greatest number? Show your work on a separate sheet of paper.

Name: _____

Related Facts

Fact Family Fun

Color the number sentences that show numbers in the Brown's fact family brown. Color the number sentences that show numbers in the Green's fact family green. Draw lines to connect the number sentences in the same fact family to lead each family home.

The Greens

The Browns

9 − 6 = 3

9 + 3 = 12

3 + 6 = 9

12 − 9 = 3

6 + 3 = 9

4 + 4 = 8

3 + 9 = 12

9 − 3 = 6

1 + 9 = 10

12 − 3 = 9

5 + 1 = 6

The Greens

The Browns

Try This!

On a separate sheet of paper, draw your own fact family house. Write the three numbers in the fact family on the roof. Write the addition and subtraction number sentences in the house.

Name: _____

Related Facts

Pairs of Number Sentences

Complete the number sentences. Draw a line to match each pair of number sentences in the same fact family.

8 + 7 = ☐   3 + 9 = ☐

9 + 3 = ☐   7 + 8 = ☐

6 + 5 = ☐   7 + 9 = ☐

9 + 7 = ☐   5 + 6 = ☐

Try This!

Complete the fact family. Use the same three numbers as in the subtraction number sentences.

14 − 6 = 8   14 − 8 = 6

☐ + ☐ = ☐   ☐ + ☐ = ☐

Name: _____

Sorting

Helping Goldilocks

Help Goldilocks sort the objects by size. Cut out the pictures. Glue each picture in the correct column.

Small	Medium	Large

Try This!

On the back of this paper, draw pictures of at least three other things that Goldilocks might have seen in the bears' house. Sort the pictures by size.

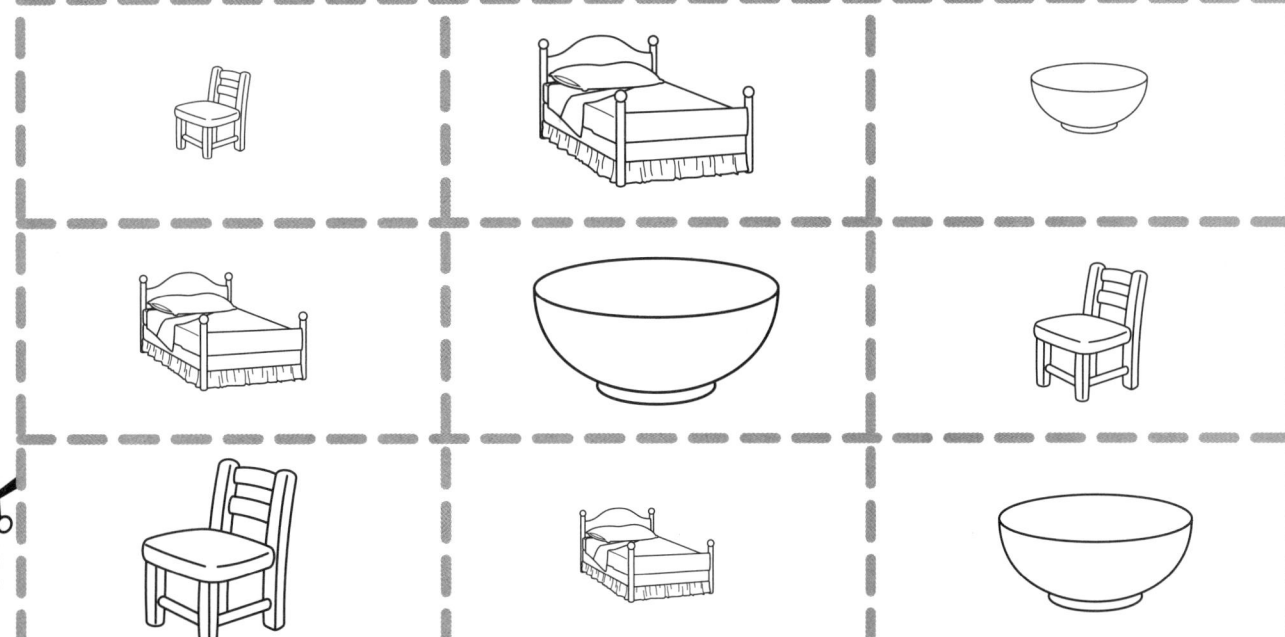

Name: _____

Sorting

Food Rules!

Write each word from the word bank in the correct food group.

milk
_____
_____
_____

meats & beans
_____
_____
_____
_____

Word Bank:
bagel
beans
butter
carrots
cheese
cherries
chicken
cottage cheese
fish
ham
lettuce
olive oil
oranges
pears
rolls
toast
yogurt

fruits
_____
_____
_____
_____

oils
_____
_____

vegetables
_____
_____
_____
_____

grains
_____
_____
_____
_____

Try This! On a separate sheet of paper, sort the same foods by another rule. Explain your sorting rule.

Name: _____

Algebra

Hats Off to Math

Draw the missing pictures. Finish the number sentences.

1. 1 + _____ = 3

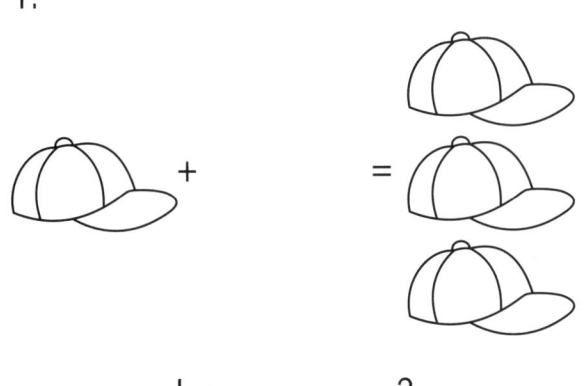

2. 3 + _____ = 5

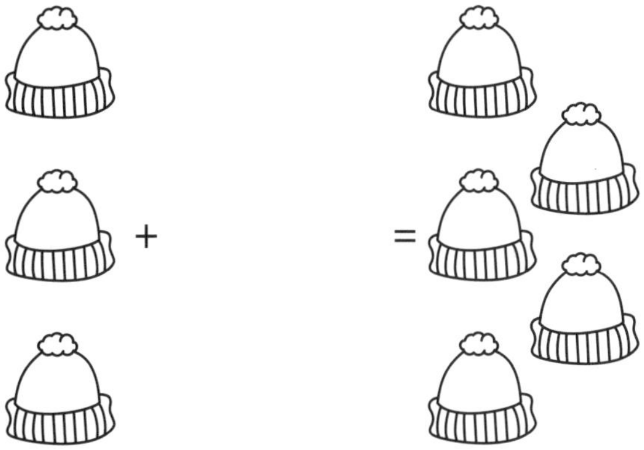

3. 5 + _____ = 8

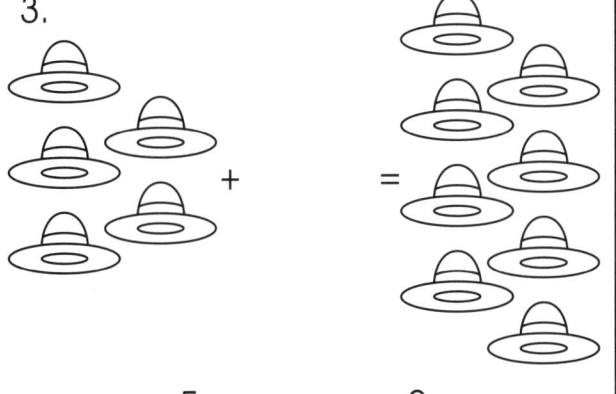

4. 3 + _____ = 6

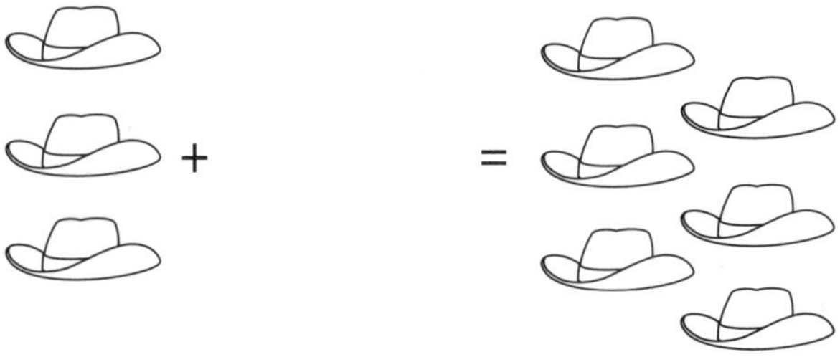

5. 2 + _____ = 7

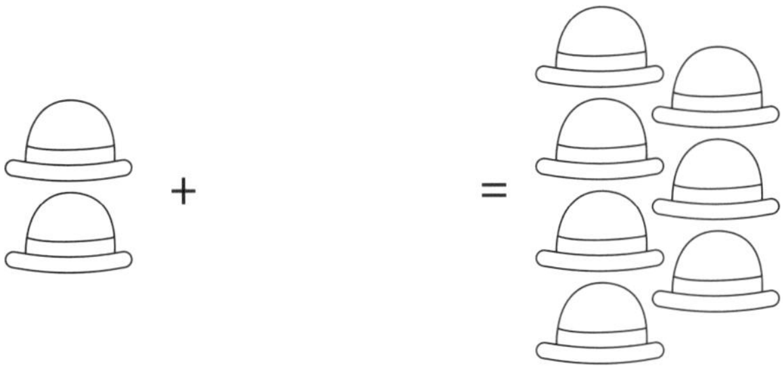

6. 4 + _____ = 5

Try This!

Above each problem, rewrite the addition sentence as a subtraction sentence.

Name: _____

Algebra

Happy About Math

Draw the missing pictures. Finish the number sentences.

1.

3 – _____ = 1

2.

10 – _____ = 7

3.

12 – _____ = 6

4.

8 – _____ = 7

Make up your own problem.

☺☺☺ – _____ = _____
☺☺

Try This!
Above each problem, rewrite the subtraction sentence as an addition sentence.

Name: _____   Unknown Variable

Something Is Missing!

Write the missing number to complete each number sentence.

6 + ☐ = 12   7 + ☐ = 12   13
                                        − ☐
                                        ―――
                                          4

20 − ☐ = 1   11 − ☐ = 2   5
                                        + ☐
                                        ―――
                                         13

15 − ☐ = 1   8 + ☐ = 11   3
                                        + ☐
                                        ―――
                                         13

7 + ☐ = 14   12 − ☐ = 3   18
                                        − ☐
                                        ―――
                                          9

Try This!

Make up two of your own problems.

☐ + ☐ = 12   ☐ + ☐ = 10

Name: _____

Even and Odd Numbers

Horses in Corrals

Cut out the horses. Glue each horse on the correct corral.

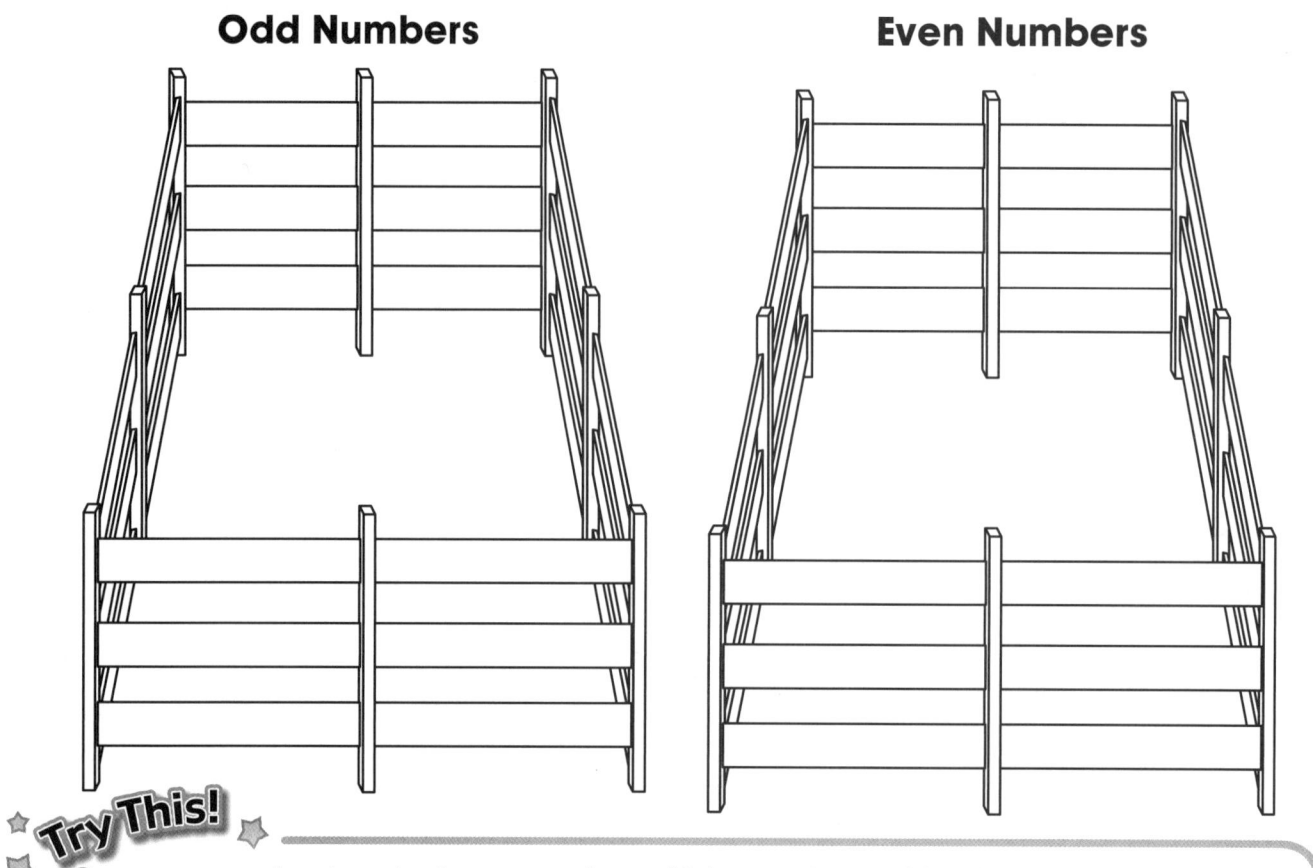

Odd Numbers **Even Numbers**

Try This!

On a separate sheet of paper, draw 13 horseshoes. Number each horseshoe. Color the even-numbered horseshoes brown and the odd-numbered horseshoes black.

cut

| 17 | 34 | 16 |
| 8 | 23 | 9 |

Name: _____   Even and Odd Numbers

Butterfly Winters

Color each even number yellow. Color each odd number black. Find the answer to the question in the picture.

What do many butterflies do each winter?

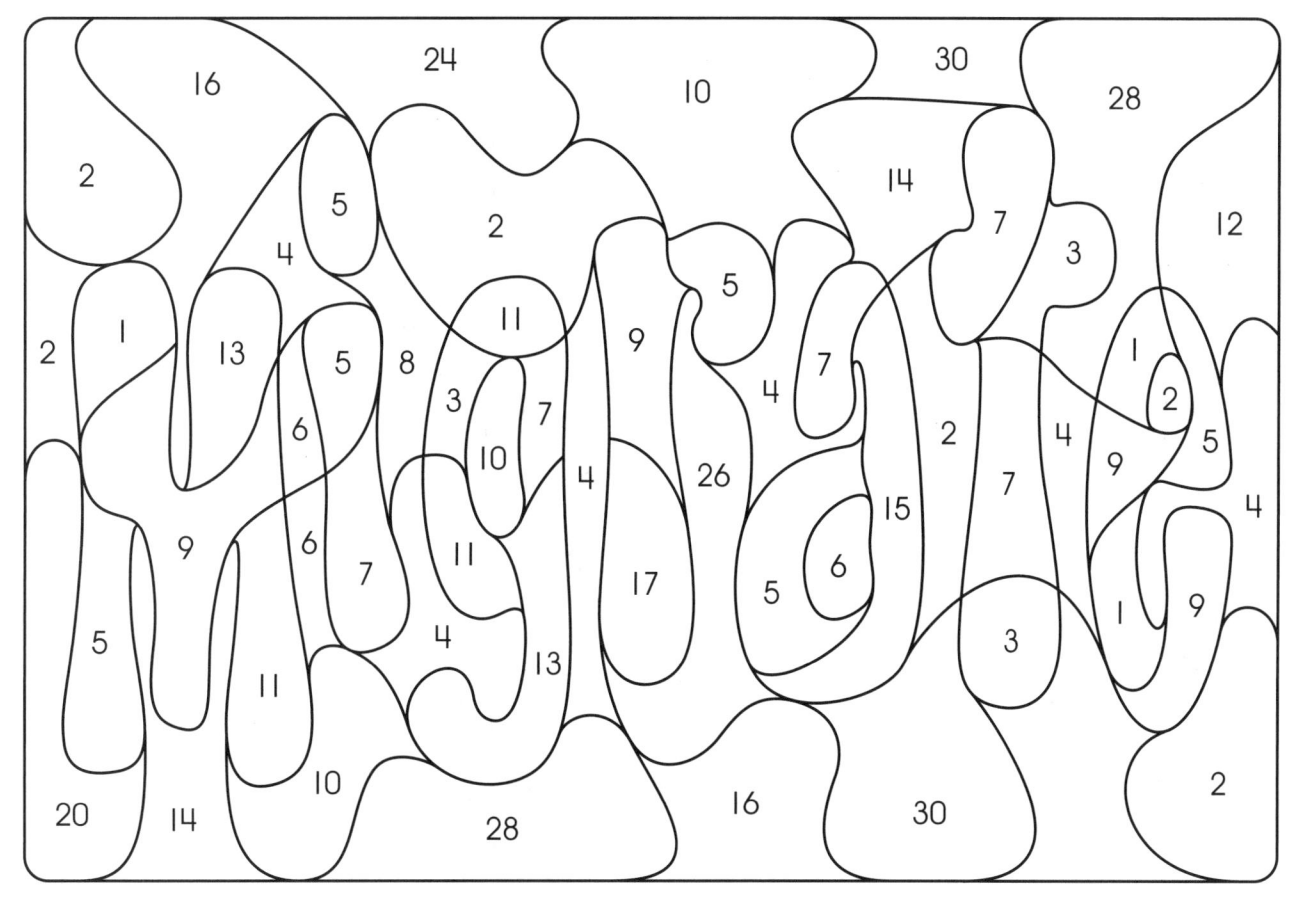

Write the word you see above: _____

What does it mean? _____

_____

Try This!

On a separate sheet of paper, describe two different ways animals prepare for winter. Give an example of an animal for each way.

Name: _____   Place Value

Tens and Ones

Write the number of objects in each set.

_____

_____

_____

_____

_____

_____

_____

_____

Write the value of each number.

29 = _____ tens and _____ ones

34 = _____ tens and _____ ones

18 = _____ ten and _____ ones

48 = _____ tens and _____ ones

Try This!

On a separate sheet of paper, draw a picture that shows 3 tens and 4 ones.

Name: _____   Place Value

Place Value Addition

Add the tens and the ones to find the two-digit sum.

2 tens and 6 ones
+ 1 ten and 3 ones
3 tens and 9 ones = 39

1 ten and 4 ones
+ 3 tens and 3 ones
☐ tens and ☐ ones = ____

1 ten and 3 ones
+ 1 ten and 1 one
☐ tens and ☐ ones = ____

2 tens and 5 ones
+ 2 tens and 0 ones
☐ tens and ☐ ones = ____

1 ten and 6 ones
+ 2 tens and 3 ones
☐ tens and ☐ ones = ____

1 ten and 4 ones
+ 3 tens and 1 one
☐ tens and ☐ ones = ____

1 ten and 5 ones
+ 2 tens and 4 ones
☐ tens and ☐ ones = ____

2 tens and 3 ones
+ 2 tens and 2 ones
☐ tens and ☐ ones = ____

Try This!

On a separate sheet of paper, make up three more addition problems that have a number in both the tens and the ones places.

Name: _____   Place Value

Building Three-Digit Numbers

Write how many hundreds, tens, and ones are in each number.

152 = _____ tens _____ hundred _____ ones

347 = _____ hundreds _____ tens _____ ones

201 = _____ tens _____ hundreds _____ one

136 = _____ ones _____ tens _____ hundred

463 = _____ hundreds _____ ones _____ tens

Try This!
Round each number above to the nearest hundred.

Name: _____   Place Value

Places Everyone!

Write each number shown.

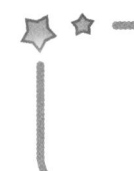

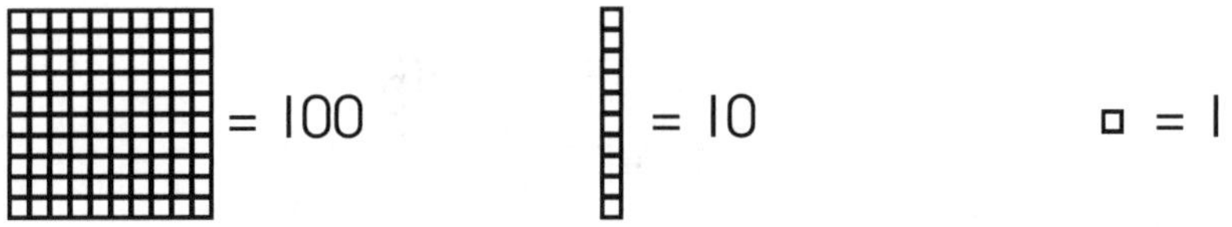

= 100 | = 10   □ = 1

1. _____

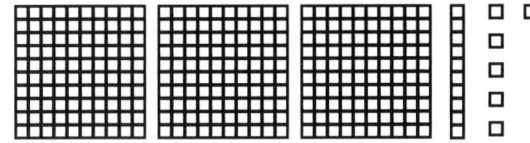

2. _____

3. _____

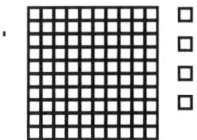

4. _____

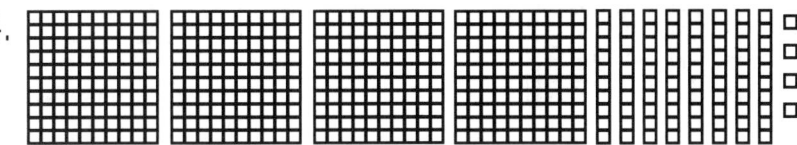

Draw how many.

5. 235

6. 182

Try This!
Write the numbers above in order from least to greatest.

Name: _____

Place Value

More Than One Way

Draw lines to match the equal numbers.

49 •

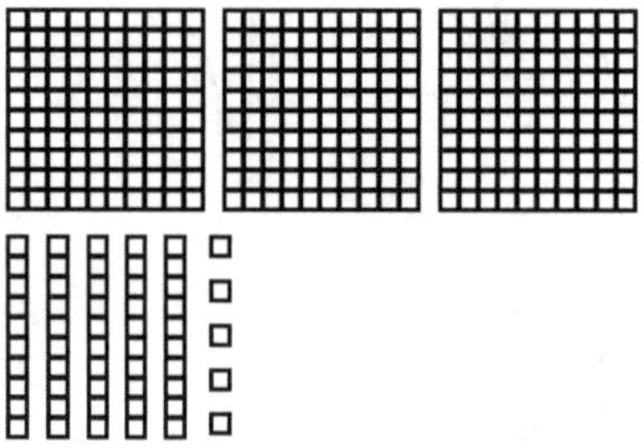

152 •

812 •

355 •

535 •

• 8 hundreds
  1 ten
  2 ones

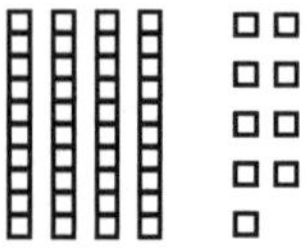

• 4 tens
  9 ones

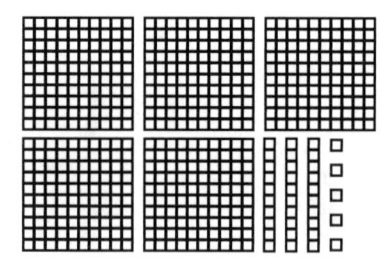

• 1 hundred
  5 tens
  2 ones

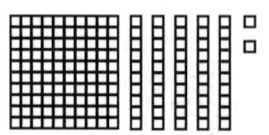

• 3 hundreds
  5 tens
  5 ones

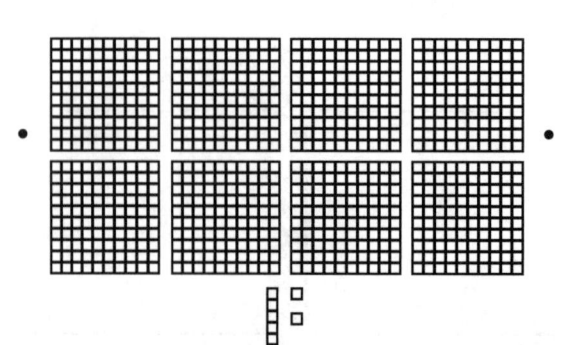

• 5 hundreds
  3 tens
  5 ones

Try This!

On a separate sheet of paper, write one number three different ways.

214

Name: _____ Two-Dimensional Shapes

Will You Find It Here?

Find the shapes. Use the code to color the shapes.

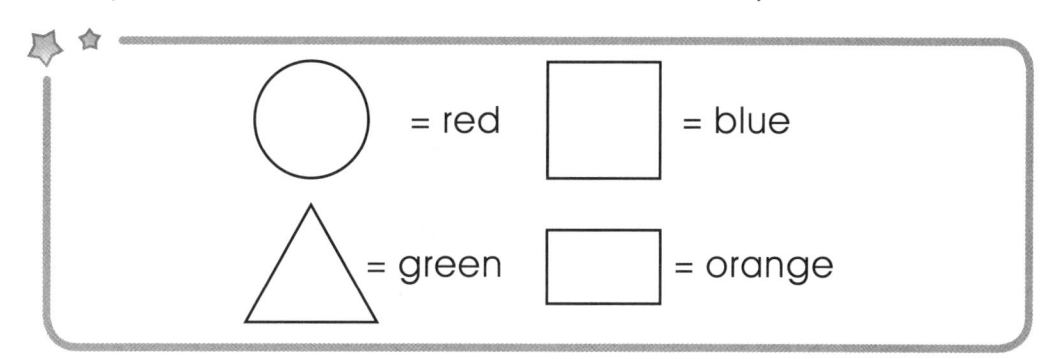

○ = red   □ = blue

△ = green   ▭ = orange

Try This!

On a separate sheet of paper, draw a map of a zoo. Include at least 10 animals that live in the grassland habitat. Label the animals.

Name: _____   Two-Dimensional Shapes

Funny Animal Shapes

Use the code to color the shapes.

squares = green   How many squares? _____

rectangles = yellow   How many circles? _____

circles = red   How many rectangles? _____

triangles = blue   How many triangles? _____

Try This!
On a separate sheet of paper, draw an animal that includes at least two of each shape. Use the above code to color your animal.

216

Name: _____   Two-Dimensional Shapes

Cabin Count

Abraham Lincoln was born in a log cabin. Look at the picture of a log cabin. How many of each shape can you find in the picture?

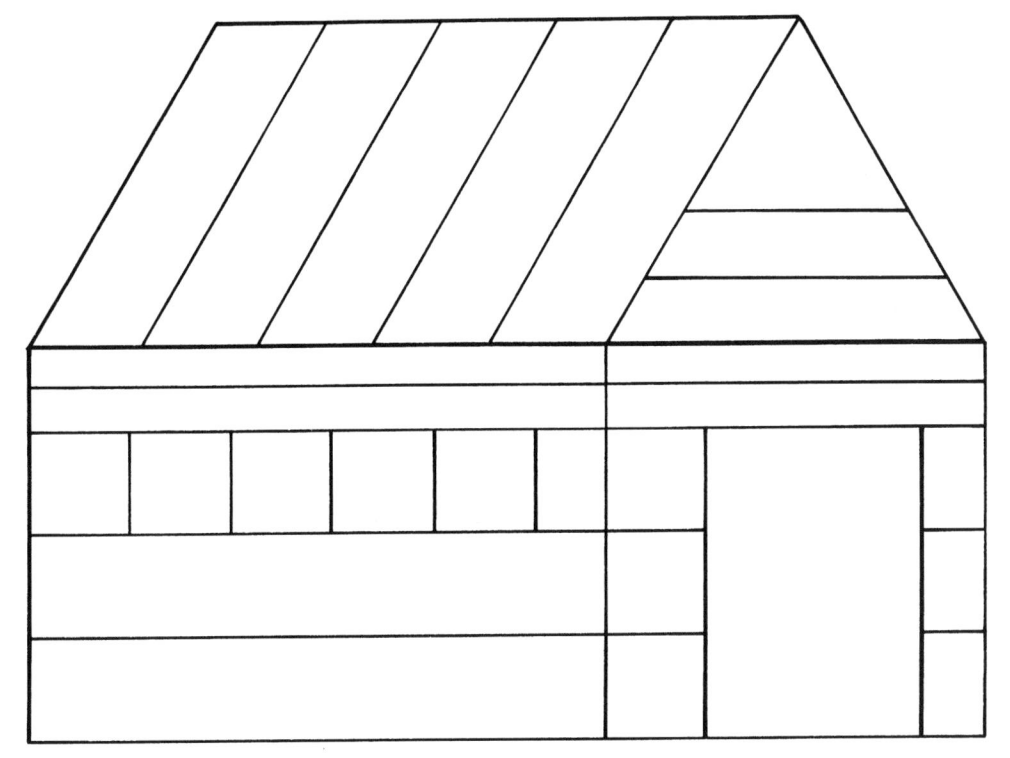

How many △ ? _____   How many ▱ ? _____   How many ▢ ? _____

Draw and color a door.

How many sides does each shape have?

△ _____   ▱ _____   ▢ _____

How many corners does each shape have?

△ _____   ▱ _____   ▢ _____

Try This!

Work with a partner to create a poster about Abraham Lincoln. Write five facts about Lincoln as a child and five facts about him as an adult.

Name: _____   Three-Dimensional Figures

The Way I See It

Label the figures. Use the code to color the figures.

> sphere = yellow   cone = red   cube = blue
>
> pyramid = green   cylinder = orange

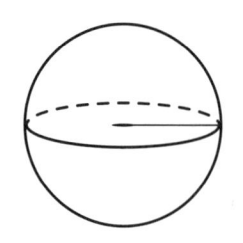

1. _____
2. _____ 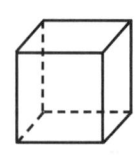
3. _____ 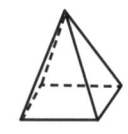
4. _____ 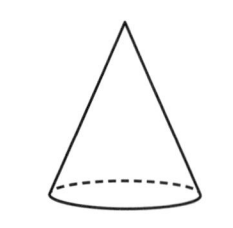
5. _____ 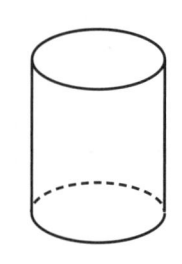
6. _____ 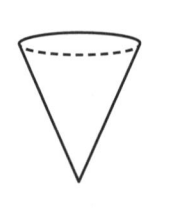
7. _____ 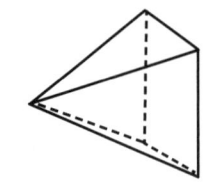
8. _____ 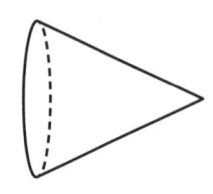
9. _____ 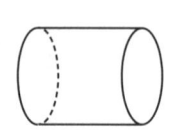
10. _____ 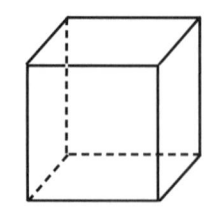
11. _____ 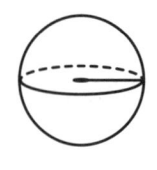
12. _____ 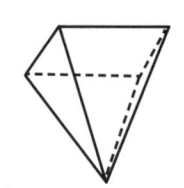

Try This!

Make a shape book. Fold sheets of paper into a booklet. Label each page with the name of a 3-D shape. Draw or glue three pictures of each shape on each page.

Name: _____

Three-Dimensional Figures

Practice in 3-D

Use the code to color the figures.

🌟🌟 ⬤ = red   △ = green   ▢ = blue   ⬜ = orange

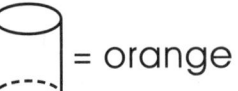

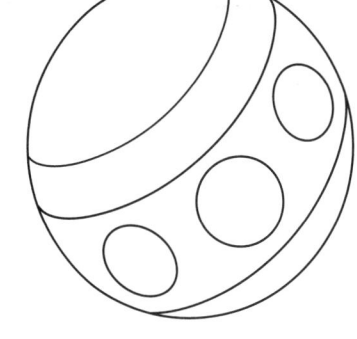

1. How many ⬤? _____
2. How many △? _____
3. How many ▢? _____
4. How many ⬜? _____

Try This!

Label each picture as *cone*, *cube*, *sphere*, or *cylinder*.

Name: _____   Three-Dimensional Figures

Explore and Explain

Complete the table.

	Number of Faces	Number of Edges	Number of Vertices (Corners)
(cone)			
(cube)			
(cylinder)			
(pyramid)			

Try This!
On a separate sheet of paper, list three real-life examples of each figure.

Name: _____   Symmetry

A Perfect Line?

Write **yes** or **no** to tell if a line of symmetry is shown.

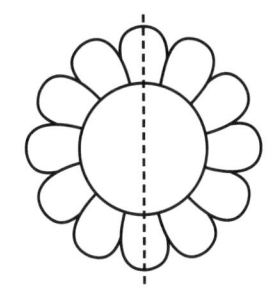

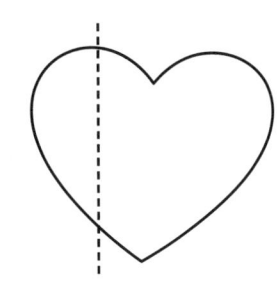

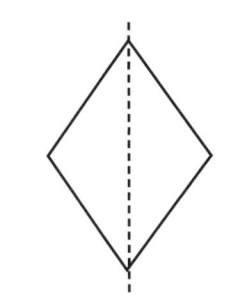

1. _____   2. _____   3. _____

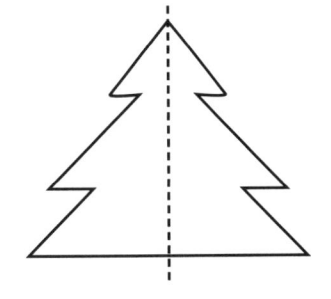

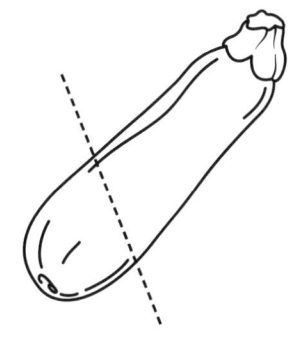

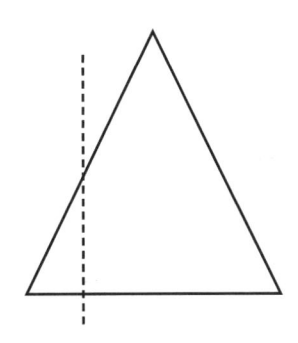

4. _____   5. _____   6. _____

Draw a line through each object to show two parts that are exactly alike.

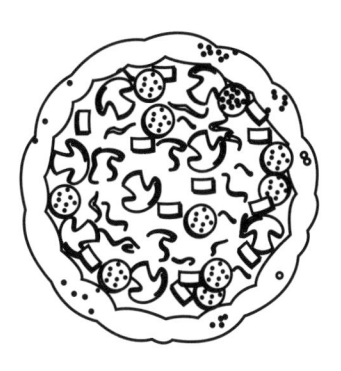

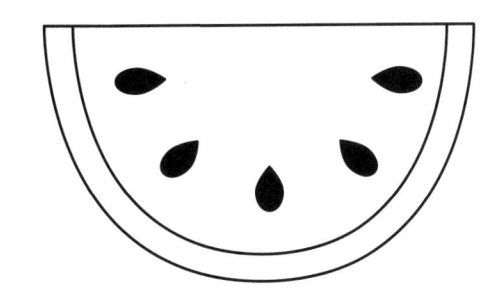

Try This!
On a separate sheet of paper, draw five shapes that do not have lines of symmetry.

Name: _____ Symmetry

The Same on Both Sides

Draw a line through each object to show two parts that are exactly alike.

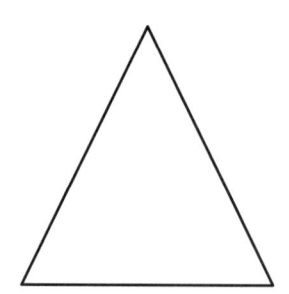

Draw the other half of each object so that the sides are exactly alike.

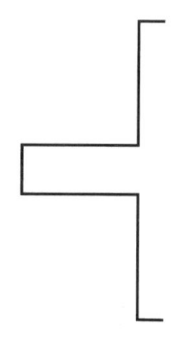

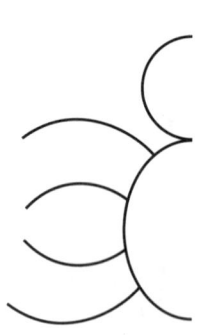

Try This!
Fold a separate sheet of paper in half. On the fold line, draw $\frac{1}{2}$ of a face, including one eye, $\frac{1}{2}$ of a nose, $\frac{1}{2}$ of a smile, one eyebrow, and one ear. Open the paper and try to draw the rest of the face using symmetry.

Name: _____   Days of the Week

These Seven Days

Read the paragraph. Answer the questions.

Seven days are in a week. Saturday and Sunday are the weekend days. You go to school the other five days. Which day do you like best?

How many days are in a week?

6   7   10

Which two days make a weekend?

_____ _____

      Saturday
      Thursday
      Sunday

Write the five days you go to school.

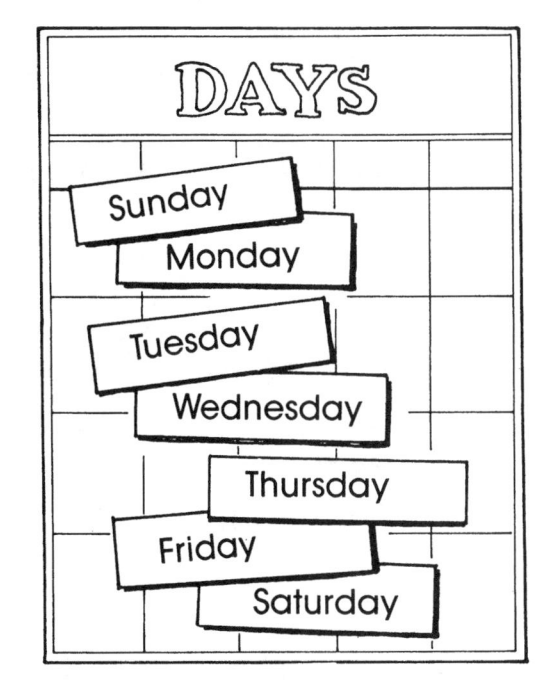

_____ _____ _____

_____ _____

Try This!

On a separate sheet of paper, draw and color what you do on a weekend. Write three sentences to describe your picture.

Name: _____   Months of the Year

This Month or Next Month

Read the paragraph. Answer the questions.

> Twelve months are in a year. The first month is January. The last month is December. Some months have 31 days. Some months have 30 days. February is the shortest month. It has 28 days. Can you name the months of the year?

January	February	March	April
May	June	July	August
September	October	November	December

How many months are in a year?   five   nine   twelve

What is the first month of the year? _____

What is the last month of the year? _____

Some months have 30 days.	YES	NO
Some months have 31 days.	YES	NO
February is the longest month.	YES	NO
February has 28 days.	YES	NO

Try This!

Write your favorite month of the year. Draw pictures of activities that you like to do during that month.

Name: _____

Seasons

Seasons of Fun

Write the season that matches each picture. Cut out the pictures. On a separate sheet of paper, glue the pictures in the correct order. Circle your favorite season.

The season is _____.

The season is _____.

The season is _____.

The season is _____.

Try This!
On the back of this paper, write three things that you like to do in your favorite season.

Name: _____

Calendar

Calendar Setup

Write the missing numbers. Cut out the days of the week. Glue them in the correct order on the calendar.

Sunday				Thursday		
			2			
	7			10		
13						19
		22				
27				31		

Try This!

On the back of this paper, write the months that could go with this calendar.

✂ cut | Saturday | Tuesday | Friday | Monday | Wednesday

Name: _____   Calendar

Calendar Exploration

Trace the number 1. Write the numbers 2 to 30 to complete the calendar. Answer the questions.

June

Sunday	Monday	Tuesday	Wednesday	Thursday	Friday	Saturday
			1			

1. On what day of the week does June end? _____

2. How many Tuesdays are in June? _____

3. How many Saturdays are in June? _____

Try This!

What other things can a calendar show? List as many things as you can think of on a separate sheet of paper.

Name: _____

Time

At This Time Today

Look at each picture. Write the word from the word bank that tells when the action in the picture happens. Write the numbers 1 to 4 to show the order that the actions happen.

afternoon   morning   night   noon

☐    1. What time of day is it? _____

☐   2. What time of day is it? _____

☐   3. What time of day is it? _____

☐   4. What time of day is it? _____

Try This!

On a separate sheet of paper, write or draw what you do each day in the morning, at noon, in the afternoon, and at night.

Name: _____ Telling Time

Don't Be Late!

Draw the clock hands to show the time.

1.

2:00

2.

11:00

3.

4:00

4.

6:00

5.

7:00

6.

9:00

Try This!

What is the difference between A.M. and P.M.? On a separate sheet of paper, write your answer and list five things you do in the A.M. and five things you do in the P.M.

Name: _____   Telling Time

Fun Time at the Fire Station

Write the digital time for each analog clock.

1.   2. 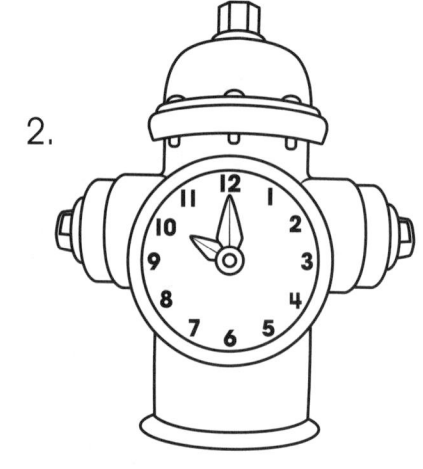 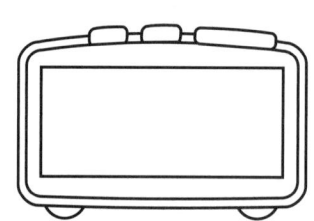   3.

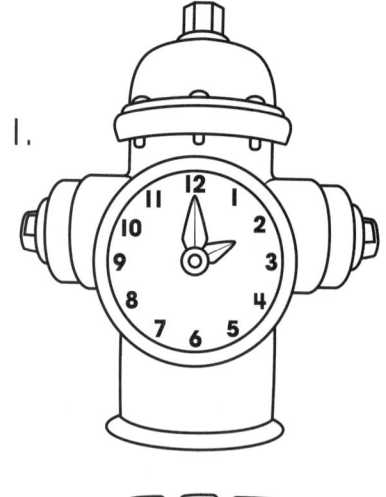

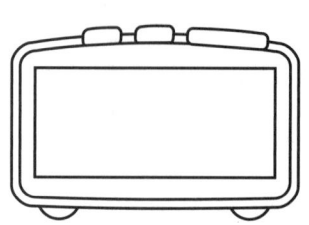

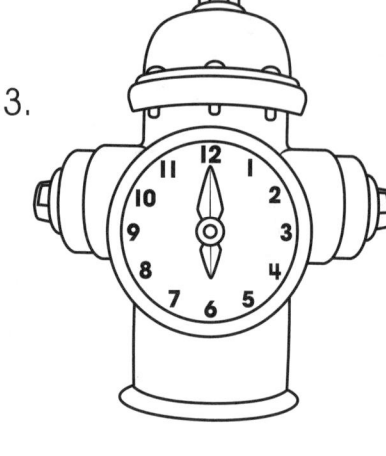

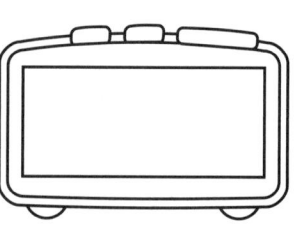

Draw the clock hands to show the time.

4.   5.   6.

1:00   9:00   5:00

Try This!

On a separate sheet of paper, write a schedule that shows at least five different times of day. Draw or write what a firefighter might do at each of those times.

Name: _____   Telling Time

Time for the Harvest

Write the time shown on each clock.

_____   _____   _____

_____   _____   _____

Try This!
On the back of this paper, sort the above foods into lists of fruits and vegetables. Add five more foods to each list.

Name: _____   Telling Time

Time for Me

Draw the clock hands to show the time.

1. 
[clock]
1:30

2. 
[clock]
11:30

3. 
[clock]
3:30

Write the time shown on each clock.

4.
[clock showing hour hand at 6]
_____

5.
[clock showing hand at 9]
_____

6.
[clock showing hand at 1]
_____

Try This!

If Sara went for a walk at 9:30 A.M. and walked for 2 hours, what time did she get home? On a separate sheet of paper, draw a clock that shows the answer.

Name: _____

Telling Time

Rock Clocks

Draw the clock hands to show the time.

1.

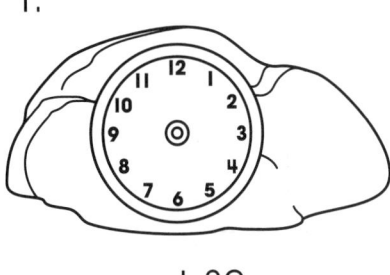

1:30

2.

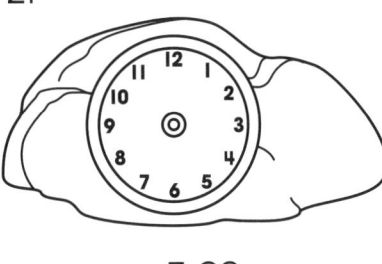

7:00

3.

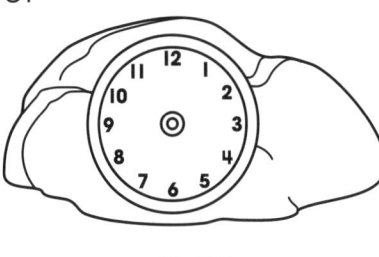

4:30

Write the time shown on each clock.

4.

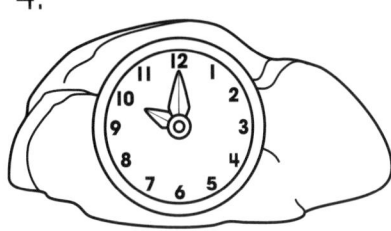

_____

5.

_____

6.

_____

Try This!
On a separate sheet of paper, write the times above in order from earliest to latest.

Name: _____

Measurement

Toothy Measures

Count how many cubes long each object is. Write the number.
Circle the things you use to take care of your teeth.

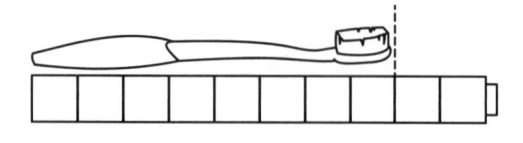

_____ cubes

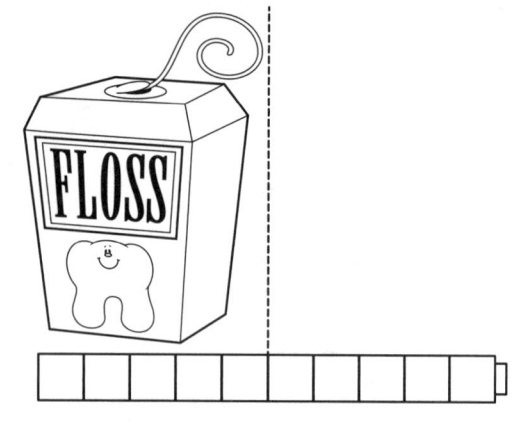

_____ cubes

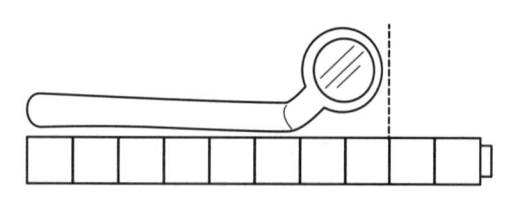

_____ cubes

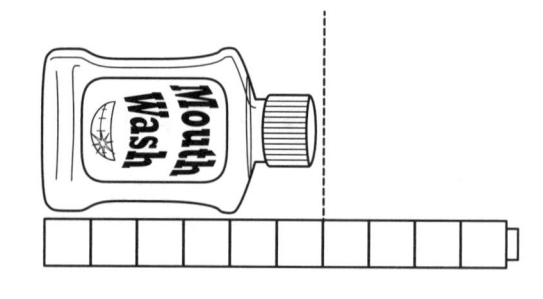

_____ cubes

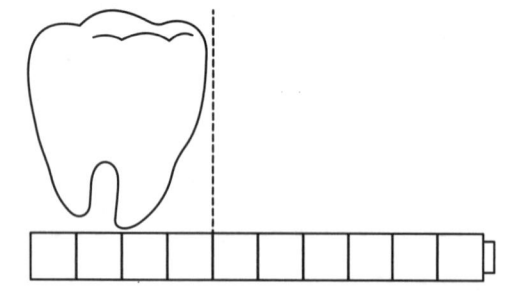

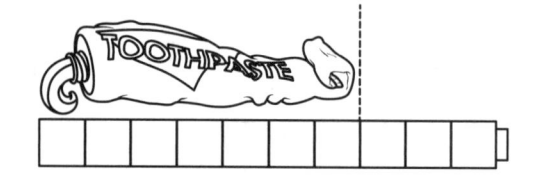

_____ cubes

_____ cubes

Try This!

How do you take care of your teeth? Explain your answer on a separate sheet of paper.

Name: _____

Measurement

The Measure of Me

Use a pencil to measure different parts of your body.

1. How long is your arm from your wrist to your elbow?

   _____ pencil lengths

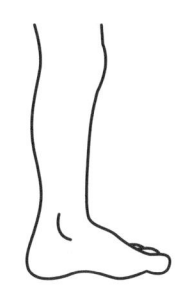

2. How long is your leg from your ankle to your knee?

   _____ pencil lengths

3. How long is it from your right shoulder to your left shoulder?

   _____ pencil lengths

4. How long is your leg from your knee to your hip?

   _____ pencil lengths

Try This!
Measure five things in the classroom with your pencil. On a separate sheet of paper, record the length of each object.

Name: _____   Measurement

Measurement Rules!

Look at each ruler. Write the length of each object. Read the units carefully.

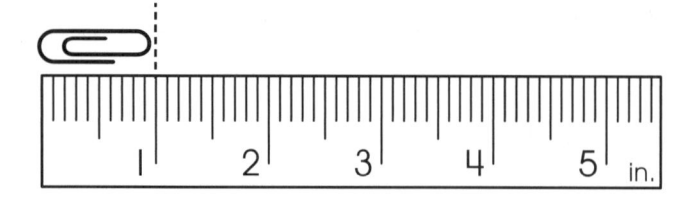

_____ inch

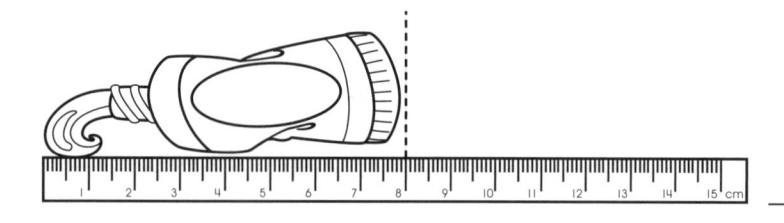

_____ centimeters

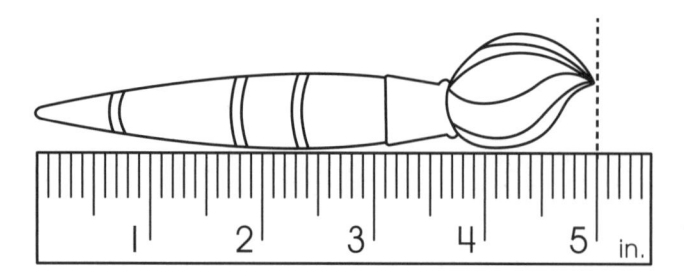

_____ inches

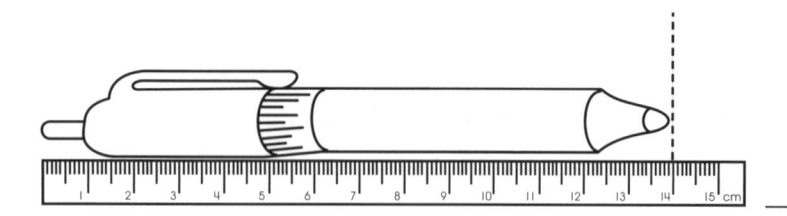

_____ centimeters

Try This!

Use a ruler to measure five objects in the classroom. On a separate sheet of paper, write the name of each object and its length in both inches and centimeters.

Name: _____   Measurement

Heavy or Not?

1. Which object weighs less than the object on the scale?

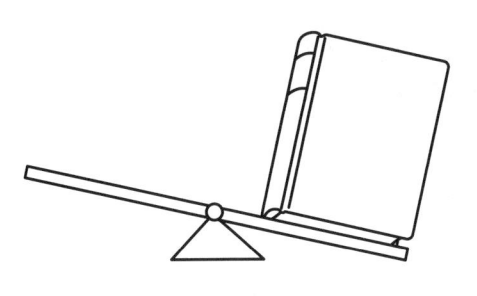

2. Which object weighs more than the toy on the scale?

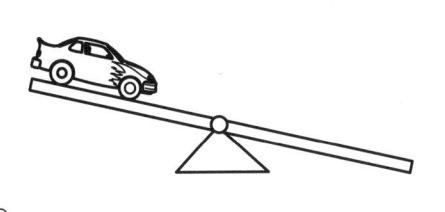

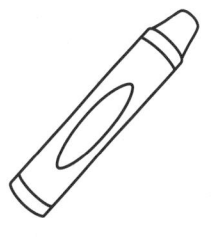

3. Which object weighs about the same as the object on the scale?

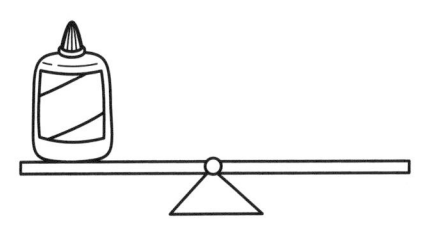

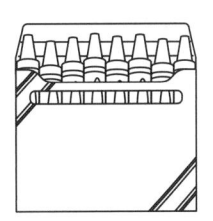

Number the objects from lightest to heaviest. Write **1** for the lightest object. Write **3** for the heaviest object.

_____   _____   _____

Try This!
On a separate sheet of paper, list five things that weigh more than you and five things that weigh less than you.

Name: _____   Money

Rain Forest Riches

Use the picture to answer the questions.

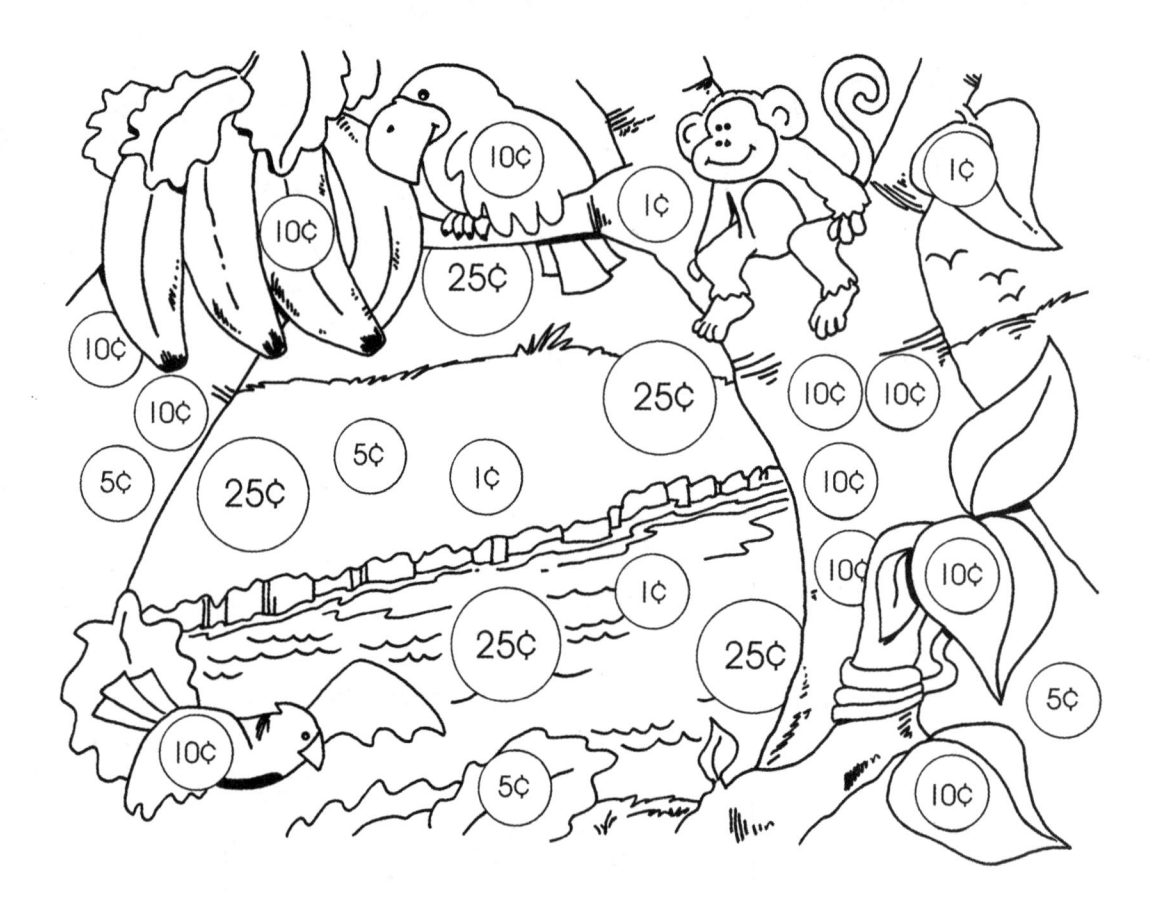

1. What is the value of all of the quarters? _____

2. What is the value of all of the nickels? _____

3. What is the value of all of the dimes? _____

4. What is the value of all of the pennies? _____

Try This!

Work with a partner to make a rain forest information poster. Draw five different kinds of animals that live in the rain forest and write three rain forest facts.

Name: _____   Money

Time to Shop

Look at each box. Circle the item you can buy with the money.

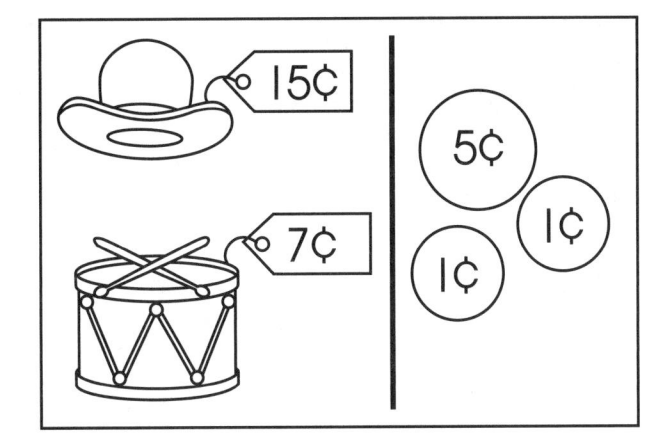

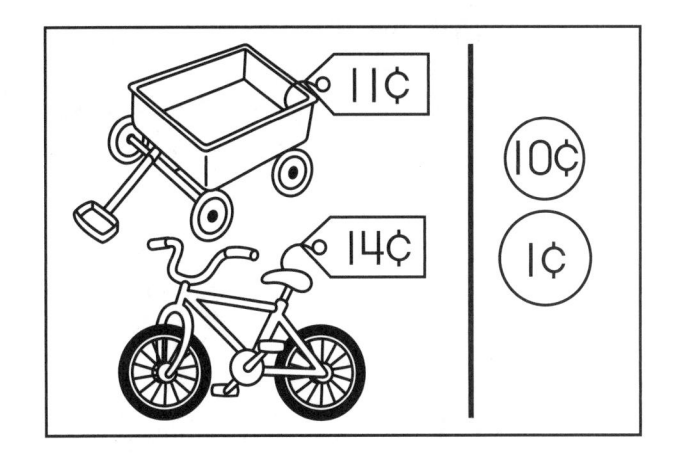

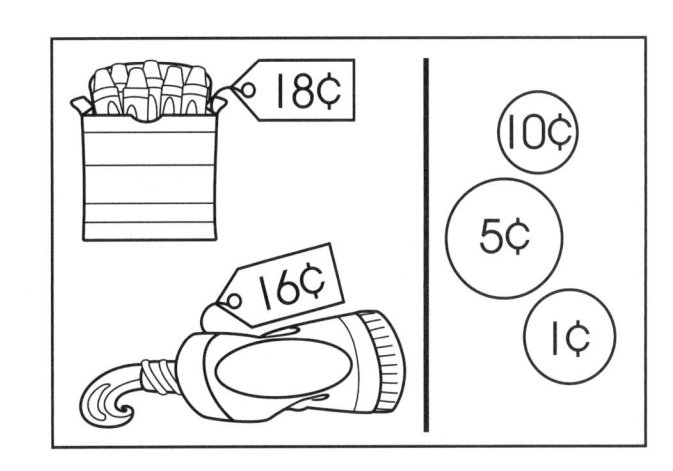

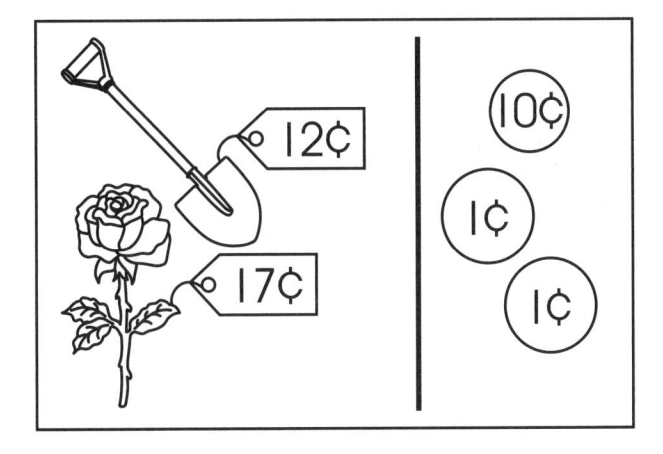

Hat 15¢ / Drum 7¢	5¢, 1¢, 1¢
Wagon 11¢ / Bicycle 14¢	10¢, 1¢
Truck 11¢ / Doll 12¢	10¢, 1¢
Basket 18¢ / Flashlight 16¢	10¢, 5¢, 1¢
Shovel 12¢ / Rose 17¢	10¢, 1¢, 1¢
Banana 17¢ / Apple 15¢	10¢, 5¢

Try This!

If you had 50¢, what three things above would you buy? How much would that cost? How much change would you get back? Answer the questions and show your work on a separate sheet of paper.

Name: _____   Money

Mouse in the Pumpkin Patch

Answer the questions.

Which pumpkin did Mouse buy with this amount of money?

(10¢) (10¢) (10¢) (10¢) (5¢) (5¢) = _____

Which pumpkin did Mouse buy with this amount of money?

(25¢) (25¢) (10¢) (10¢) (5¢) (1¢) = _____

Which two pumpkins did Mouse buy with this amount of money?

(25¢) (25¢) (10¢) (10¢) (10¢) (10¢) (10¢) = _____

Which pumpkin did Mouse buy with this amount of money?

(25¢) (10¢) (1¢) (1¢) = _____

A – 19¢
B – 37¢
C – 50¢
D – 48¢
E – 76¢
F – 24¢

Try This!

How much money would you need to buy all of the pumpkins? Answer the question and show your work on a separate sheet of paper.

Name: _____   Charts and Graphs

Vacation Reading

The Perez family read during their vacation. Use the graph to answer the questions.

Books Read on Vacation

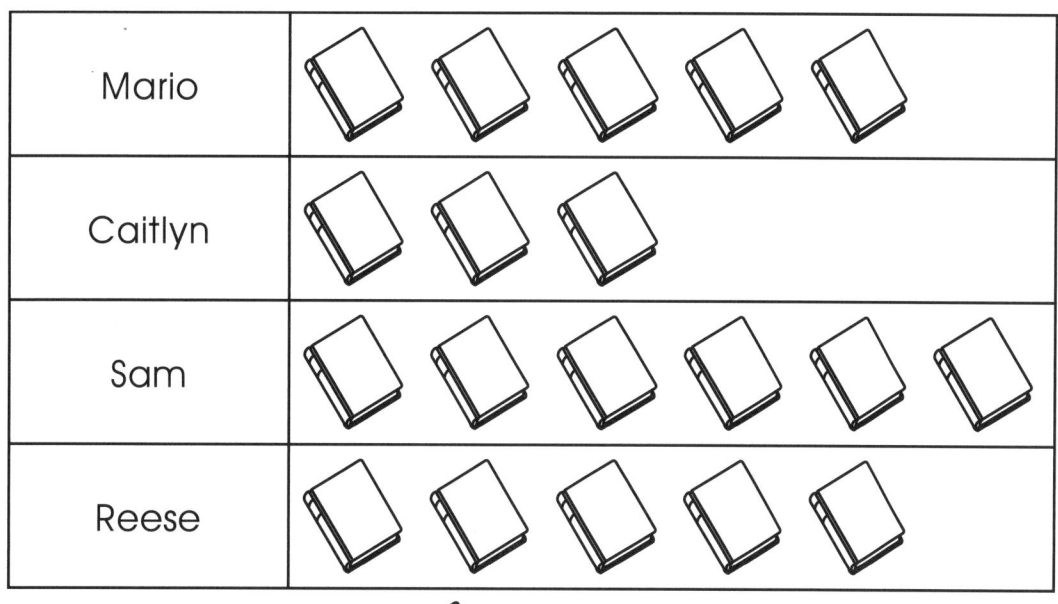

Mario	📖 📖 📖 📖 📖
Caitlyn	📖 📖 📖
Sam	📖 📖 📖 📖 📖 📖
Reese	📖 📖 📖 📖 📖

📖 = 1 book

1. Who read 6 books while on vacation? _____

2. Who read the least number of books? _____

3. How many books did Mario read? _____

4. How many books did Sam and Reese read altogether? _____

5. How many more books did Sam read than Reese? _____

6. How many books did the family read altogether? _____

Try This!

On a separate sheet of paper, use crayons or markers to draw the cover of your favorite book. Write the title on the cover and write four or five sentences about your favorite part. Share your book cover with a friend.

Apple Orchard Trip

Mr. Kim's first-grade class went to the apple orchard. Use the graph to answer the questions.

Apple Picking

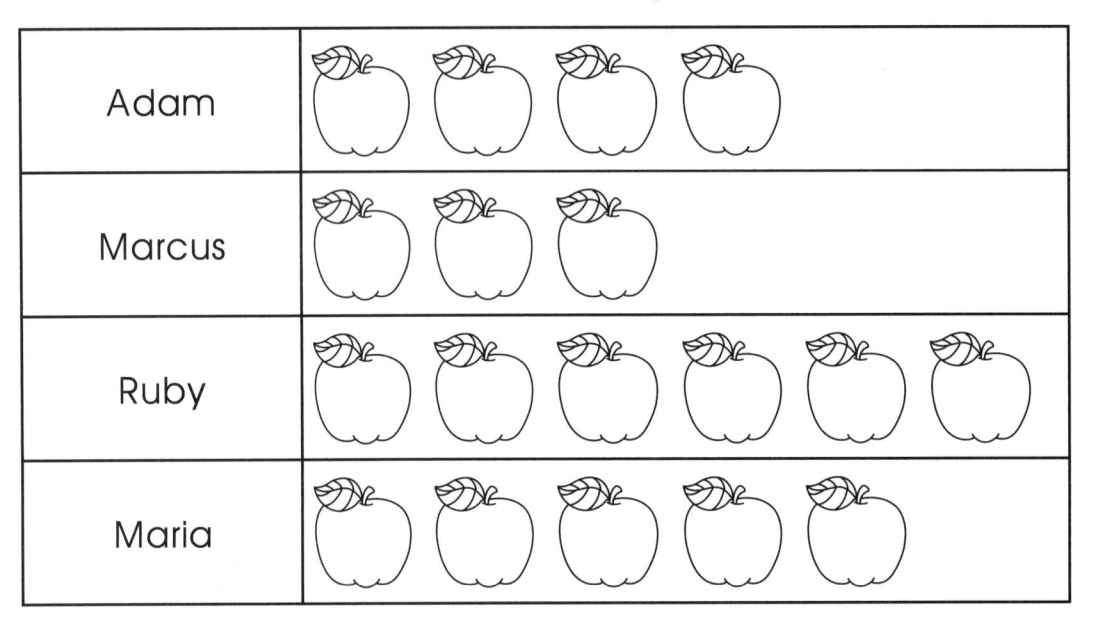

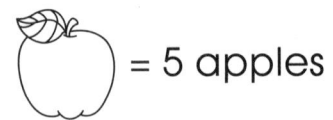

Adam	🍎 🍎 🍎 🍎
Marcus	🍎 🍎 🍎
Ruby	🍎 🍎 🍎 🍎 🍎 🍎
Maria	🍎 🍎 🍎 🍎 🍎

🍎 = 5 apples

1. Who picked 30 apples? _____

2. How many apples did Adam pick? _____

3. Who picked the most apples? _____

4. How many more apples did Maria pick than Adam? _____

5. How many apples did Maria and Marcus pick altogether? _____

6. How many apples did the class pick altogether? _____

Try This!

If each apple tree had 15 apples picked from it, how many trees did Mr. Kim's class pick apples from? Answer the question and show your work on a separate sheet of paper.

Name: _____   Charts and Graphs

Fund-Raiser Fun

Washington Elementary School sold raffle tickets. Use the graph to answer the questions.

Tickets Sold

Kindergarten	4 tickets
First Grade	7 tickets
Second Grade	5 tickets
Third Grade	2 tickets
Fourth Grade	4 tickets
Fifth Grade	3 tickets

🎟 = 10 tickets

1. How many tickets did fifth grade sell? _____

2. Which grade sold 20 tickets? _____

3. Which two grades sold the same amount of tickets?

   _____ , _____

4. How many fewer tickets did fifth grade sell than first grade? _____

5. Which grade sold the most tickets? _____

Try This!

How many tickets did the school sell in all? Write a number sentence to show your answer.

Name: _____   Charts and Graphs

How We Travel

Mr. Jacob's class made a graph about how they traveled while on vacation. Use the graph to answer the questions.

How We Travel on Vacation

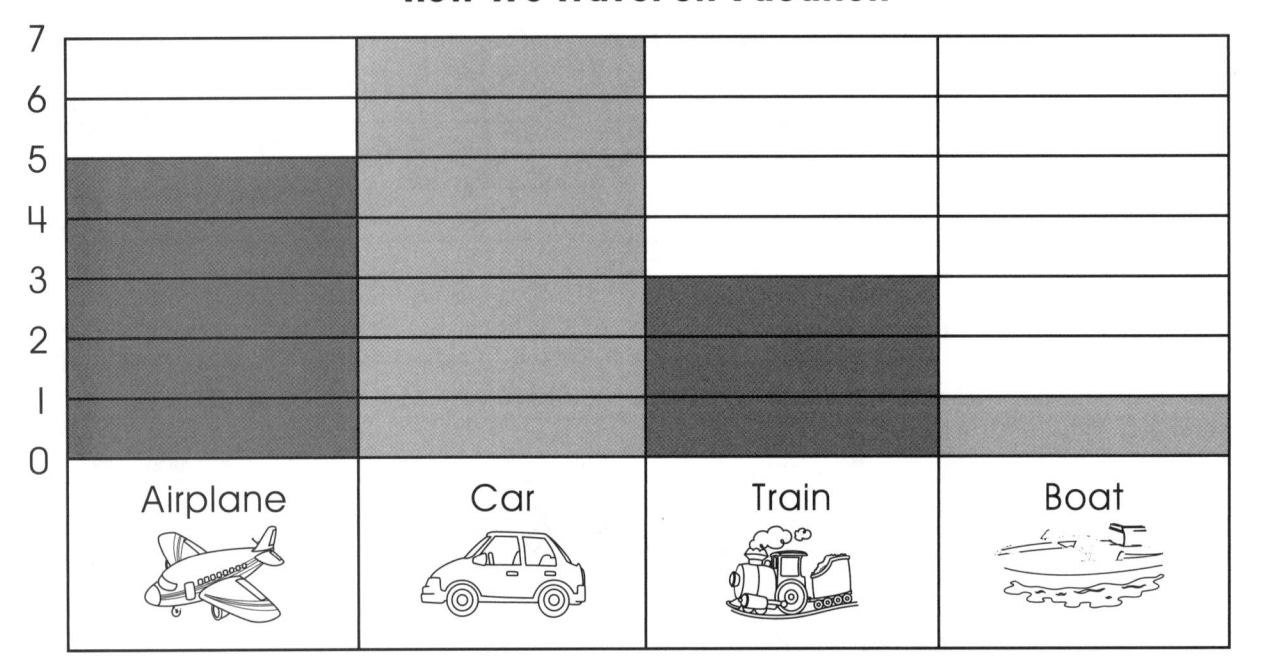

	Airplane	Car	Train	Boat
7				
6		▓		
5	▓	▓		
4	▓	▓		
3	▓	▓	▓	
2	▓	▓	▓	
1	▓	▓	▓	▓
0				

1. How many students traveled by train? _____

2. How did most students travel on vacation? _____

3. What kind of travel was used the least? _____

4. How many more students traveled by car than by airplane? _____

5. How many students traveled by airplane and train combined? _____

Try This!

If you could travel anywhere, where would you go and how would you get there? Answer the question in three to four sentences on a separate sheet of paper.

Name: _____   Charts and Graphs

Zoo Animal Count

The city zoo made a graph to show the animals that can be found at the zoo. Use the graph to answer the questions.

Animals at the City Zoo

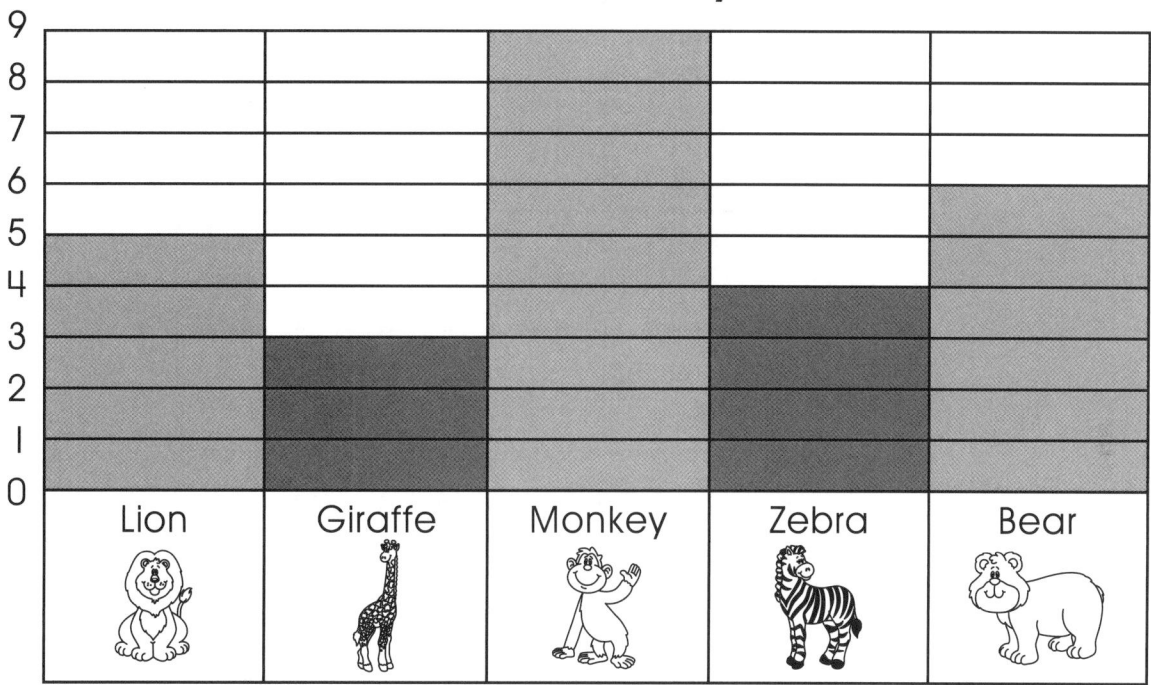

1. How many zebras are at the zoo? _____

2. The zoo has 6 of what kind of animal? _____

3. Does the zoo have more lions or bears? _____

4. How many giraffes and monkeys are at the zoo altogether? _____

5. How many more monkeys than giraffes are at the zoo? _____

6. How many animals are at the zoo altogether? _____

Try This!

On a separate sheet of paper, write three facts about each animal above.

Name: _____

Charts and Graphs

Sports Are Fun!

Ask seven classmates which sport they like best. In the table below, make a tally mark beside the sport each one likes. Count the tally marks. Color the graph.

Sport		
Baseball	⚾	
Basketball	🏀	
Football	🏈	
Soccer	⚽	

(bar graph with y-axis 0–7 and x-axis: Baseball, Basketball, Football, Soccer)

Try This!

On a separate sheet of paper, create a graph about favorite pets. To help you complete the graph, ask seven classmates about their favorite pets.

Name: _____   Charts and Graphs

Pet Tally

Ms. Smith's first-grade class worked together to complete a tally chart about their pets. Each student made only one tally. Use the chart to answer the questions.

My Pet

Pet	Tally
Dog	¦¦¦¦ ¦¦
Cat	¦¦¦
Fish	¦¦
Bird	¦
Other	¦¦¦¦
None	¦¦

1. How many students have a dog? _____

2. Only one student has a pet _____.

3. How many more students have a dog than a cat? _____

4. How many students do not have a pet? _____

5. How many students are in Ms. Smith's class? _____

Try This!

On a separate sheet of paper, draw a picture of your pet or a pet you would like to have. Write three sentences about what makes your pet special.

Name: _____   Charts and Graphs

Drink Tally

Ask 10 classmates which drink they like best. In the table below, make a tally mark beside the drink each one likes. Use the chart to answer the questions.

Favorite Kind of Drink

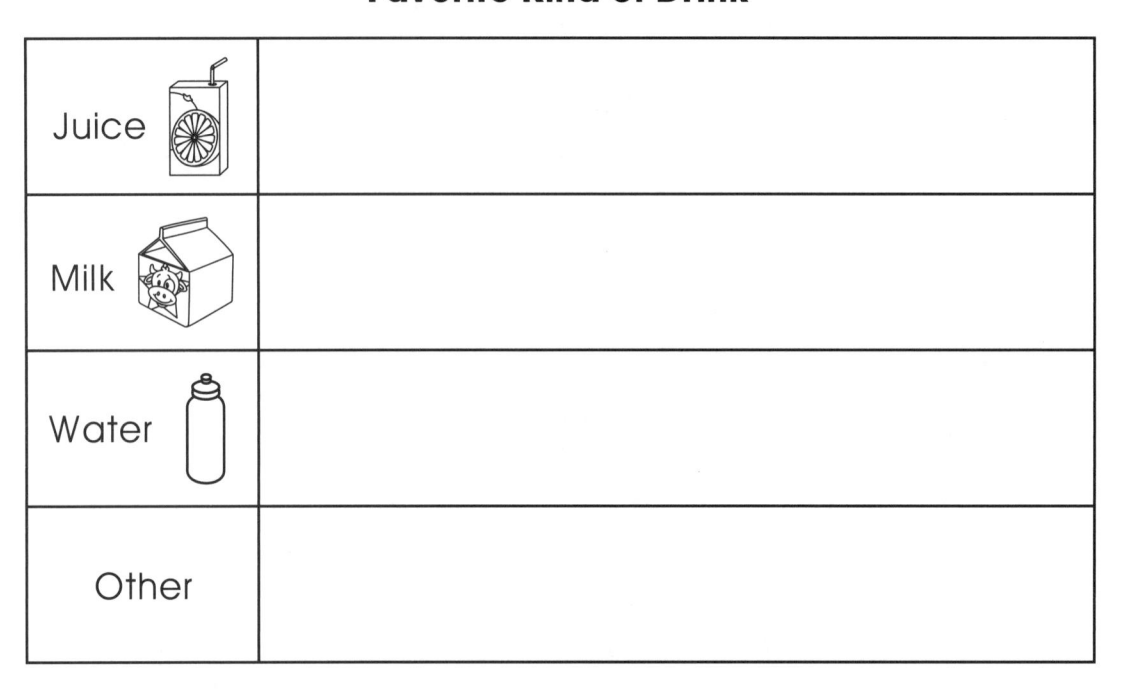

Juice	
Milk	
Water	
Other	

1. How many students like milk? _____

2. How many students like juice? _____

3. Do more students like water or milk? _____

4. How many students altogether like water and juice? _____

Try This!

On a separate sheet of paper, create your own tally chart. Think of a topic and ask 10 classmates to help you complete the chart.

Name: _____   Charts and Graphs

Tasty Fruits

Each first-grade student at Washington Elementary School has chosen a kind of fruit to have at a school party. Use the chart to answer the questions.

Fruit	Number of Students
Grapes	47
Apples	32
Pears	17
Oranges	10
Blueberries	5

1. Which kind of fruit did the most students choose? _____

2. Which kind of fruit did the fewest students choose? _____

3. How many more students chose grapes than apples? _____

4. How many more students chose oranges than blueberries? _____

5. How many more students chose grapes than pears? _____

6. What is the total number of students that chose pears or oranges? _____

Try This!

How many first-grade students go to Washington Elementary School?

Name: _____   Charts and Graphs

A Day at the Park

Jerome asked all of the kids at the playground where their favorite places to play are. He recorded the information in a chart. Use the chart to answer the questions.

Favorite Play Place	Number of Kids
Basketball Court	20
Seesaw	8
Slide	16
Swings	28
Other	10

1. Which place to play was chosen by the fewest kids? _____

2. Which place to play was chosen by the most kids? _____

3. How many more kids like to play at the basketball court than on the seesaw? _____

4. What is the total number of kids that chose the slide or the seesaw? _____

5. What is the total number of kids that chose the basketball court or the swings? _____

Try This!

On a separate sheet of paper, draw a picture of what you think would be the best park ever. Write three sentences that explain what makes your park the best.

Name: _____   Venn Diagrams

Brothers and Sisters

Ms. Keith's first-grade class completed a Venn diagram about whether the students have siblings. Use the diagram to answer the questions.

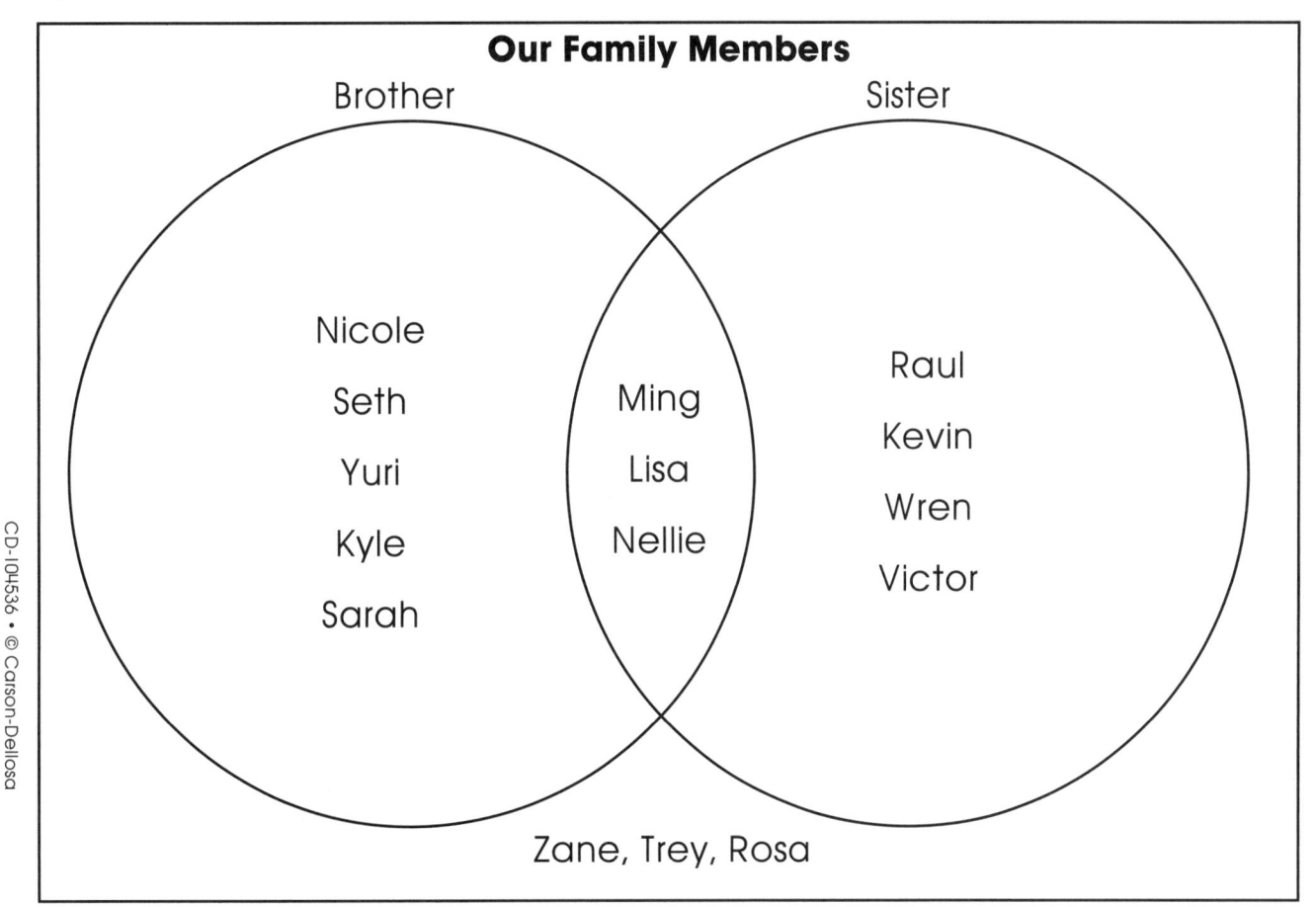

Our Family Members

Brother — Sister

- Nicole
- Seth
- Yuri
- Kyle
- Sarah

Ming
Lisa
Nellie

- Raul
- Kevin
- Wren
- Victor

Zane, Trey, Rosa

1. How many students have a brother? _____

2. How many students have a sister? _____

3. How many students have a brother and a sister? _____

4. How many students have neither a brother nor a sister? _____

5. How many students are in Ms. Keith's class? _____

Try This! _____
What makes a good brother or sister? List five characteristics of a good sibling.

Name: _____   Venn Diagrams

Land or Sea

Use the Venn diagram to answer the questions.

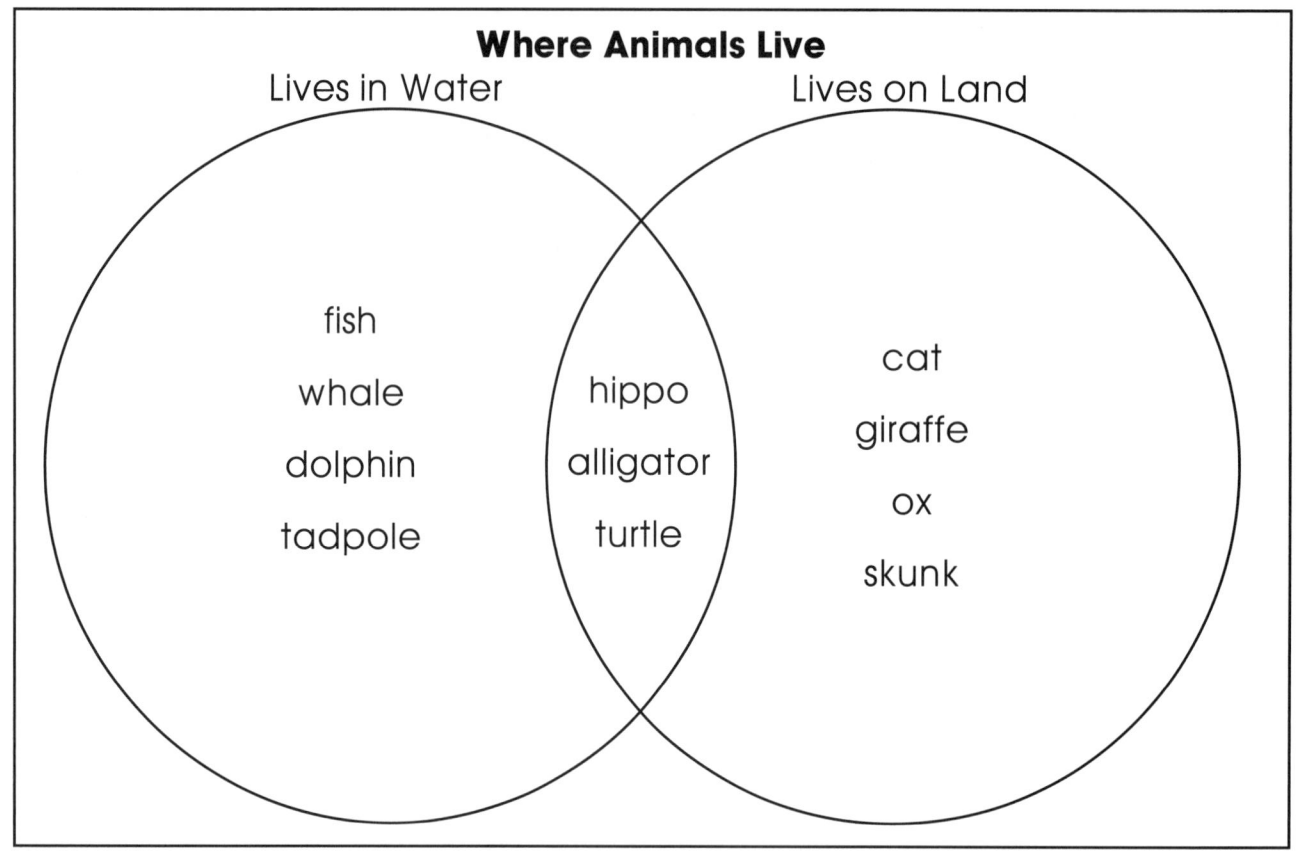

Where Animals Live

Lives in Water — Lives on Land

- Water only: fish, whale, dolphin, tadpole
- Both: hippo, alligator, turtle
- Land only: cat, giraffe, ox, skunk

1. Name two animals that live in the water. _____ _____

2. Name two animals that live on land. _____ _____

3. Where does a turtle live? _____

4. Write each animal name below on the Venn diagram in the correct spot:

   camel   cow   frog   jellyfish   octopus

Try This!

On a separate sheet of paper, draw the habitat for one of the animals above.

Name: _____

Making Predictions

It Takes This Long

Predict about how long it would take to do each activity. Circle the correct answer.

1. Bake a cake.

   1 second
   1 minute
   1 hour

2. Tie your shoes.

   1 second
   1 minute
   1 hour

3. Take a breath.

   1 second
   1 minute
   1 hour

Try This!

On a separate sheet of paper, list three things that take about one minute to do.

Name: _____

Making Predictions

Classroom Predictions

Predict the measurement of each object. Use cubes to measure the object.

1. How long is your shoe?

   Predict: _____

   Count: _____

2. How tall is your chair?

   Predict: _____

   Count: _____

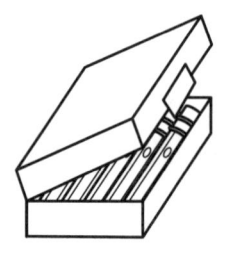

3. How many cubes can fit in a pencil box?

   Predict: _____

   Count: _____

4. How wide is your desk?

   Predict: _____

   Count: _____

Try This!

Choose three objects in the classroom to measure. On a separate sheet of paper, predict how many inches long each object is. Use a ruler to measure the objects. Write how long each object is.

Name: _____   Probability

Spin the Spinner!

Color the spinner. Answer the questions.

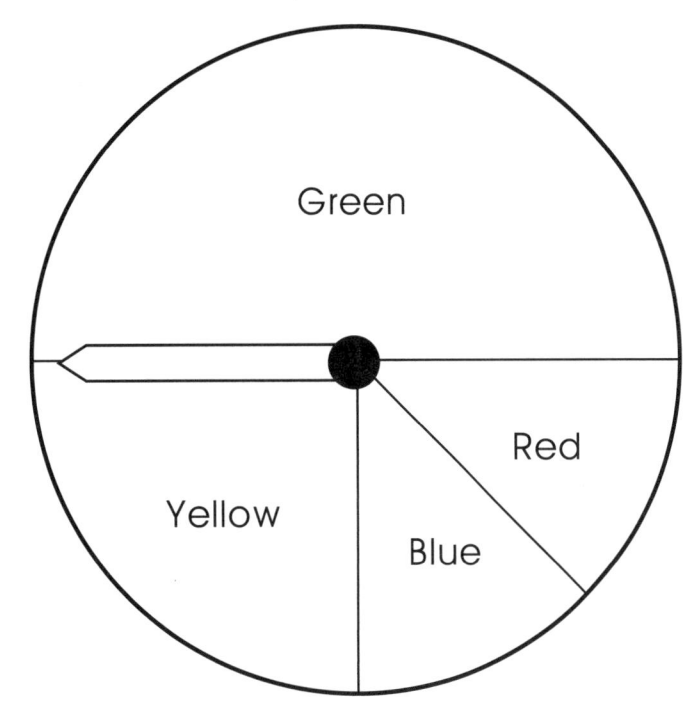

1. What color will the spinner probably land on the most often?

   _____

2. What color will the spinner probably land on the least often?

   _____

3. Will the spinner be more likely to land on red or yellow?

   _____

4. Will the spinner be more likely to land on blue or green?

   _____

Try This!

Create a spinner using a paper plate, a brass paper fastener, and a construction paper arrow. Color your spinner to match the one above. Spin the arrow 10 times. On a separate sheet of paper, record how often the spinner lands on each color.

Name: _____   Probability

Jelly Bean Probability

Color the jelly beans. Answer the questions.

4 jelly beans red   5 jelly beans green
3 jelly beans blue   2 jelly beans yellow
6 jelly beans orange

1. If you were to pick without looking, are you more likely to pick a green or yellow jelly bean? _____

2. If you were to pick without looking, what color of jelly bean are you most likely to pick? _____

3. If you were to pick without looking, what color of jelly bean are you least likely to pick? _____

Try This!
On a separate sheet of paper, write the probability of picking each color.

Name: _____

Word Problems

Ten-Frame Addition

Use red and yellow counters to help you solve the problems.

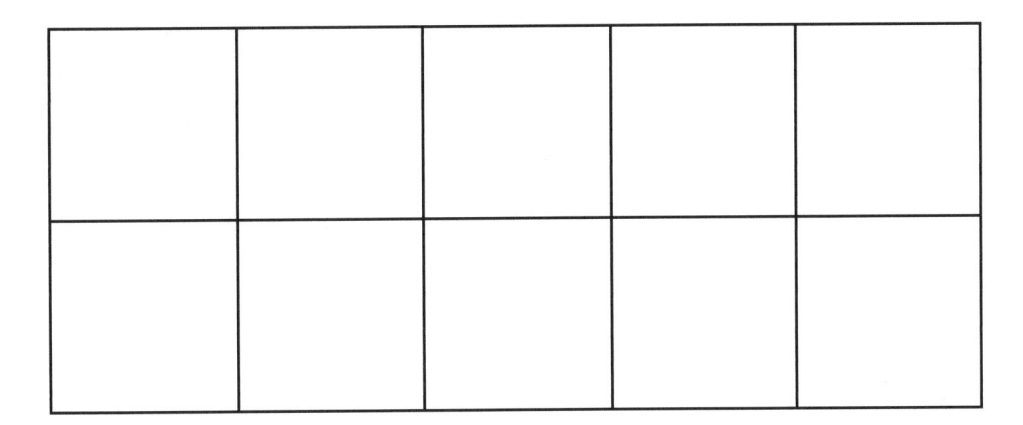

1. John had 4 marbles. His friend gave him 3 marbles. How many marbles does John have in all?

   _____ marbles

2. Carla swam 4 laps in the pool this morning. After lunch, she swam 3 more laps. How many laps did she swim in all?

   _____ laps

3. Bryan has 2 pet fish. His sister has 3 pet fish. How many fish do they have altogether?

   _____ fish

4. Keisha read 5 pages of her book last night. She read 4 more pages this morning. How many pages did she read in all?

   _____ pages

Try This!
On a separate sheet of paper, show a different way to solve each problem. Explain using words or pictures.

Name: _____

Word Problems

Tasty Problems

Draw pictures to help you solve the problems. Write **healthy** under each box that shows healthful food choices.

1. Claire ate 1 banana and 7 grapes for breakfast. How many pieces of fruit did she eat in all?

   _____ pieces of fruit

   _____

2. Jay ate 4 pieces of cake last week and 4 pieces of cake this week. How much cake did he eat in all?

   _____ pieces of cake

   _____

3. Amad ate 2 vegetable servings on Tuesday and 5 vegetable servings on Wednesday. How many vegetable servings did Amad eat altogether?

   _____
   vegetable servings

   _____

4. Ella drank 8 glasses of water yesterday and 8 glasses of water today. How much water did she drink in all?

   _____
   glasses of water

   _____

Try This!

How many fruits and vegetables do you eat in a day? On a separate sheet of paper, list all of the fruits and vegetables you ate yesterday. Then, write your own word problem about the list.

Name: _____

Word Problems

Want It or Need It?

Solve the problems. Write **need** or **want** to describe what is being bought.

1. Mom bought 24 strawberries and 12 carrots at the grocery store. How much food did she buy in all?

   _____ pieces of food

   _____

2. Lamar bought 2 packs of baseball cards. Each pack has 24 cards. How many cards does he have in all?

   _____ baseball cards

   _____

3. Penny bought 23 pencils and 32 erasers. How many things did she buy in all?

   _____ things

   _____

4. Jose bought 12 bars of soap and 11 pairs of socks. How many things did Jose buy in all?

   _____ things

   _____

Try This!
On a separate sheet of paper, draw a picture of your bedroom. Then, list five things in your bedroom that are needs and five things that are wants.

Name: _____

Word Problems

Pictures and Numbers

Solve the problems. Show your work with numbers or pictures.

1. Kayla's family went on a road trip. They drove 54 miles on Friday and 25 miles on Saturday. How far did they drive?

   _____ miles

2. Nick read 48 pages last week and 51 pages this week. How many pages did he read altogether?

   _____ pages

3. Kayla saw 24 ducks and 32 turtles at the lake. How many animals did she see in all?

   _____ animals

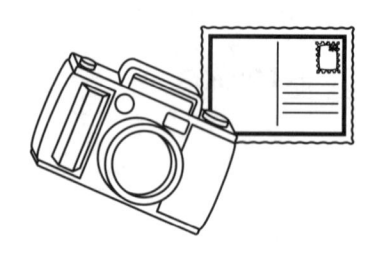

4. Aiden went on vacation. He took 36 pictures and bought 12 picture postcards. How many pictures does he have in all?

   _____ pictures

Try This!

On a separate sheet of paper, write four word problems. Ask a friend to solve the problems.

Name: _____   Word Problems

Ten-Frame Subtraction

Use red and yellow counters to solve the problems.

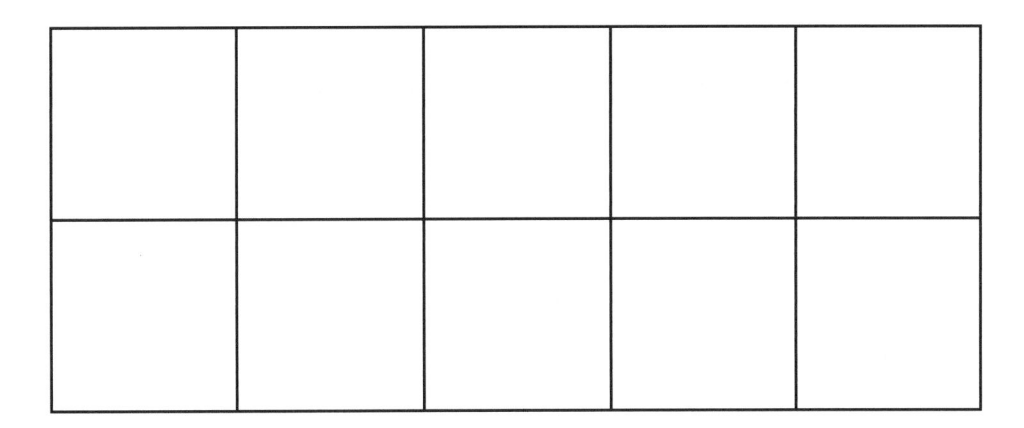

1. Mia baked 6 cookies. She gave 3 cookies to her brother. How many cookies does she have left?

   _____ cookies

2. Mark has 5 toy cars. He lost 1 car. How many cars does he have left?

   _____ cars

3. Nora took 8 pictures. She mailed 5 pictures to her grandmother. How many pictures does she have left?

   _____ pictures

4. Tripp took 4 bottles of water to his soccer game. He gave away 2 bottles of water. How many bottles of water does he have left?

   _____ bottles of water

Try This!
On a separate sheet of paper, rewrite each problem as an addition problem.

Name: _____

Word Problems

Seasonal Subtraction

Draw pictures to help you solve the problems. Write the name of each season being described.

1. Greg made 10 snowballs. He gave 5 of them to his sister. How many snowballs does he have left?

   _____ snowballs

   Season: _____

2. Holly made 7 sand castles while on vacation at the beach. The ocean washed away 4 of them. How many sand castles are left?

   _____ sand castles

   Season: _____

3. Leo raked 12 piles of leaves. His sister put 8 of the piles in bags. How many piles of leaves are left?

   _____ piles of leaves

   Season: _____

4. Malia picked 8 flowers. She gave 6 of them to her mom. How many flowers does Malia have left?

   _____ flowers

   Season: _____

Try This!

On a separate sheet of paper, write the seasons in order. Write your favorite thing to do in each season.

Name: _____   Word Problems

Pumpkin Problems

Draw pictures to help you solve the problems.

1. Farmer John counted 8 blossoms on the plants. Then, 2 blossoms fell off. How many blossoms are left?

   ☐ _____ blossoms

2. Farmer John planted 15 pumpkin seeds. Birds ate 4 seeds. How many seeds are left?

   ☐ _____ seeds

3. Farmer John counted 11 pumpkins. He picked 7. How many pumpkins are left?

   ☐ _____ pumpkins

4. Farmer John's 14 pumpkin plants each have 1 ladybug on them. Then, 9 ladybugs fly away. How many plants now have ladybugs on them?

   ☐ _____ plants

Try This!

Write the numbers 1 to 4 in the boxes to show the growth cycle of the pumpkin.

Name: _____   Word Problems

Celebrating Cinco de Mayo

Solve the problems. Show your work.

1. The parents worked to make a piñata for the class. The piñata has 49 prizes in it. The class has 24 students in it. How many more prizes than students are there?

2. Yasmin's teacher gave her 28 stickers to decorate her sombrero. Yasmin gave 16 of the stickers to her best friend. How many stickers does Yasmin have left?

3. Ms. Friedman made 56 tortillas for the fiesta. The students ate 34 tortillas. How many tortillas are left?

4. The students made 54 tissue-paper flowers. The students gave 32 of the flowers to the teachers in the school. How many tissue-paper flowers are left?

Try This!

Look at question 1. If each student gets the same number of prizes, how many will each get? How many will be left over? Answer the questions on a separate sheet of paper.

Name: _____

Word Problems

A Sea of Subtraction

Solve the problems. Show your work.

1. We saw 26 dolphins playing in the water.
   We saw 13 swim away.
   How many dolphins are left?

2. There were 48 fish in the coral.
   Then, 12 swam away.
   How many fish are left?

3. I watched 24 sharks race in the water.
   I watched 12 stop to watch fish.
   How many sharks are still racing?

4. A total of 86 jellyfish swam around a sunken ship. A group of 42 swam into the ship. How many jellyfish are still swimming around the ship?

Try This!

Work with a partner to make an ocean information poster. Draw five or more animals that live in the ocean and write three reasons why the oceans are important.

Name: _____

Word Problems

Working in Gardens

Read each problem. Decide if you need to add or subtract to find the answer. Solve the problem.

1. Cameron saw 6 birds in the garden. He saw 3 fly away. How many birds are left?

   _____ birds

2. Larissa planted 6 tulip bulbs. Her mom planted 6 more. How many tulips did they plant in all?

   _____ tulips

3. Mary picked 10 tomatoes. She gave 3 to her neighbor. How many tomatoes are left?

   _____ tomatoes

4. Daniel watered 6 pumpkin plants and 6 pepper plants. How many plants did he water in all?

   _____ plants

Try This!
On a separate sheet of paper, explain how all of the problems are alike.

Name: _____

Word Problems

Cleaning Up with Addition and Subtraction

Read each problem. Decide if you need to add or subtract to find the answer. Solve the problem.

1. In the sink are 12 dirty cups and 13 dirty plates. How many dirty dishes are in the sink in all?

   _____ dirty dishes

2. Jan vacuumed for 32 minutes. Her sister dusted for 21 minutes. How much longer did Jan work than her sister?

   _____ minutes

3. Dad recycled 24 bottles and 35 cans. How many things did he recycle in all?

   _____ things

4. Aunt Linda washed 24 windows at her house and 12 windows at our house. How many more windows did she wash at her house?

   _____ windows

Try This!

On a separate sheet of paper, list five ways you help take care of your home. Explain why it is important to keep a home clean.

Name: _____   Word Problems

Number Line Helper

Use the number line to help you solve the problems.

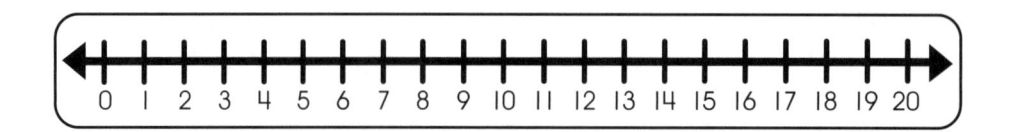

0 1 2 3 4 5 6 7 8 9 10 11 12 13 14 15 16 17 18 19 20

1. Lita had 8 dolls. Her friend gave her 2 more dolls. How many dolls does Lita have now?

   _____ dolls

2. Pete watched 5 hours of TV last week. This week, he watched 3 fewer hours of TV. How many hours of TV did he watch this week?

   _____ hours

3. Rashad read 9 books last month. He read 7 books this month. How many books did he read altogether?

   _____ books

4. Beth picked 18 flowers. She gave away 9 flowers. How many does she have left?

   _____ flowers

Try This!
On a separate sheet of paper, write two word problems that can be solved using a number line. Ask a friend to solve the problems.

Name: _____   Word Problems

A World of Patterns

Read and answer the problems.

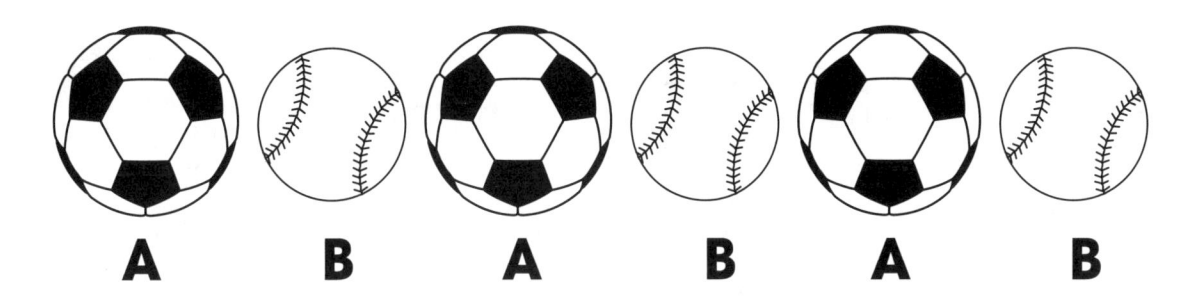

A   B   A   B   A   B

1. Jared made an **AB** pattern using shapes and the colors red and blue. Draw what it might look like.

2. Pam made an **ABC** pattern using different kinds of fruit. Draw what it might look like.

3. Andy made an **ABBA** pattern using flowers and butterflies. Draw what it might look like.

Try This!
On a separate sheet of paper, tell where you might see patterns in the world. Explain with words or pictures.

Name: _____

Word Problems

Shopping for Father's Day

Use the items below to answer the questions.

flowers 54¢ 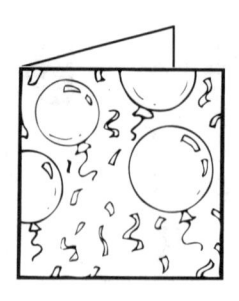   card 22¢ 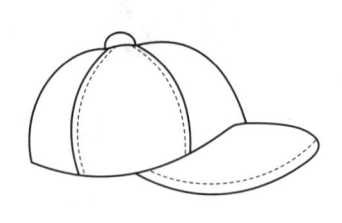   hat 73¢    book 35¢

1. Ava wants to buy her dad flowers and a hat for Father's Day. How much money will she need?

2. Brian has 38¢. What two things can he buy? How much money will he have left?

3. Dave had 68¢. He bought flowers for his dad. How much money does he have left?

4. Molly's dad loves to read. How many books can Molly buy if she has 74¢? How much money will she get back?

Try This!

Work with a partner to brainstorm a list of five things you can give a family member that do not cost any money. Write your list on a separate sheet of paper.

Name: _____

Word Problems

Healthy Ways

Use the items below to answer the questions.

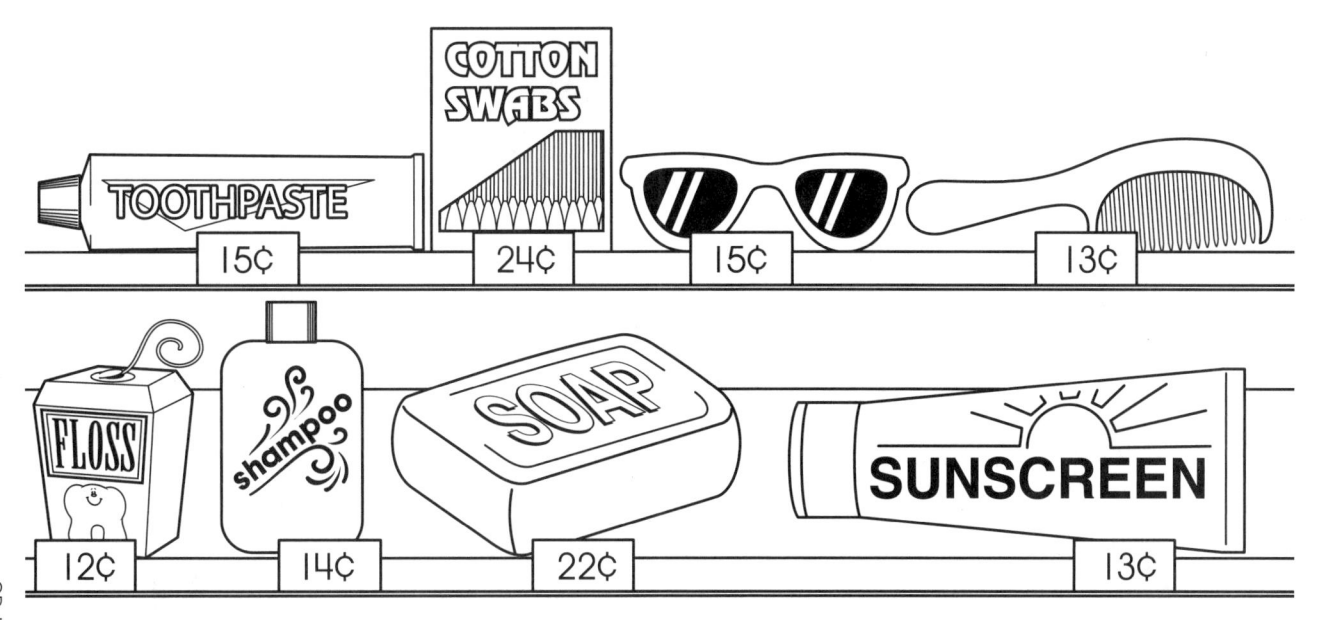

TOOTHPASTE 15¢ | COTTON SWABS 24¢ | (sunglasses) 15¢ | (comb) 13¢

FLOSS 12¢ | shampoo 14¢ | SOAP 22¢ | SUNSCREEN 13¢

1. Kelly needs to buy more toothpaste and dental floss. She has 30¢. How much will she spend, and how much change will she get back?

2. Charlotte needs to buy cotton swabs and soap. How much will this cost?

3. Matt's hair is a mess. What 2 things should he buy to help clean and tidy his hair? How much will this cost?

4. Lily is going to the beach. What 2 things should she buy to protect her skin and eyes? How much will this cost?

Try This!

On a separate sheet of paper, write three ways you take care of your body.

Name: _____

Word Problems

Wonderful Weather Time

Solve the problems.

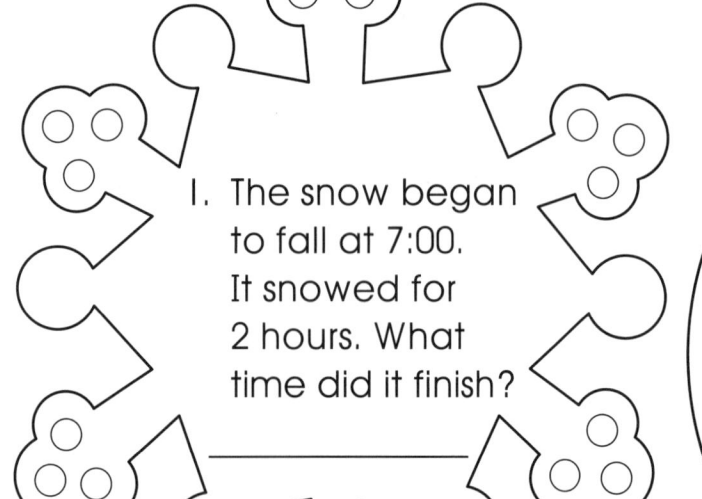

1. The snow began to fall at 7:00. It snowed for 2 hours. What time did it finish?

   _____

2. It rained from 11:00 A.M. to 1:30 P.M. How many hours did it rain?

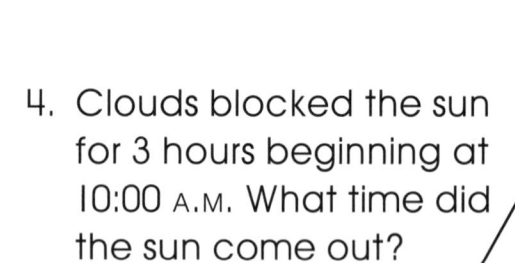

   _____

3. It began to storm at 10:30. It stopped 30 minutes later. What time did the storm stop?

   _____

4. Clouds blocked the sun for 3 hours beginning at 10:00 A.M. What time did the sun come out?

   _____

Try This!

How does the weather change over time? On a separate sheet of paper, draw what the weather might be like at 1:00 P.M. on January 1, April 1, July 1, and October 1.

Name: _____

Word Problems

Time for Sports!

Solve the problems.

1. Tia has soccer practice at 3:30. Practice lasts 60 minutes. What time does Tia's soccer practice finish?

   _____

2. Shay runs at 7:00 every morning. Her run lasts 30 minutes. What time does Shay finish?

   _____

3. Parker finished football practice at noon on Saturday. Practice lasted 2 hours. What time did it begin?

   _____

4. Miguel has a tennis match at 10:30. He plays for 1 hour. What time does he finish?

   _____

Try This!

What is your favorite sport? Answer the question on a separate sheet of paper and write three sentences to explain why the sport is your favorite.

Name: _____   Word Problems

February Activity Planner

Use the calendar to solve the problems.

February

Sunday	Monday	Tuesday	Wednesday	Thursday	Friday	Saturday
					1	2
3	4	5	6	7	8	9
10	11	12	13	14 ♥	15	16
17	18	19	20	21	22	23
24	25	26	27	28		

1. Sally went to the museum on the last Saturday of the month. What is the date Sally went to the museum?

   _____

2. It will be Valentine's Day in 9 days. What day of the week is it?

   _____

3. Valentine's Day was 1 week ago. What day of the week is it?

   _____

4. It is the third Tuesday of the month. Carter's birthday will be in 3 days. What day of the week is Carter's birthday?

   _____

Try This!
Choose one holiday that happens in February to tell more about. On a separate sheet of paper, draw a picture and write five things that tell more about that holiday.

Name: _____ Everyday Math

Math in Our World

Look at each picture. Write about two ways that math is being used. Use the math words in the word bank to help you.

addition	graphs	patterns
fractions	measurement	subtraction
geometry (shapes)	money	time

_____
_____
_____
_____
_____
_____

Try This!

Work with a partner to make a "Math in Our World" book. Show a different math word on each page and an example of how it is used in the world.

275

Name: _____   Everyday Math

Math and Me

Draw a line to match each picture to the type of math being used.

- Money -

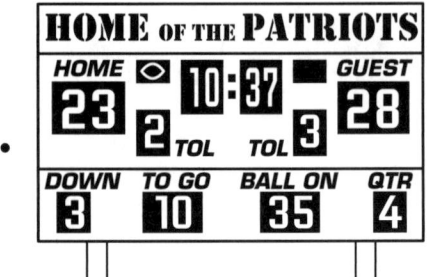

- Fractions -

- Time -

- Graphs -

- Counting -

- Measurement -

Draw a picture that shows when you use math. List the math skills you are using.

Try This!
On a separate sheet of paper, explain your favorite way to use math outside of school. Draw a picture to illustrate your use of math.

Mathematical Concepts Assessment Record

Check the box when a student has mastered that skill.

Student Names	Counts, reads, and writes whole numbers to 100	Demonstrates the meaning of addition and subtraction	Uses estimation strategies in computation and problem solving	Uses number sentences with operational symbols and expressions to solve problems	Uses direct comparison and nonstandard units to describe the measurements of objects	Identifies, describes, and compares triangles, rectangles, squares, and circles	Organizes, represents, and compares data by category on simple graphs and charts	Describes and extends simple repeating patterns (e.g., rhythmic, numeric, color, and shape)	Tells time at the hour and the half hour	Solves problems involving applications of time (clock and calendar)	Solves problems and justifies reasoning
1.											
2.											
3.											
4.											
5.											
6.											
7.											
8.											
9.											
10.											
11.											
12.											
13.											
14.											
15.											
16.											
17.											
18.											
19.											
20.											
21.											
22.											
23.											
24.											
25.											
26.											
27.											
28.											
29.											
30.											

Name: _____   Writing Rubric

Writing Rubric

	Yes	Not Yet	Comments
Prewriting Skills			
Does the student . . .			
know how to hold a writing instrument correctly?			
know that written words stand for spoken words?			
know that letters make words?			
know that words are different lengths?			
use letter- and numeral-like forms to convey meaning?			
write from left to right and top to bottom?			
Writing Mechanics			
Does the student . . .			
write uppercase letters?			
write lowercase letters?			
write numerals?			
mix uppercase and lowercase letters?			
spell words phonetically?			
Composition Skills			
Does the student . . .			
write in complete sentences?			
use uppercase and lowercase letters correctly?			
leave spaces between words?			
order words correctly to convey meaning?			
use punctuation marks correctly?			
make corrections/revisions to his or her own writing?			
Applying Meaning			
Does the student . . .			
write to demonstrate learning?			
appear to be self-motivated to write?			
generate ideas for writing?			
name several different purposes for writing?			
correctly read his or her own writing?			

Name: _____   Reading Rubric

Reading Rubric

	Yes	Not Yet	Comments
Basic Concepts of Books and Print			
Does the student . . .			
know that books have titles, authors, and illustrators?			
make predictions from the title, the cover, and the illustrations?			
differentiate between pictures and text?			
know that text and pictures are related?			
follow print from left to right and top to bottom?			
know that words convey meaning?			
know that there are spaces between words?			
Retelling Stories			
Does the student . . .			
begin the story with an introduction?			
name the main character(s)?			
name other characters?			
make a statement about the setting?			
refer to the problem or the goal of the main character(s)?			
recall major episodes in the story?			
explain the solution to the problem or the goal?			
tell the story's ending?			
retell the story in the order that it was presented?			
Comprehension Skills			
Does the student . . .			
follow spoken directions?			
make inferences?			
identify characters in the story?			
recognize the sequence of events?			
identify the story's setting?			
understand characters' feelings?			
Appreciation			
Does the student . . .			
participate in shared reading?			
enjoy shared reading experiences?			
appreciate stories and literature?			
relate stories to personal experiences?			
express what he or she likes/dislikes about the story?			
choose to spend time reading independently?			

Name: _____   Parent/Guardian Correspondence Log

Parent/Guardian Correspondence Log

Student's Full Name _____

Nickname (if any) _____   Date of Birth _____

Father's Name _____	Mother's Name _____
Address _____	Address _____
Phone (Daytime) _____	Phone (Daytime) _____
Phone (Evening) _____	Phone (Evening) _____
Phone (Cell) _____	Phone (Cell) _____
E-mail _____	E-mail _____

Date	Form of Communication	Comments	Follow-Up

Name: _____

Weekly Homework Assignments

Keep track of your homework in each subject. Have your parent initial the form each day.

	Monday	**Tuesday**	**Wednesday**	**Thursday**	**Friday**
Reading					
Writing					
Language Arts					
Spelling					
Math					
Science					
Social Studies					
Other					
Special Reminders					
Initials					

Name: _____   Substitute Teacher Information

Substitute Teacher Information

Here is some information about the school, the faculty, and the staff that you may find helpful.

My Name and Room Number _____

Teacher Assistant(s) _____

Classroom Pet(s) _____

Other Teacher(s), Specialist(s), or Volunteer(s) Who Work in the Classroom and When
_____
_____

Grade-Level Teachers and Room Numbers
_____
_____
_____
_____
_____
_____

Principal _____

Assistant Principal _____

Administrative Assistant _____

Guidance Counselor _____

Other Office Personnel _____

PE Teacher _____

Music Teacher _____

Art Teacher _____

Foreign Language Teacher _____

Computer Lab Teacher or Monitor _____

Media Specialist _____

Other Specialists _____

Important School Rules/Policies _____

Other Necessary School Information _____
_____

Name: _____   Substitute Teacher Class Procedures

Substitute Teacher Class Procedures

Things to Know:
Room Number _____   Grade Level _____

School Starts _____   School Ends _____
Teacher to Ask for Help/Room Number _____
Students to Ask for Help _____
Morning Procedures:
    Lockers/Cubbies _____
    Student Work _____
    Attendance _____
    Announcements _____
    Other _____
Schedule:

Time	Subject/Activity	Special Notes

Restroom Procedure: _____
Lunch Procedure: _____
Recess Procedure: _____
Dismissal Procedures:
    Lockers/Cubbies _____
    Walkers _____
    Car Riders _____
    Bus Riders _____
    Other _____

Students Changing Classrooms

Name	Time	Destination	Will Return

Name: _____

Missing Assignments

Student's Name _____ Date(s) absent _____

We missed you! Here's what you missed:

Subject   Assignment   Completed

_____
_____
_____
_____
_____

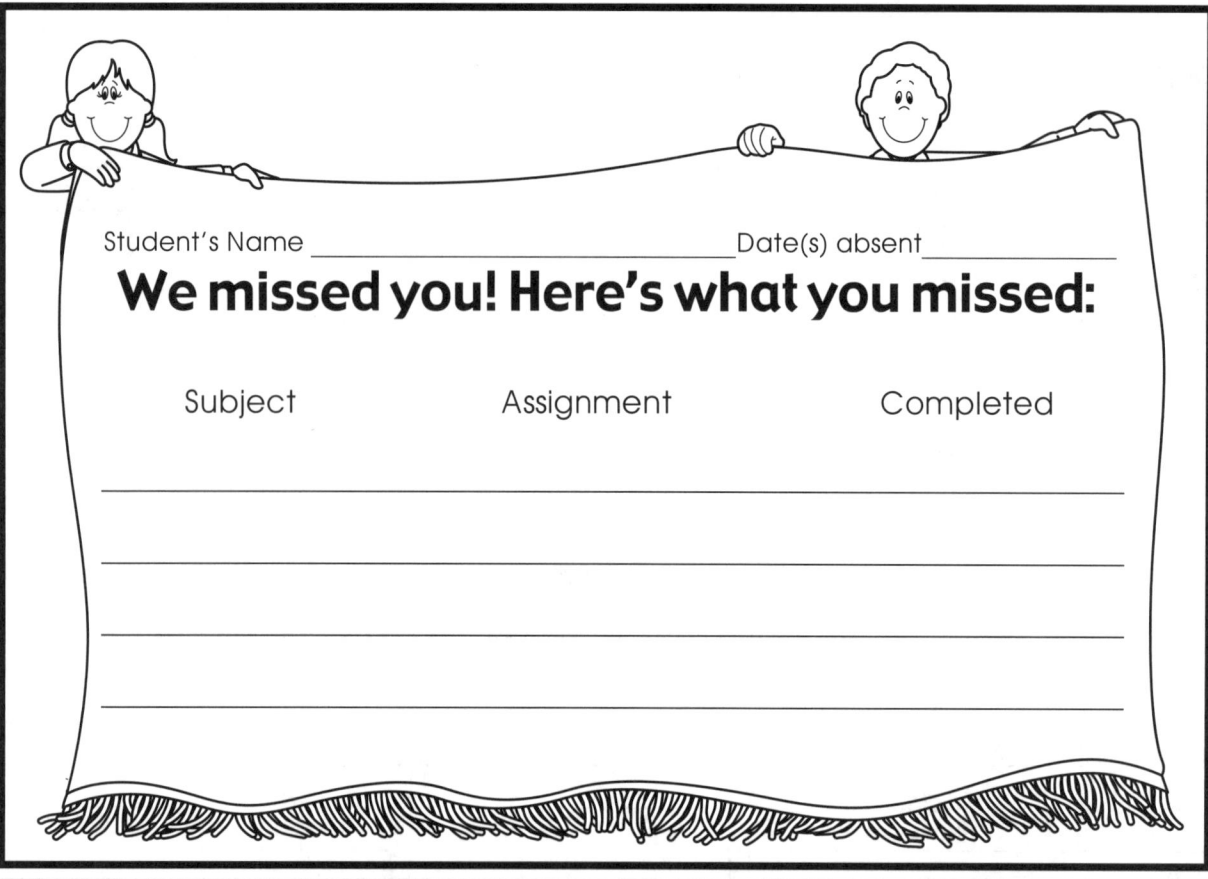

Student's Name _____ Date(s) absent _____

Oops! You have some missing assignments.

Please complete the following work and hand it in by _____.

Subject   Assignment   Completed   Original Due Date   Completed

_____
_____
_____

Name: _____   Volunteer Request

Volunteer Request

Much of the fun and learning throughout the school year is possible because of volunteers. We would love for you to share your time and talents volunteering in our classroom or in other areas of the school. Please check off your interests or suggest your own ideas for volunteering.

Thank you!

_____

Your Name _____

Child's Name _____

Best Days/Times for You to Volunteer _____

Best Time and Method of Communication _____

Volunteer Opportunities

_____ holiday parties (any in particular?) _____

_____ field trips (any in particular?) _____

_____ lunchroom

_____ cultural festivals

_____ field day

_____ class projects

_____ tutoring (any particular subjects?) _____

_____ teacher help (making copies, putting up displays, etc.)

_____ supplying materials

_____ reading to students

_____ computer help

_____ teach/share a special skill/interest

_____ other _____

A Note from the Teacher

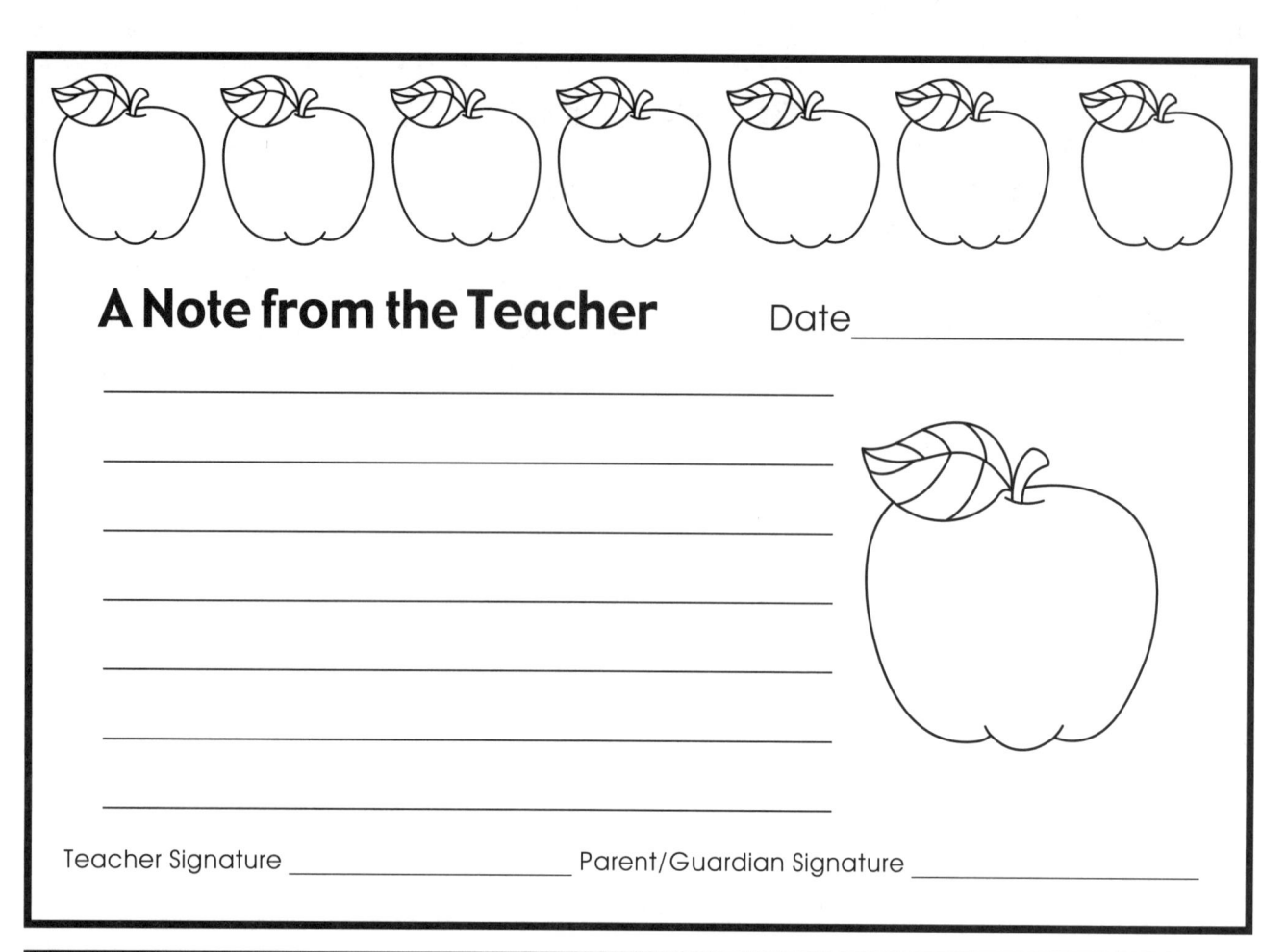

Date _____

_____
_____
_____
_____
_____
_____

Teacher Signature _____   Parent/Guardian Signature _____

A Note from the Teacher

Date _____

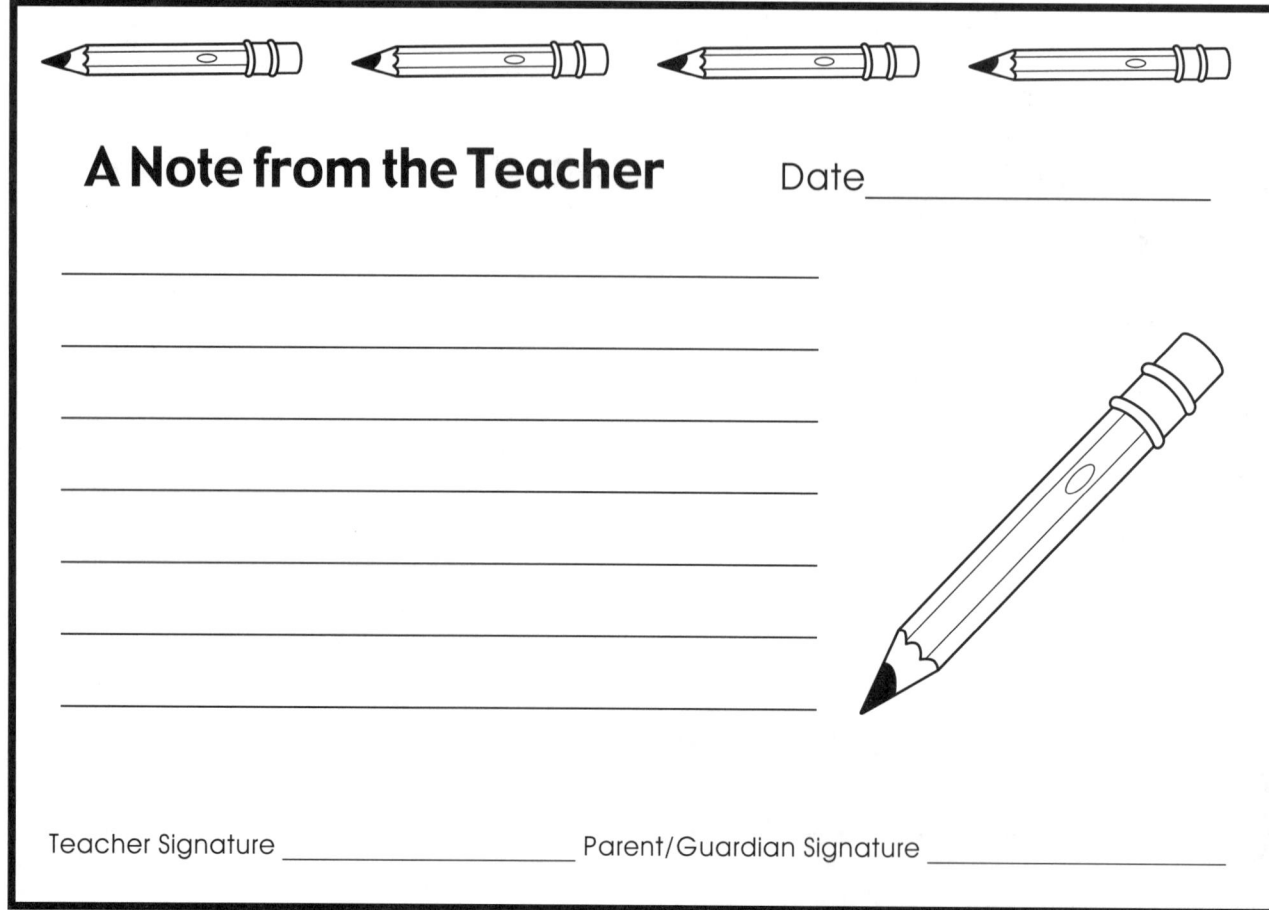

_____
_____
_____
_____
_____
_____

Teacher Signature _____   Parent/Guardian Signature _____

Good Citizen

Happy Birthday!

Good Work!

STAR STUDENT

YOU DID IT!

Name _____

For _____

_____

Signed _____

Date _____

THREE CHEERS FOR YOU!

Name _____

For _____

_____

Signed _____

Date _____

_____ Shows
Tremendous Teamwork!

Signed _____ Date _____

Thanks for Your Helping Hand!

Name _____

For _____
_____

Signed _____

Date _____

Answer Key

Page 9
One syllable: cat, bird, fish; two syllables: turtle, spider, rabbit; answers will vary.

Page 10
muffin, hungry, kitchen, mixer; answers will vary.

Page 11
K, S, E; answers will vary.

Page 12
uppercase: G, D, R, L, K, A; lowercase: t, b, i, e, q, h; answers will vary.

Page 13
Row 1: c, d, f; Row 2: m, b, g; answers will vary; bird, cat, duck, fox, goat, mouse

Page 14
Box 1: b, bear; d, dog; f, fox; g, goat; Box 2: q, queen; v, vest; w, web; z, zipper; answers will vary; answers will vary.

Page 15
Row 1: s, c, m; Row 2: f, y, b; Row 3: k, z, w; answers will vary.

Page 16
Row 1: bed, bird, answers will vary; Row 2: dog, duck, answers will vary; Row 3: goat, gum, answers will vary; Row 4: moon, milk, answers will vary; Row 1: d, d, b, answers will vary; Row 2: d, g, k, answers will vary; Row 3: t, m, g, answers will vary; Row 4: m, n, k, answers will vary.

Page 17
Row 1: t, s, p; Row 2: r, t, n; n, g, x; answers will vary.

Page 18
red star: bed; yellow stars: tub, bib; blue star: cat; green stars: egg, frog; answers will vary; answers will vary.

Page 19
Scott–bat; Nell–ball; Nick–block; Taylor–bear; Dion–train; Sam–drum; answers will vary.

Page 20
Row 1: g, b, s and l; Row 2: t, m and p, r and g; box, sun, fan; answers will vary.

Page 21
Row 1: box–circle, mop–circle, dog–circle; Row 2: bed–do nothing, cat–color, tub–do nothing; Row 3: gas–color, pin–do nothing, log–circle; answers will vary.

Page 22
Row 1: cat–color, fan–circle, top–circle; Row 2: web–circle, sun–circle, wig–circle; Row 3: mop–circle, hen–color, six–circle; answers will vary.

Page 23
Row 1: pan–color, glue, fan–color, Row 2: bat–color, wig–circle, crab–color; Row 3: pin–color, answers will vary; answers will vary; circle wig, pin.

Page 24
color: jet, net, vest, web; answers will vary.

Page 25
Row 1: u, e, i; Row 2: i, a, i; Row 3: e, u, i; answers will vary.

Page 26
Row 1: bed, mop–color, top–color; Row 2: man, rock–color, lock–color; answers will vary.

Page 27
Path should go through bus, dug, nut, mug, truck, gum, rug, duck, hug, brush, cup, plug, tug, up, luck; short a: bag, ant, hat, pan; short e: egg, ten; short i: pin, big; short o: top; short u: bus, dug, nut, mug, truck, gum, rug, duck, hug, brush, cup, plug, tug, up, luck

Answer Key

Page 28

fan, can, crab, pin, crib, pan, fish, mitt, mat, man; fan, can, pan, man

Page 29

i; a; o; e; u; fish–bowl; bat–cave; fox–woods; hen–nest; duck–pond

Page 30

order of train cars: cave, hay, nail, rain, snake, vase; red–hay; yellow–nail, rain; green–cave, snake, vase; answers will vary.

Page 31

Jean, sees, key, tree; Dean, reads, seas; she, eat, meat, beans; he, see, stream; Pete, dream, sheep; answers will vary.

Page 32

hive, prize, knight, stripes, kite, nine, ties; answers will vary.

Page 33

green–seal, sheep, pea; yellow–bike, tie, five; answers will vary.

Page 34

color: comb, cone, nose, rose, hose; answers will vary; nose, rose, hose rhyme.

Page 35

Row 1: fruit; Row 2: glue, tube, ruler; Row 3: flute, tuba; circle; Row 2; answers will vary.

Page 36

red: snake; green: bee; orange: mice, lion, firehouse, tiger; yellow: goat, crow, toad; blue: mule; turn left on Friends Way, turn right on Main Street, turn right on Firehouse Drive. Firehouse is on the right.

Page 37

Row 1: ee, a, i; Row 2: a, o, a; Row 3: i, u, a; red–whale, hay, grapes, rake; orange–bone; green–bee; blue–flute; yellow–bike, nine; whale, bike, bone, grapes, nine, flute, rake

Page 38

☺, ☹, ☺, ☺, ☹, ☹; long i–fly, try, bye; long e–baby, berry, funny

Page 39

Apples on tree: red–nail, kite, cake, snake, tie; yellow–cat, bed, mug, sun, wig; Apples in basket: red–ruler; yellow–hat, tub; Apples on ground: red–bone, five; yellow–mop; 8 clouds

Page 40

Needs: fruit, soap, bed, coat; Wants: pet, game, gum, doll; red: fruit, soap, coat, game; blue: bed, pet, gum, doll; answers will vary.

Page 41

flag–red; block–blue; clock–green; clover–green; blanket–blue; fly–red; answers will vary; answers will vary.

Page 42

pl, gl, pl, gl, pl, pl; gray: glue, glove; blue: plant, plum, plug, plate; glove, glue, plant, plate, plug, plum

Page 43

Row 1: globe; Row 2: blimp; Row 3: clock, cloud; fl; gl; cl; pl; answers will vary.

Page 44

1. pr, cr, yes; 2. cr, cr, no; 3. pr, pr, yes; 4. gr, br, yes; 5. fr, gr, yes; 6. cr, tr, yes; answers will vary.

Page 45

print, present, prince, prize, pretzel

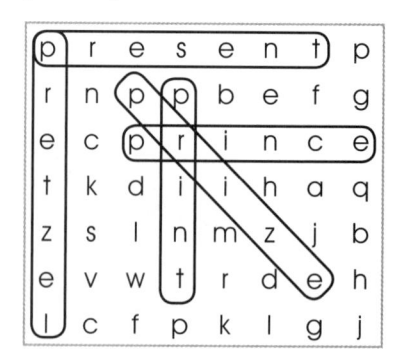

Answer Key

Page 46
trampoline–tr; present–pr; frog–fr; crab–cr; grapes–gr; brain–br; dress–dr; br; pr; cr; dr; answers will vary.

Page 47
snake, stool; swan, sky; skunk, skates; squirrel, swing

living	nonliving
snake	stool
swan	sky
skunk	skates
squirrel	swing

Page 48
sp; sc; sw; st; sn; sl; answers will vary.

Page 49
1. sk; 3. sm; 4. st; 6. st; 7. sm; 8. sn; 9. sp; 10. sw; 11. stamp; 12. spider; 13. snow; 14. sky; answers will vary.

Page 50
1. flag; 2. clown; 3. train; 4. hand; 5. ant; 6. desk; 7.–9. Answers will vary; answers will vary.

Page 51
color: nice/rice, sky/fly, clock/sock; went/tent, soon/moon; answers will vary but may include fish, right, trace; answers will vary.

Page 52
1. sun; 2. tree; 3. mop; 4. mat; answers will vary.

Page 53
top–hop, take–lake, hole–pole, leg–egg, meet–eat, him–swim; answers will vary.

Page 54
cat, mat, nap, lap; answers will vary.

Page 55
fire–wire, flame–game, truck–stuck, smell–bell, match–catch; answers will vary; answers will vary.

Page 56
flight–night, rocket–pocket, sky–fly, fun–sun, far–star, trip–ship, mark–dark, fast–blast

Page 57
CH: watch, match, sandwich; CH: check, cherries, chair; answers will vary.

Page 58
pink: shoe, shark; brown: brush, fish; yellow: tree, whistle; answers will vary; answers will vary.

Page 59
three, thimble, thorn, thermometer; answers will vary.

Page 60
1. ch; 2. ch; 3. sh; 4. th; 5. wh; 6. th; sh; th; wh; ch; th; sh; answers will vary.

Page 61
yellow: sandwich, couch, chair; red: trash, dish; green: teeth, moth; brown: whale, whisk; answers will vary.

Page 62
1. wrong, 2. bring, 3. rang, 4. strong, 5. stung, 6. wing

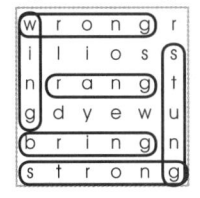

Page 63
bubble: whisk, strong, wheat, moth, thumb, dish; sh, wh, ng, ch, th, wh; answers will vary.

Page 64
red: brush; green: thumb; yellow: cheese, couch; pink: ring, swing; digraph at the beginning: thumb, cheese; digraph at the end: brush, couch, ring, swing; answers will vary.

Page 65
/ow/ as in cow: crown, brown, gown, town; /ow/ as in snow: throw, crow, blow, mow; sentences will vary; answers will vary.

Page 66
stones to color: moon, spoon, igloo, baboon, pool, school, spool, broom, tool, snoop, boot, moose, goose, stool; answers will vary.

Answer Key

Page 67

underline: hay, snail, coat, yawn, beans, mouse, knee, crow; words will vary; answers will vary.

Page 68

skirt; shirt; dirt; hair; circle: bird; skirt; or, ar; answers will vary.

Page 69

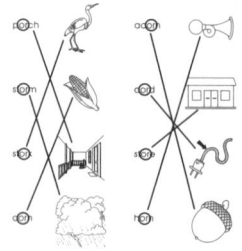

acorn, cord, corn, horn, porch, store, stork, storm

Page 70

turtle, nurse, turnip, purse; 1. turkey; 2. nurse; 3. return; 4. hurt; 5. turn; answers will vary.

Page 71

brown: car, barn, yarn, star; yellow: corn, fork, horn; green: skirt, bird; purple: nurse, purse, turkey, curtain; answers will vary.

Page 72

1. red; 2. yellow; 3. orange; 4. purple; 5. green; 6. brown; 7. white; 8. black; green

Page 73

in, on, in, up; answers will vary.

Page 74

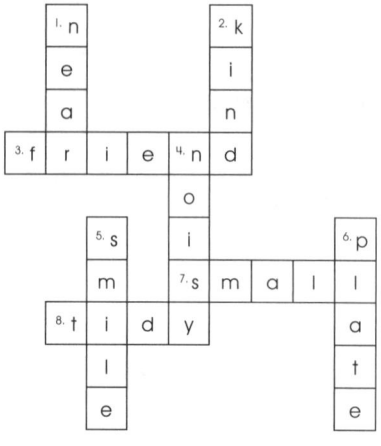

Across: 3. friend; 7. small; 8. tidy
Down: 1. neat; 2. kind; 4. noisy; 5. smile; 6. plate

Answers will vary.

Page 75

loud–noisy; neat–tidy; giggle–laugh; messy–sloppy; happy–glad; ill–sick; angry–mad; below–under; answers will vary.

Page 76

left–right; night–day; dry–wet; happy–sad; drawings will vary; answers will vary but may include nice, down, cold.

Page 77

in–out, little–big, hard–soft, cold–hot, back–front, empty–full; answers will vary.

Page 78

red: shut/close; smart/clever; blue: wet/dry; silly/serious; front/back; cold/hot; answers will vary but may include kind, mean and neat, messy; answers will vary.

Page 79

dog + house; lady + bug; fish + bowl; sand + box; rain + bow; suit + case; cup-cake, sun-shine, fire-fly, sail-boat; drawings will vary.

Page 80

toothbrush, goldfish, pancake, swimsuit, airplane, raindrop; answers will vary.

Page 81

1. room = bedroom;
2. book = notebook;
3. side = outside;
4. nut = peanut;
5. boat = sailboat;
6. thing = something;
7. light = stoplight;
8. shine = sunshine;
answers will vary.

Page 82

1. shouldn't; 2. can't; 3. won't; 4. didn't; 5. isn't; 6. don't; 7. couldn't; 8. doesn't; 9. do not; 10. have not; 11. would not; answers will vary.

Answer Key

Page 83
1. We're; 2. I'll; 3. She's; 4. I'm; 5. He'll; 6. I've; answers will vary.

Page 84
1. I'll; 2. you're; 3. he's; 4. we've; 5. I'm (or won't); 6. won't (or I'm); answers will vary.

Page 85
1. seed; 2. sprout; 3. plant; 4. flower; answers will vary.

Page 86
sunny, snowy, cloudy, rainy, foggy; sentences will vary; answers will vary.

Page 87
2, 1, 3; drawings will vary but should show baby birds learning to fly or leaving the nest; answers will vary.

Page 88
1. tree with leaves falling on ground; 2. boy raking leaves into piles; 3. rake propped against open bags full of leaves; 4. leafless tree with cinched bags of leaves on ground below; answers will vary.

Page 89
Logan got a new bike. He rode his bike to the park. He rode back home. He put his new bike away. Answers will vary.

Page 90
Boy with finished art–last; boy drawing–then; boy hanging up finished art–next; boy arriving at table–first; answers will vary.

Page 91
2, 4, 3, 1; drawings will vary but may include a rainbow with the sun shining; answers will vary.

Page 92
6, 1, 5, 4, 3, 2; answers will vary.

Page 93
Answers will vary.

Page 94
Answers will vary.

Page 95
Answers will vary.

Page 96
Answers will vary.

Page 97
Answers will vary.

Page 98
1. r; 2. o; 3. w; row, row, row, row, row; answers will vary.

Page 99
4, 2, 3, 1; answers will vary.

Page 100
eight; web; home; insects; drawings will vary; answers will vary.

Page 101
feelings; sad; happy; angry; drawings will vary; drawings will vary.

Page 102
yes, yes, yes, no; drawings will vary.

Page 103
Joe went to the park. Tara loves to play dress-up. Answers will vary.

Page 104
1. true; 2. false; 3. true; 4. true; answers will vary.

Page 105
1. nonfiction; 2. fiction; 3. fiction; 4. nonfiction; 5. fiction; 6. nonfiction; 7. nonfiction; 8. fiction; 9. fiction; answers will vary.

Page 106
1. groceries; 2. cans; 3. off; 4. clothes; 5. running; square around 1, 4; circle around 2; triangle around 3, 5

Page 107
1. long; 2. There; 3. help; 4. can; Some dogs will play fetch. Answers will vary.

Page 108
egg; caterpillar; leaf; change; green; butterfly; answers will vary.

Answer Key

Page 109

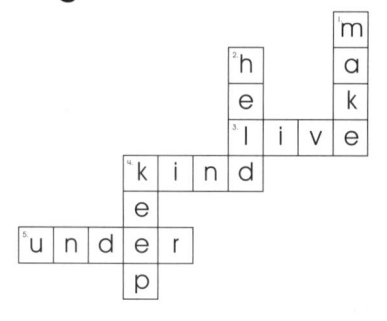

Answers will vary.

(Crossword: make, help, live, kind, keep, under, up)

Page 110
1. woods, farm, desert, city; 2. red, gray, white; 3. hunt for it; 4. a den; answers will vary.

Page 111
1. the city; 2. place them in a big box; 3. give them away; answers will vary.

Page 112
1. S; 2. D; 3. S; 4. D; 5. S; answers will vary; answers will vary.

Page 113
1. C, E; 2. C, E; 3. C, E; 4. Answers will vary; answers will vary.

Page 114
1. rain, wet; 2. sun; hot; 3. seed, plant; answers will vary; answers will vary.

Page 115
1. They got on the bus. 2. They all got off the bus. Answers will vary; answers will vary.

Page 116
It is time to get up. It is time to go to school. It is time to eat lunch. It is time to go home from school. Answers will vary.

Page 117
1. cow; 2. snake; 3. ox; 4. horse; 5. tiger; 6. rat; 7. dog; 8. camel; 9. raccoon; "ILLIGATOR"; answers will vary.

Page 118
head: hat, cap; feet: shoe, sock; hands: ring, glove; answers will vary.

Page 119
two legs: man, bird; four legs: dog, horse; six legs: ant, ladybug; answers will vary.

Page 120
person: girl, firefighter; place: school, farm; thing: key, book; answers will vary.

Page 121
1. bus, home, school; 2. chef, pizza, lunch; 3. firefighter, fire; 4. school librarian, book; 5. nurse, temperature; answers will vary.

Page 122
horses, boxes, shoes, dishes, matches, pumpkins, drums, tables, bears; illustrations will vary; answers will vary.

Page 123
1. boxes; 2. dishes; 3. cars; 4. moon; answers will vary.

Page 124
1. ride; 2. swing; 3. jump; 4. cries; 5. sits; 6. cooks; answers will vary.

Page 125
1. swim; 2. sew; 3. cook; 4. drive; 5. works; 6. feeds; 7. plants; answers will vary.

Page 126
nouns: apple, cat, toy; verbs: swim, drive, run; answers will vary.

Page 127
1. washed; 2. stirred; 3. poured; 4. helped; answers will vary.

Page 128
1. is; 2. is; 3. are; 4. am; 5.–7. Answers will vary; answers will vary.

Page 129
1. were; 2. was; 3. was; 4. was; 5. was; 6. was; 7. were; 8. were; answers will vary.

Page 130
1. big; 2. fuzzy; 3. tiny; 4. three; 5.–8. Answers will vary; answers will vary.

Page 131
they, they, we, she, it, he; answers will vary.

Answer Key

Page 132

1. She; 2. Dr. Sharma; 3. Do, Paul Brown; 4. We, Atlanta, December; 5. May, Sunday; 6. On, Tuesday; sentences will vary; answers will vary.

Page 133

1. Is, ?; 2. Did, ?; 3. How, ?; 4. Will, ?; 5. Answers will vary; answers will vary.

Page 134

1. ?; 2. .; 3. ?; 4. .; 5. Answers will vary; answers will vary.

Page 135

1. ?; 2. ?; 3. .; 4. .; 5. ?; 6. ?; 7. .; 8. ?; answers will vary.

Page 136

Bats are the only flying mammals. Some bats live in caves. I love to read about bats. Do all bats eat insects? Some bats eat frogs or small fish. Drawings will vary; answers will vary.

Page 137

1. Answers may include dogs, puppies, animals. 2. door; 3.–4. Answers will vary; answers will vary.

Page 138

first, last, next; answers will vary.

Page 139

Answers will vary.

Page 140

Answers will vary.

Page 141

Answers will vary.

Page 142

Answers will vary.

Page 143

Answers will vary.

Page 144

Check that colors match number code. There are 3 twos; answers will vary.

Page 145

Check that colors match number code. 5 ones, 8 twos, 6 threes, 2 fours, 5 fives, 5 sixes, 3 sevens, 9 eights, 17 nines, 8 tens; answers will vary.

Page 146

5, 10, 3; drawings will vary; 31

Page 147

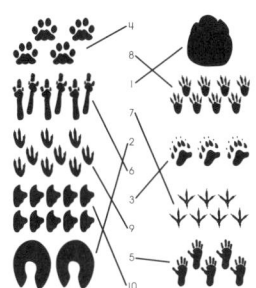

4–four, 8–eight, 1–one, 7–seven, 2–two, 6–six, 3–three, 9–nine, 5–five, 10–ten

Page 148

Page 149

Page 150

1. 1; 2. 0; 3. 5; 4. 3; drawings will vary; 20, 19, 18, 17, 16, 15, 14, 13, 12, 11, 10, 9, 8, 7, 6, 5, 4, 3, 2, 1

Page 151

9; 1; 4; 5; 3; 7; Saturday; answers will vary.

Page 152

1. 5; 2. 1; 3. 10; 4. 4; 3 objects; 7 objects; answers will vary.

Page 153

1. circle 3, cross out 10; 2. circle 2, cross out 9; 3. circle 3, cross out 20; 4. circle 9, cross out 18; 5. circle 9, cross out 36; 6. circle 23, cross out 42; 1. 3, 4, 8, 10; 2. 2, 5, 7, 9; 3. 3, 5, 6, 7, 12, 16, 20; 4. 9, 10, 11, 14, 18; 5. 9, 10, 13, 15, 36; 6. 23, 28, 34, 38, 42

Answer Key

Page 154
1. 1 butterfly; 2. 2 books; 3. 2 glasses; 4. 5 pencils; 5. 4 spoons; 6. 1 shoe; 1. <; 2. >; 3. >; 4. >; 5. <; 6. >

Page 155
1. 3 starfish; 2. 2 scooters; 3. 3 bugs; 4. 4 cheese wedges; 5. 2 hot air balloons; 6. 5 guitars; 1. >; 2. <; 3. <; 4. >; 5. >; 6. <

Page 156
1. >; 2. <; 3. <; 4. >; 5. <; 6. >; 7. >; 8. <; 9. >; 10. >; 11. <; 12. <; drawings will vary.

Page 157
Check that train cars match the code.

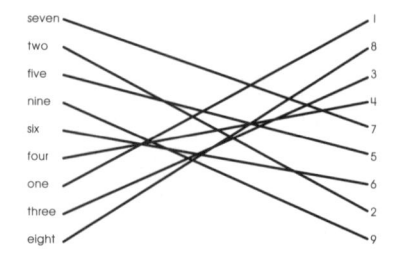

Page 158
1. one; 2. six; 3. three; 4. zero; 5. five; 6. ten; 7 dots; 2 dots; 9 dots; zero, one, two, three, five, six, seven, nine, ten

Page 159
first, second, third, fourth, fifth; fifth

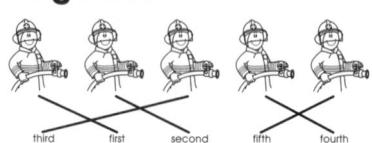

Page 160
Check that answers match directions. Answers will vary.

Page 161
Answers will vary.

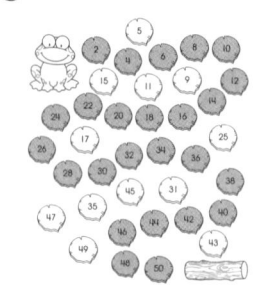

Page 162
52, 54, 56, 58, 60, 62, 64, 66, 68, 70, 72, 74, 76, 78, 80, 82, 84, 86, 88, 90, 92, 94, 96, 98, 100; answers will vary.

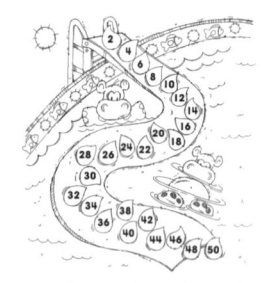

Page 163
5, 10, 15, 20, 25, 30, 35, 40, 45, 50; answers will vary.

Page 164
10, 15, 20, 25, 30, 35, 40, 45, 50; answers will vary.

Page 165

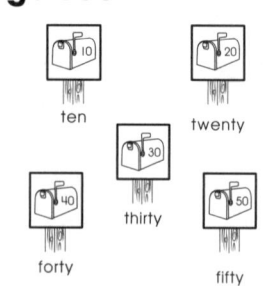

Page 166
1. 3; 2. 4; 3. 4; 4. 5; 5. 3; 6. 6; answers will vary.

Page 167
1. 4; 2. 6; 3. 7; 4. 5; 5. 2; 6. 5; 1. 6 + 4 = 10, 2. 4 + 6 = 10, 3. 3 + 7 = 10, 4. 5 + 5 = 10, 5. 8 + 2 = 10, 6. 5 + 5 = 10

Page 168
Answers will vary but may include:

Answers will vary.

Page 169
1. 1/2; 2. 1/4; 3. 3/4; 4. 1/3; 5.–6. Check that fractions are colored correctly; 1/4, 2/4, 3/4

Page 170
two, three, four, four, two, two, three, two; each part should be labeled 1/4.

Page 171
Clockwise: 3, 5, 4, 3, 4, 5; answers will vary.

Answer Key

Page 172

orange: 4 + 4 = 8, 0 + 0 = 0, 2 + 2 = 4, 5 + 5 = 10, 1 + 1 = 2, 3 + 3 = 6, 0 + 0 = 0, 2 + 2 = 4; blue: 1 + 2 = 3, 4 + 3 = 7, 3 + 1 = 4, 1 + 5 = 6, 3 + 5 = 8, 4 + 2 = 6, 2 + 3 = 5, 3 + 0 = 3, 2 + 1 = 3, 5 + 2 = 7, 1 + 4 = 5, 0 + 4 = 4, 1 + 3 = 4; 0 + 0 = 0, 1 + 1 = 2, 2 + 2 = 4, 3 + 3 = 6, 4 + 4 = 8, 5 + 5 = 10, 6 + 6 = 12, 7 + 7 = 14, 8 + 8 = 16, 9 + 9 = 18, 10 + 10 = 20

Page 173

yellow: 0 + 0 = 0, 1 + 0 = 1, 0 + 1 = 1, 1 + 0 = 1; blue: 2 + 1 = 3, 3 + 0 = 3; orange: 2 + 2 = 4, 3 + 1 = 4, 4 + 0 = 4, 1 + 3 = 4, 1 + 4 = 5; purple: 5 + 2 = 7, 4 + 3 = 7, 6 + 1 = 7, 7 + 0 = 7, 3 + 3 = 6, 4 + 2 = 6, 6 + 0 = 6, 5 + 2 = 7; answers will vary.

Page 174

8 + 2 = 10, 9 + 6 = 15, 2 + 2 = 4; 1 + 2 = 3, 6 + 7 = 13, 5 + 6 = 11, 3 + 2 = 5, 6 + 8 = 14, 5 + 5 = 10, 6 + 6 = 12, 6 + 3 = 9, 3 + 4 = 7, 6 + 2 = 8, 1 + 1 = 2, 1 + 5 = 6; answers will vary.

Page 175

top to bottom, left to right: 11, 6, 12, 12, 9, 9, 18, 5, 13, 8; black: 11, 12, 12, 18, 13; brown: 6, 9, 9, 5, 8; answers will vary.

Page 176

13, 14, 11, 13, 11, 12, 13, 17; 11, 11, 12, 13, 13, 13, 14, 17; answers will vary.

Page 177

top to bottom, left to right: 58, 46, 88, 48, 75, 97, 19; red: 58, 88, 75, 97; blue: 46, 19, 48; answers will vary.

Page 178

top to bottom, left to right: 58, 74, 28, 77, 76, 24, 68, 58, 69, 45, 97, 99, 49, 59, 69, 99; red: 77, 69, 45, 97, 99, 49, 59, 69, 99; yellow: 58, 74, 28, 76, 24, 68, 58; answers will vary.

Page 179

top to bottom, left to right: 31, 73, 60, 46, 52, 71, 40, 58; HONEST ABE; answers will vary.

Page 180

top to bottom, left to right: 0, 5, 7, 1, 3, 2, 3, 4, 3, 3, 3, 7, 0, 2, 3, 3, 1, 2, 4, 1, 2, 5, 8, 2, 4, 6; yellow: 7 – 5, 7 – 4, 10 – 7, 3 – 0, 9 – 6, 4 – 1, 6 – 3, 8 – 5, 5 – 3, 2 – 0, 3 – 1, 6 – 4; 9 – 6 = 3

Page 181

top to bottom, left to right: 4, 2, 3, 2, 1, 2, 1, 3, 1; red: 4 – 3, 2 – 1, 3 – 2; orange: 4 – 2, 3 – 1, 5 – 3; yellow: 5 – 2, 4 – 1; brown: 5 – 1; 8 – 3 = 5

Page 182

1. 11, circle 13 – 2, 15 – 4, 13 – 2, 14 – 3, 12 – 1; 2. 10, circle 13 – 3, 12 – 2, 15 – 5, 13 – 3, 11 – 1; 3. 13, circle 15 – 2, 18 – 5, 14 – 1; 4. 12, circle 18 – 6, 13 – 1, 20 – 8, 15 – 3; 5. 14, circle 15 – 1, 18 – 4; answers will vary.

Page 183

top to bottom, left to right: 15, 12, 4, 3, 9, 11, 18, 7; NINA, PINTA, and SANTA MARIA; answers will vary.

Page 184

top to bottom, left to right: 14, 13, 2, 6, 8, 10, 19, 1; A PAIR OF SCISSORS; answers will vary.

Page 185

top to bottom, left to right: 32, 52, 13, 21, 41, 22, 23, 61, 10; drawings will vary.

Page 186

top to bottom, left to right: 17, 22, 34, 51, 22, 17, 51, 34; 12 + 17 = 29, 23 + 22 = 45, 65 + 34 = 99, 36 + 51 = 87, 65 + 22 = 87, 22 + 17 = 39, 25 + 51 = 76, 33 + 34 = 67

Answer Key

Page 187
top to bottom, left to right: 52, 9, 36, 35, 19, 18; answers will vary.

Page 188
2. 11 − 4 = 7; 3. 12 − 7 = 5; 4. 7 + 6 = 13; 5. 5 + 5 = 10; 6. 8 + 6 = 14; answers will vary.

Page 189
Marcus: 3 + 2 = 5, 5 + 5 = 10, 9 + 1 = 10, 2 + 6 = 8, 5 + 4 = 9, 6 + 4 = 10, 5 + 2 = 7, 5 + 3 = 8, 2 + 7 = 9; Mona: 3 − 3 = 0, 9 − 4 = 5, 10 − 8 = 2, 10 − 3 = 7, 8 − 2 = 6, 7 − 3 = 4, 6 − 3 = 3; answers will vary.

Page 190
Answers may include:
1. 6 + 2 = 8, 8 − 2 = 6, 8 − 6 = 2; 2. 5 + 7 = 12, 12 − 5 = 7, 12 − 7 = 5; 3. 2 + 1 = 3, 3 − 1 = 2, 3 − 2 = 1; 4. 4 + 2 = 6, 6 − 4 = 2, 6 − 2 = 4; 5. 5 + 6 = 11, 11 − 6 = 5, 11 − 5 = 6; 6. 4 + 3 = 7, 7 − 3 = 4, 7 − 4 = 3; answers will vary.

Page 191
top to bottom, left to right: 10, 12, 13, 11, 4, 19, 5, 15, 6, 3, 8, 17; A NORTH POLE AND A SOUTH POLE; answers will vary but may include paper clip, refrigerator, canned food, scissors, door key, wood, glass, cotton, water, plastic.

Page 192
top to bottom, left to right: 12, 15, 16, 12, 10, 11, 10, 5, 12; answers will vary.

Page 193
Answers will vary.

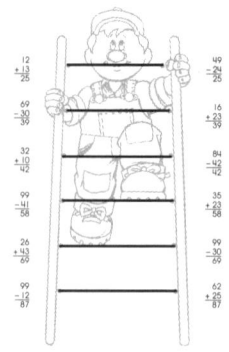

Page 194
top to bottom, left to right: 25, 21, 3, 14, 59, 10, 32, 6, 27; circle: apple, bread, strawberry, milk, lettuce, yogurt; box: cookie, soft drink, ice-cream cone; answers will vary.

Page 195
leaf, flower, flower; flower, leaf, flower; corkscrew vine, corkscrew vine, leaf; answers will vary; ABB; ABA; AAB

Page 196
large heart, small heart; large heart, upside-down large heart, small heart; large heart, small heart facing left, small heart facing left, large heart; small heart, large heart, upside-down small heart; answers will vary.

Page 197
basketball, golf ball; baseball, soccer ball, golf ball; basketball, soccer ball, soccer ball, basketball; answers will vary; answers will vary.

Page 198
1. 4 strawberries, 5 strawberries;
2. 8 strawberries, 10 strawberries;
3. 7 strawberries, 9 strawberries;
4. Answers will vary; answers will vary.

Page 199
1. 7 seeds, 9 seeds;
2. 8 petals, 10 petals;
3. 20, 25; 4. Answers will vary; 1, 2, 4, 6, 8, 10 and 1, 2, 4, 8, 16, 32

Page 200
2 + 8 = 10, 8 + 2 = 10, 10 − 2 = 8, 10 − 8 = 2; 3 + 4 = 7, 4 + 3 = 7, 7 − 3 = 4, 7 − 4 = 3; 2 + 3 = 5, 3 + 2 = 5, 5 − 2 = 3, 5 − 3 = 2; 5 + 3 = 8, 3 + 5 = 8, 8 − 3 = 5, 8 − 5 = 3; answers will vary. 9 + 1 = 10, 8 + 2 = 10, 7 + 3 = 10, 6 + 4 = 10, 5 + 5 = 10

Page 201
Greens: 9 − 6 = 3, 3 + 6 = 9, 6 + 3 = 9, 9 − 3 = 6; Browns: 9 + 3 = 12, 12 − 9 = 3, 3 + 9 = 12, 12 − 3 = 9; answers will vary.

Answer Key

Page 202

8 + 7 = 15 and 7 + 8 = 15; 9 + 3 = 12 and 3 + 9 = 12; 6 + 5 = 11 and 5 + 6 = 11; 9 + 7 = 16 and 7 + 9 = 16; 6 + 8 = 14 and 8 + 6 = 14

Page 203

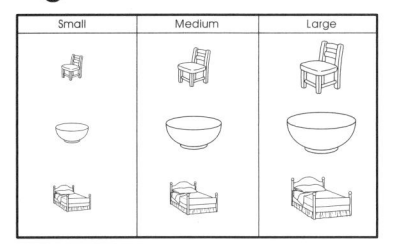

Answers will vary.

Page 204

milk: cheese, cottage cheese, yogurt; meats & beans: beans, chicken, fish, ham; fruits: cherries, oranges, pears; oils: butter, olive oil; vegetables: carrots, lettuce; grains: bagel, rolls, toast; answers will vary.

Page 205

1. 2; 2. 2; 3. 3; 4. 3; 5. 5; 6. 1; 1. 3 – 2 = 1 or 3 – 1 = 2; 2. 5 – 3 = 2 or 5 – 2 = 3; 3. 8 – 5 = 3 or 8 – 3 = 5; 4. 6 – 3 = 3; 5. 7 – 5 = 2 or 7 – 2 = 5; 6. 5 – 4 = 1 or 5 – 1 = 4

Page 206

1. 2; 2. 3; 3. 6; 4. 1; answers will vary; 1. 1 + 2 = 3 or 2 + 1 = 3; 2. 3 + 7 = 10 or 7 + 3 = 10; 3. 6 + 6 = 12; 4. 1 + 7 = 8 or 7 + 1 = 8

Page 207

Row 1: 6, 5, 9; Row 2: 19, 9, 8; Row 3: 14, 3, 10; Row 4: 7, 9, 9; answers will vary.

Page 208

odd numbers: 17, 23, 9; even numbers: 34, 16, 8; answers will vary.

Page 209

MIGRATE; to move from one area to another because of the season; answers will vary.

Page 210

top to bottom, left to right: 6, 15, 12, 10, 8, 13, 10, 13; 2 tens and 9 ones; 3 tens and 4 ones; 1 ten and 8 ones; 4 tens and 8 ones; drawings will vary.

Page 211

top to bottom, left to right: 4 tens and 7 ones = 47; 2 tens and 4 ones = 24; 4 tens and 5 ones = 45; 3 tens and 9 ones = 39; 4 tens and 5 ones = 45; 3 tens and 9 ones = 39; 4 tens and 5 ones = 45; answers will vary.

Page 212

top to bottom: 5 tens, 1 hundred, 2 ones; 3 hundreds, 4 tens, 7 ones; 0 tens, 2 hundreds, 1 one; 6 ones, 3 tens, 1 hundred; 4 hundreds, 3 ones, 6 tens; 200, 300, 200, 100, 500

Page 213

1. 316; 2. 85; 3. 104; 4. 484;
5.

6.

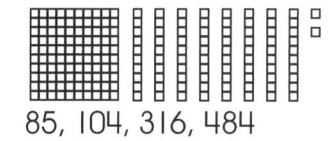

85, 104, 316, 484

Page 214

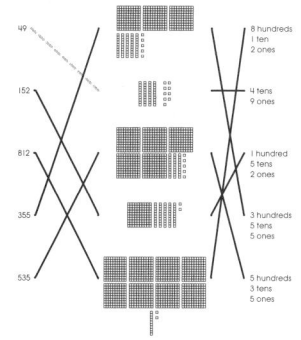

Answers will vary.

Page 215

Check that colors match the geometric code; answers will vary.

Page 216

Check that colors match the geometric code. 13 squares, 7 circles, 14 rectangles, 18 triangles; answers will vary.

Answer Key

Page 217

3; 6; 9; answers will vary; 3; 4; 4; 3; 4; 4; answers will vary.

Page 218

Check that colors match the code. 1. sphere; 2. cube; 3. pyramid; 4. cone; 5. cylinder; 6. cone; 7. pyramid; 8. cone; 9. cylinder; 10. cube; 11. sphere; 12. pyramid; answers will vary.

Page 219

red: baseball, globe, beach ball; blue: gift box, ice cube; green: ice-cream cone, party hat, cone; orange: soup can, towel roll; 1. 3; 2. 3; 3. 2; 4. 2; top to bottom, left to right: cone, cylinder, sphere, cone, cube, cylinder, sphere, cube, cone, sphere

Page 220

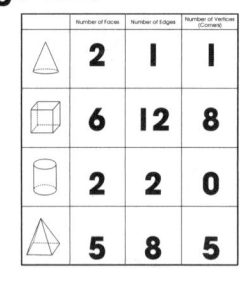

	Number of Faces	Number of Edges	Number of Vertices (Corners)
△	2	1	1
⬛	6	12	8
⬭	2	2	0
△	5	8	5

Answers will vary but may include cone: ice-cream cone, traffic cone, party hat; cube: box, die, ice cube; cylinder: paper towel roll, pipe (plumbing), aerosol can; square pyramid: roof, lampshade, pyramids in Egypt.

Page 221

1. yes; 2. no; 3. yes; 4. yes; 5. no; 6. no; answers will vary; answers will vary.

Page 222

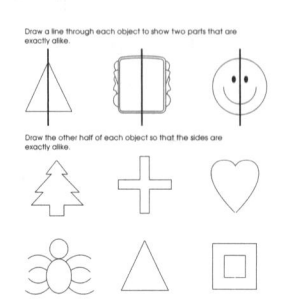

Answers will vary.

Page 223

7; Saturday, Sunday; Monday, Tuesday, Wednesday, Thursday, Friday; answers will vary.

Page 224

twelve; January; December; yes, yes, no, yes; answers will vary.

Page 225

spring; autumn; summer; winter; glue pictures in the following order: spring, summer, autumn, winter; answers will vary.

Page 226

Sunday	Monday	Tuesday	Wednesday	Thursday	Friday	Saturday
			1	2	3	4	5
6	7	8	9	10	11	12
13	14	15	16	17	18	19
20	21	22	23	24	25	26
27	28	29	30	31		

January, March, May, July, August, October, December

Page 227

Sunday	Monday	Tuesday	Wednesday	Thursday	Friday	Saturday
				1	2	3	4
5	6	7	8	9	10	11
12	13	14	15	16	17	18
19	20	21	22	23	24	25
26	27	28	29	30		

1. Thursday; 2. 4; 3. 4; answers will vary but may include birthdays, holidays, seasons.

Page 228

1. night; 2. morning; 3. noon; 4. afternoon; answers will vary.

Answer Key

Page 229

2:00; 11:00; 4:00
6:00; 7:00; 9:00
Answers will vary.

Page 230

1. 2:00; 2. 10:00; 3. 6:00;
1:00; 9:00; 5:00
Answers will vary.

Page 231

1. 10:30; 2. 12:30; 3. 5:30;
4. 7:30; 5. 9:30; 6. 3:30;
fruits: apple, peach, pear, tomato; vegetables: corn, pumpkin; answers will vary.

Page 232

1:30; 11:30; 3:30
4. 6:30; 5. 8:30; 6. 12:30
11:30 A.M.

Page 233

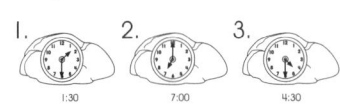

1:30; 7:00; 4:30
4. 10:00; 5. 3:30; 6. 9:30;
1:30; 3:30; 4:30; 7:00; 9:30; 10:00

Page 234

8; 5; 8; 6; 4; 7; circle: toothbrush, floss, mouthwash, toothpaste; answers will vary.

Page 235

Answers will vary.

Page 236

1 inch; 8 centimeters; 5 inches; 14 centimeters; answers will vary.

Page 237

1. scissors; 2. soccer ball; 3. crayon box; 1, 3, 2; answers will vary.

Page 238

1. $1.25; 2. 20¢; 3. $1.10; 4. 4¢; answers will vary.

Page 239

top to bottom, left to right: drum (7¢); wagon (11¢); truck (11¢); paint (16¢); shovel (12¢); apple (15¢); answers will vary.

Page 240

C; F; E and F; B; 19¢ + 37¢ + 50¢ + 48¢ + 24¢ + 76¢ = 254¢ or $2.54

Page 241

1. Sam; 2. Caitlyn; 3. 5; 4. 11; 5. 1; 6. 19; answers will vary.

Page 242

1. Ruby; 2. 20; 3. Ruby; 4. 5; 5. 40; 6. 90; 6

Page 243

1. 30; 2. third; 3. kindergarten and fourth grade; 4. 40; 5. first; 40 + 70 + 50 + 20 + 40 + 30 = 250

Page 244

1. 3; 2. car; 3. boat; 4. 2; 5. 8; answers will vary.

Page 245

1. 4; 2. bear; 3. bears; 4. 12; 5. 6; 6. 27; answers will vary.

Page 246

Answers will vary.

Page 247

1. 7; 2. bird; 3. 4; 4. 2; 5. 19; answers will vary.

Page 248

Answers will vary.

Page 249

1. grapes; 2. blueberries; 3. 15; 4. 5; 5. 30; 6. 27; 111

Page 250

1. seesaw; 2. swings; 3. 12; 4. 24; 5. 48; answers will vary.

Page 251

1. 8; 2. 7; 3. 3; 4. 3; 5. 15; answers will vary.

Answer Key

Page 252

1. Answers will vary but may include fish, whale, dolphin, tadpole, hippo, alligator, turtle. 2. Answers will vary but may include hippo, alligator, turtle, cat, giraffe, ox, skunk. 3. both land and water; 4. water: jellyfish, octopus; both: frog; land: camel, cow; answers will vary.

Page 253

1. 1 hour; 2. 1 minute; 3. 1 second; answers will vary.

Page 254

Answers will vary.

Page 255

1. green; 2. red or blue; 3. yellow; 4. green; answers will vary.

Page 256

1. green; 2. orange; 3. yellow; 4/20 red; 3/20 blue; 5/20 green; 2/20 yellow; 6/20 orange

Page 257

1. 7; 2. 7; 3. 5; 4. 9; answers will vary.

Page 258

1. 8, healthy; 2. 8; 3. 7, healthy; 4. 16, healthy; answers will vary.

Page 259

1. 36, need; 2. 48, want; 3. 55, need; 4. 23, need; answers will vary.

Page 260

1. 79; 2. 99; 3. 56; 4. 48; answers will vary.

Page 261

1. 3; 2. 4; 3. 3; 4. 2; 1. 3 + 3 = 6; 2. 4 + 1 = 5; 3. 3 + 5 = 8; 4. 2 + 2 = 4

Page 262

1. 5, winter; 2. 3, summer; 3. 4, autumn; 4. 2, spring; spring, summer, autumn, winter; answers will vary.

Page 263

1. 6; 2. 11; 3. 4; 4. 5; 1. 3; 2. 1; 3. 4; 4. 2

Page 264

1. 25; 2. 12; 3. 22; 4. 22; 2 each with 1 left over

Page 265

1. 13; 2. 36; 3. 12; 4. 44; answers will vary.

Page 266

1. 3; 2. 12; 3. 7; 4. 12; All were in a garden.

Page 267

1. 25; 2. 11; 3. 59; 4. 12; answers will vary.

Page 268

1. 10; 2. 2; 3. 16; 4. 9; answers will vary.

Page 269

Answers will vary.

Page 270

1. $1.27 or 127¢; 2. book – 3¢ left or card – 16¢ left; 3. 14¢; 4. 2 and 4¢ back; answers will vary.

Page 271

1. 27¢ and get 3¢ back; 2. 46¢; 3. shampoo and comb, 27¢; 4. sunglasses and sunscreen, 28¢; answers will vary.

Page 272

1. 9:00; 2. 2 1/2 hours; 3. 11:00; 4. 1:00 P.M.; answers will vary.

Page 273

1. 4:30; 2. 7:30; 3. 10:00 A.M.; 4. 11:30; answers will vary.

Page 274

1. February 23; 2. Tuesday; 3. Thursday; 4. Friday; answers will vary.

Page 275

Answers will vary but may include: measurement, addition; measurement, money; time, money; answers will vary.

Page 276

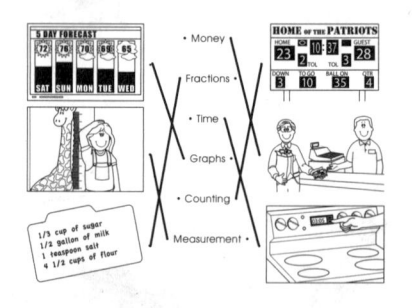

Answers will vary.